Kings and Bishops in England, 1066–1216

C000180710

Kings and Bishops in Medieval England, 1066–1216

ROGER WICKSON

First published 2015 by
PALGRAVE

Palgrave in the UK is an imprint of Macmillan Publishers Limited, registered in England, company number 785998, of 4 Crinan Street, London, N1 9XW.

Palgrave Macmillan in the US is a division of St Martin's Press LLC, 175 Fifth Avenue, New York, NY 10010.

Palgrave is the global imprint of the above companies and is represented throughout the world.

Palgrave® and Macmillan® are registered trademarks in the United States, the United Kingdom, Europe and other countries.

ISBN 978–1–137–43117–2 hardback
ISBN 978–1–137–43116–5 paperback

This book is printed on paper suitable for recycling and made from fully managed and sustained forest sources. Logging, pulping and manufacturing processes are expected to conform to the environmental regulations of the country of origin.

A catalogue record for this book is available from the British Library.

A catalog record for this book is available from the Library of Congress.

Printed in China

Contents

Preface

This book makes no claim to be an original work in that it is entirely derived from the work of distinguished and masterly historians. I am not a scholar, but throughout my teaching career, which began in 1963 and continues, in my retirement, to this day, I believe that I have been effective in communicating the scholarship of others. The claim to originality that I do make for the book is that while there are works of great learning and scholarship on the subject, no previous attempt has been made to communicate this important aspect of history to those coming to medieval history for the first time. I have written it for the sixth-former, the university student and the general reader with an interest in church history for whom the Middle Ages are unfamiliar.

I have aimed throughout to make the reader aware of the contemporary sources, particularly monastic chroniclers with all their biases and prejudices, that are essential for knowledge of the period and reasonably accessible. I have also tried to draw the attention of readers to the masters of the period from the great William Stubbs and F.W. Maitland of the nineteenth century, who still have much to offer, to the present day. I hope that readers of this book will be encouraged to turn to them.

It is a matter of sadness and regret to me that so few sixth-formers study medieval history at A level. My love of the Middle Ages began at the age of 11 at Whitgift School when we were taught by a formidable master named Ken Bell. However, I then had to wait until I went to Cambridge in 1959 before I learnt any medieval history again. At A level we studied the almost inevitable Tudors. I hope very much that the commemoration this year of the 800th anniversary of *Magna Carta* will encourage more young people to study medieval history in the future.

I was fortunate to be at Cambridge when some of the greatest medievalists were lecturing: Christopher Cheney, David Knowles, Edward Miller and Walter Ullmann. I was particularly fortunate in my supervisor at Sidney Sussex College, R.C. 'Otto' Smail. Otto was a fine medievalist, an awesome teacher and a great college man. He was my guide, counsellor and friend until his death in 1986. I would like to dedicate this book to his memory and to that of those sixth-formers who gave me such pleasure when I taught them medieval history at Ardingly College from 1966 to 1977.

This book arises from a series of classes that I ran in retirement as a part-time tutor in the University of Keele's Department of Continuing and Professional Education. I am very grateful to those members of the 'older generation' who attended these classes.

I am indebted to the distinguished medievalists who have each read chapters of the book and commented fully and helpfully on them – David Bates, who supported the suggestion of such a book when I first put it to him; David Carpenter; Anne Duggan; Henrietta Leyser; Philip Morgan and Graeme White. No blame can be attached to them for any errors that remain. Finally I must thank my wife, Sue, whose computer skills have made life very much easier for me.

Roger Wickson
February 2015

Abbreviations

ASC	*The Anglo-Saxon Chronicles*, ed. and trans. Michael Swanton (Phoenix, 2000)
CTB	*The Correspondence of Thomas Becket, Archbishop of Canterbury 1162–79*, ed. and trans. Anne Duggan, 2 vols, Oxford Medieval Texts (Oxford University Press, 2000)
ECP	Z.N. Brooke, *The English Church and the Papacy from the Conquest to the Reign of John* (Cambridge University Press, 1952)
EEA	*English Episcopal Acta* (British Academy Series), ed. various
EHD	*English Historical Documents*, vol. ii 1042–1189, ed. D.C. Douglas and G.W. Greenaway (Eyre & Spottiswoode, 1953, reprinted 1961)
EHR	*English Historical Review*
EHNA	Eadmer, *History of Recent Events in England*, trans. Geoffrey Bosanquet (The Cresset Press, 1964)
GS	*Gesta Stephani*, ed. and trans. K.R. Potter, Nelson Medieval Texts (Nelson, 1955)
HC	Hugh the Chantor, *The History of the Church of York 1066–1127*, Nelson Medieval Texts (Nelson, 1961)
HH	Henry of Huntingdon, *The History of the English People 1000–1154*, ed. and trans. Diana Greenway, Oxford World's Classics (Oxford University Press, 2002)
HM-H	Henry Mayr-Harting, *Religion, Politics and Society in Britain 1066–1272* (Pearson Education, 2011)
JMH	*Journal of Medieval History*
LTB	*The Lives of Thomas Becket*, ed. and trans. Michael Staunton, Manchester Medieval Sources (Manchester University Press, 2001)
MV	*Magna Vita S. Hugonis: The Life of St Hugh of England*, ed. and trans. Decima Douie and Hugh Farmer, 2 vols, Nelson Medieval Texts (Nelson, 1961–2)
NMT	*Nelson Medieval Texts*
ODNB	*Oxford Dictionary of National Biography*, ed. H.C.G. Matthew and B. Harrison (Oxford University Press, 2004)
OMT	*Oxford Medieval Texts*
OV	*The Ecclesiastical History of Orderic Vitalis*, ed. and trans. Marjorie Chibnall, 6 vols, Oxford Medieval Texts (Oxford University Press, 1969–80)

RH	Roger of Howden, *The Annals*, vol. 2, parts i 1181–92 and ii 1192–1201, trans. Henry T. Riley (Llanerch Press)
RW	Roger of Wendover, *Flowers of History*, vol. 2, parts i 1170–1215 and ii 1215–1235, trans. J.A. Giles (Llanerch Press)
SC	William Stubbs, *Select Charters* (Oxford University Press, 1913)
SLI	*Selected Letters of Pope Innocent III concerning England (1198–1216)*, ed. and trans. C.R. Cheney and W.H. Semple, Nelson Medieval Texts (Nelson, 1953)
WMGP	William of Malmesbury, *The Deeds of the Bishops of England*, trans. David Preest (Boydell Press, 2002)
WMGR	William of Malmesbury, *A History of the Norman Kings 1066–1125*, ed. Joseph Stevenson, trans. John Sharp (Llanerch Press)
WMH	William of Malmesbury, *Historia Novella*, ed. K.R. Potter, Nelson Medieval Texts (Nelson, 1955)
WMVW	William of Malmesbury, *Vita Wulfstani*, trans. J.H.F. Peile (Llanerch Press)
WNHEA	William of Newburgh, *The History of English Affairs*, ed. and trans. P.G. Walsh and M.J. Kennedy (Aris & Phillips, 1988)

Introduction

Anglicana ecclesia

'*In primis concessisse quod Anglicana ecclesia libera sit*' ('In the first place we have granted that the English church shall be free'). King John's first undertaking in *Magna Carta* was to guarantee the freedom of the English church. To understand the nature of the relationship of the kings of England with their bishops it is important to understand what is meant by the English church in this period and to be aware of how it related to the rest of the Christian church. The word 'church' has two senses apart from the building. First, and broadly, it is the community of all faithful Christians, 'the blessed company of all faithful people'. In medieval Europe this included, theoretically at least, everybody except Jews, heretics and followers of Islam. It does not mean, of course, that everyone was particularly pious, devout or virtuous, but that certain assumptions about life in this world and existence after death were shared by everybody with a greater or lesser degree of sophistication according to their intelligence, education and social status and upbringing. A second meaning of the word 'church' is that group of people, known as clerics or clergy, who were qualified, as a consequence of education and certain rites and practices, to lead and organise the Christian life of the community. This group of men (for they were all men) was seen as a class apart from the laity, the ordinary men, women and children of whatever class or background who made up the majority of the Christian community. The words *Anglicana ecclesia* certainly do not mean 'the Anglican church' or 'the Church of England' but simply that part of the Latin Christian church which happens to be in that part of the western world known as England.

That is, perhaps, a somewhat abstract concept of *Anglicana Ecclesia*. Henry Mayr-Harting has pointed out that it is highly unlikely that the church in this period was seen as a single entity. The monks of Christ Church, Canterbury often used the phrase, but when they did so they were thinking above all of their own organisation, whose interests they were determined to protect by projecting them onto a broader canvas, the whole English church.[1]

This book will examine the relationship between the kings, the men who claimed that they had ultimate authority over all the people of England, and the bishops, the men who claimed that they had spiritual authority over all the people of England including the king. In doing so it draws upon a range of sources, primary and secondary. The primary sources are mainly those which exist in readily available translations. They are largely narrative accounts of events and must be read in conjunction with letters and sources illustrative of administrative and judicial activity. Of great value to students of this period are the second and third volumes of *English Historical Documents* (*EHD*). Many of the secondary sources used were written in the twentieth century by outstanding historians and have become classics of historical study. All later historians have stood on the shoulders of these giants and a number of works written in the last ten years have been used (see Recommended Reading).

The Christian church is an enduring legacy of the Roman Empire. The Christian faith was born in one of its distant outposts. This empire left a three-fold legacy to the world deriving from the reign of Constantine in the fourth century AD. First, Western Christendom and its sacred language Latin; second, Eastern or Byzantine Christendom and its sacred language Greek; and third, the non-Christian faith and way of life of Islam which, after its birth in the Middle East, erupted into lands once under Roman control. Western Christendom corresponded with the western Roman Empire as established by Constantine and his successors in the fourth and fifth centuries. The people who feature in this book, clergy and laymen, were members of Western Christendom, an earthly concept made up of fallible human beings, a mundane reflection of the spiritual reality that existed in heaven, the *Respublica Christiana*. Only those judged to be worthy were admitted to heaven; the rest had less agreeable fates.

As Christianity spread it developed an institutional structure which reflected the administrative structure of the Empire. It was positively hierarchical. As well as the distinction made between the laity and the clergy the clergy were divided into a hierarchy of seven orders, the major orders of bishop, priest, deacon and sub-deacon and the three minor orders of acolyte, lector and doorkeeper. Before being admitted to an order the aspiring clerk was tonsured, and theoretically the tonsure was made bigger as the clerk went up the orders. The tonsure of monks was bigger than the clerical tonsure. The three lower orders could be conferred by someone acting on behalf of a bishop; only a bishop could confer the higher orders. This was meant to be a gradual process, but when it suited a ruler the leap from sub-deacon to bishop could be remarkably swift. 'Archdeacon' and 'archbishop' were not orders but offices.

The western church was a community of dioceses and parishes. The origins of medieval, and indeed modern, ecclesiastical organisation go back to Roman times; the diocese corresponded with the Roman *civitas*, several dioceses becoming grouped into provinces under the authority of a senior bishop or 'metropolitan'. The diocese was the area over which a bishop had authority and the principal ecclesiastical town in each diocese, from which the diocese took its name, was the bishop's see. The see was the cathedral town and in the cathedral was the bishop's throne, the *cathedra*, which symbolised his authority and on which he alone could sit. At the time of the Norman Conquest there were 17 English dioceses, which increased to 19 in the reign of Henry I with the foundation of Ely and Carlisle. They varied considerably in size and wealth, from the rich and powerful Canterbury, York, Winchester, London and Durham, territorially huge Lincoln to the decidedly modest Rochester. After the Conquest a number of sees were transferred to more important towns. There were no further creations until the Reformation. There were two metropolitan provinces in England, Canterbury and York. Canterbury was far more extensive than York which, following the creation of Carlisle, consisted of only three dioceses. Nevertheless the archbishop of York claimed parity with Canterbury and, as we shall see, a feature of the period following the Conquest was the struggle between the respective archbishops for ultimate authority, the primacy.

The religious life of those who were not attached to cathedrals or members of religious communities came to be focused on the parish, with its church and priest. The formation of the parish came long after the diocese and was not fully under way before the eleventh century and complete by the thirteenth.[2] Before that the dominant church below the cathedral was the minster. Minsters were served by communities of priests who had responsibility for the pastoral care of people in a wide area. During the eleventh and twelfth centuries many local stone churches were built, the old minsters were eclipsed and their parishes divided between smaller, local churches. Baptism and burial took place in the parish church with its font and cemetery, the rector or vicar officiating. The rector might well be an absentee, not necessarily a clerk in holy orders, who enjoyed the revenues attached to the church while employing a vicar to act on his behalf – vicariously – often for a very modest income. Many churches were acquired by monastic communities which enjoyed the income while appointing a parson, who either paid a rent while retaining a small allowance or received a modest stipend. There was often friction between the head of a monastic community and the bishop of its diocese about who had authority over monastic parishes, with some abbots claiming exemption from episcopal control.

The concept of apostolic succession was vital. The bishop was the living representative of Christ's apostles. At a time when the oral legacy was as important as the written, it was essential that a bishop should have received instruction directly from one of the apostles or from someone who had received instruction from an apostle. In order to transfer the original authority of the apostles to those living decades and centuries after them some tangible contact was required. This was the laying-on of hands, a symbolic act which enabled a bishop and the members of his diocese to believe that he had had actual physical contact, albeit indirectly, with Christ's apostles and so Christ himself. As the representative of the apostles only the bishop could admit to full membership of the church by confirmation, exclude from it by excommunication, consecrate other bishops and ordain into the higher orders. Those who had been duly ordained were authorised to perform baptisms and burials and administer the Eucharist. There was other work for bishops to perform: pastoral, liturgical and sacramental, building and maintaining buildings, caring for sacred equipment.

In matters of belief and doctrine Christendom came to be far from united. A series of councils was held from the fourth to eighth centuries to define Christian doctrine. As a consequence the orthodox doctrine of the Catholic, or universal, church was established and those who refused to concur with it were condemned as heretics, those who had erred, without hope of salvation. Catholic orthodoxy was reinforced by the specific law of the church known as canon law, which came to be enforced in its own courts. The outcome of the different attempts to define Catholic doctrine was that in the course of the Middle Ages many who believed themselves to be Christians were, in the eyes of the authorities of the Roman church, heretics denied any hope of salvation. Moreover, doctrinal issues came to aggravate the tension between the Western and Eastern Roman Christian Churches.

Since the legitimisation of Christianity in the Roman Empire evangelists and missionaries had gradually, and with many setbacks, converted pagans throughout the Empire and beyond. The majority were uneducated, unsophisticated and illiterate. Inevitably the intellectually complex doctrines of scholars and theologians were beyond the grasp of many, and were simplified and modified while often merging with pre-Christian pagan ideas and practices. In an illiterate society the visible and tangible were of great importance, hence the significance attached to relics, ritual, liturgy, symbols and sacraments. Concepts that a modern, educated mind might regard as metaphors, allegories or speculation were believed in as realities. Miracles and portents, like Haley's comet seen in 1066, may well have been physical phenomena with rational explanations, but were interpreted as evidence of the work of a supernatural power.

Christian beliefs

Fundamental was the belief that life on earth was a preparation for life after death. The nature of that life would be determined by the way that earthly life was conducted. It was believed that forces of evil, led by Satan, were for ever on the lookout to lead human beings astray and enjoy their sufferings in Hell. For most people Hell was a reality which was understood in extremely graphic terms. In the mid-eleventh century John, the abbot of Fécamp, wrote a harrowing and terrifying account of the fate of those condemned to a permanent existence in Hell.[3] For those who could not read there were plenty of church wall paintings to serve as appalling warnings. At death every human being would be judged. Some would go directly to Heaven, others to Hell, and those judged to be worthy of a period of testing would go to Purgatory. Life in Purgatory was only slightly less wretched than that in Hell. The thirteenth-century chronicler Roger of Wendover[4] described it at considerable length. Ultimately, earthly time would end, but no one knew when. However, there was no doubt that the material world was finite, and when it had passed the spiritual worlds of Heaven and Hell would remain. At the end of time Jesus would return and all human beings, no matter when and where they had lived, would be called to the final judgement, Domesday.

The sacraments provided the means of expressing religious life and feeling in words and gestures. By the twelfth century the number of ceremonies considered sacraments was seven: baptism, confirmation, Eucharist, penance, extreme unction, marriage, holy orders. Persons, places and objects might be set aside exclusively for God's use. As a consequence of certain rituals a man became a king, a bishop or a priest; bread and wine became the body and blood of Christ; a mundane cup could become a chalice; a piece of ground a plot reserved for Christian burial; a building a church. All were sacred. To defile the sacred in any way was to be guilty of sacrilege, an offence against God with serious consequences for the life of the offender in this world and the next.

To be valid these ceremonies had to be performed correctly. They were therefore written down in liturgical books that were used by those in holy orders for the spiritual health of those in their care. Liturgies were not confined to the seven sacraments; many occasions from life to death had to be marked by a religious service. Few people could actually read or even understand the words of the services, which were conducted in Latin in the west and Greek in the east, but they could become so familiar with the sounds that they would know them by heart and they would become equally familiar with the gestures or rituals associated with them. Eternal life in Heaven was the goal of all, but to lead a reasonably good life was no guarantee of salvation. It was therefore necessary for ordinary people to have mediators and advocates who would act and pray on their behalf. Relics, that is, tangible objects associated with a holy person, were believed to have considerable efficacy. Most sought-after were the remains of a saintly body, the blood, the skeleton or some of the bones, even bits of hair or flesh, perhaps of a most intimate nature, like Christ's foreskin. But also important were material objects that a saint had left behind. Most sacred of all were fragments of the True Cross on which Christ had been crucified and the Holy Lance which had pierced his side.

Monasticism

It was believed that the way of life that would bring a man or woman closest to God was that of the monastery or convent. The eleventh and twelfth centuries saw a considerable rise in the numbers of men and women living in monasteries. Most monks and nuns, but there were significantly fewer nuns than monks, were Benedictines, their way of life and structure of their communities based on the sixth-century *Rule of St Benedict*. Monasteries, like many churches, were founded and supported by aristocratic endowments. Those who were rich enough to do so could put considerable wealth into these institutions as a form of afterlife insurance policy, and they regarded their foundations as their personal property. In return they expected members of 'their' community to pray and say masses for them not only while they lived, but after death. A great landmark in the history of monasticism was the foundation of the monastery of Cluny in Burgundy by William of Aquitaine in 910. For two centuries Cluniac foundations dominated western monasticism until in the twelfth century their supremacy was challenged and supplanted by the foundation of Cistercian houses. The success of monasticism was grounded in the belief in the efficacy of prayer. This belief was shared by clergy and laity, and few doubted that prayer worked, even if they were hazy about how it actually did so. Christians were confident that if they prayed for one another, living and dead, God would listen. The most effective at praying on behalf of others were the monastic communities. They were specialists in liturgy, and liturgical services were required to fill one-third of every 24 hours. In the eleventh century devotion to the liturgy dominated every other aspect of Cluniac life, with increasing importance attached to saying masses for the dead. Some of the most distinguished popes and bishops in this period were monks.

A very important feature of the twelfth century was the decline of Cluny as the dominant force in Western monasticism and the rapid growth, expansion and impact of new religious orders, especially the Cistercians, particularly under the influence of Bernard of Clairvaux. This had a significant impact on the relationship of some kings with some of their bishops. Bernard did not ever visit England but his authority was felt through his protégés and his letters. David Knowles cited a number of occasions on which he intervened in English affairs and he was a stern mentor of Eugenius III, pope in the later part of Stephen's reign (1145–53).[5]

Another form of religious order that became prominent in the twelfth century was that of the Augustinian canons. Augustinian houses were commonly founded as collaborative ventures, often in towns. Like monks the canons lived in a community according to a rule, *The Rule of St Augustine*, but theirs was not an enclosed community and the canons went out into the world, perhaps running cathedrals or large churches, organising schools like the distinguished school of St Victor in Paris and playing a significant pastoral role in the locality. A few houses existed in England before 1100 but they increased significantly in the reign of Henry I, supported by Henry and his wife Matilda, some senior royal officials and a number of bishops. Henry appointed two Augustinian canons to bishoprics, the saintly and learned Robert of Bethune to Hereford and the austere ascetic Athelwold in 1133 as the first bishop of the newly created diocese of Carlisle.

Cynics suggest that Henry was keen to endow communities of Augustinians because they were less expensive to establish than houses of enclosed orders while giving the founder all the spiritual benefits of providing for a religious community. This is a harsh judgement, as Henry was a generous supporter of the Cluniacs and he founded, or strictly speaking re-founded Reading Abbey as a great abbey following Cluniac observance. Moreover, following the death of William Giffard in 1129 he nominated Henry of Blois, brother of the future King Stephen, as bishop of Winchester, an office he held in plurality with that of abbot of the Cluniac abbey of Glastonbury.

The papacy

Two figures claimed to be at the head of the Christian world: the bishop of Rome, who became known as the pope, and the emperor. For more than three hundred years after 476 the west had been without an emperor until the coronation of

Charlemagne in 800. His empire in its fullest extent did not long survive him. In 962 the German king Otto I restored the imperial title, albeit as ruler of a much reduced empire, and in the period at which we are looking western emperors were rulers of a conglomeration of states known, for convenience, as Germany. No German king could call himself emperor without a papal coronation, and for much of our period popes and emperors coexisted in a state of tension.

With hindsight it may seem inevitable that Rome became the capital city of Christendom. In reality it was not so. Not until the sixth century was the title 'pope', which simply means 'father', used exclusively for the bishop of Rome. Periodically Rome was eclipsed by other cities, like Milan under Ambrose in the second half of the fourth century. Later there were times when popes had to flee Rome and set themselves up, often insecurely, in other parts of Italy or in France. From time to time two men, each with their own supporters, were demanding recognition as the rightful pope. The claim of the Roman church to supremacy was derived from Christ's words to Peter quoted in St Matthew's Gospel: 'You are Peter and upon this rock I will build my church and I will give to you the keys of the kingdom of Heaven.' Two great popes in the early Middle Ages played essential parts in establishing papal authority. Leo the Great (441–61) stressed the identity of the papacy as the unworthy heir of St Peter. He emphasised the importance of the apostolic tradition and saw the papacy as the head of an *imperium* which was not of this world. At this crucial period in Rome's history he could not cut himself off from worldly affairs and the burden of secular responsibility became greater over a century later during the pontificate of Gregory the Great (590–604). Italy was then the desert which the Emperor Justinian called a peace. It was in effect a Greek colony and Rome was eclipsed by Ravenna. Gregory was a reluctant pope who saw himself as *servus servorum dei*, servant of the Roman people undertaking civic responsibilities like maintaining water supplies and caring for the sick and needy. By reorganising the papal states he greatly increased their revenue and gave the church an organisation independent of the Empire or other lay power. He extended Rome's authority by sending missionaries to claim or reclaim pagan lands, as he did with Augustine's mission to England.

Even so, for much of the first millennium the popes were in reality little more than local bishops, with the office reaching its nadir in the tenth century when the papacy became in effect the plaything of the Roman aristocracy. Some popes were downright scandalous, like John XII, who became pope at the early age of 18, 12 years below the minimum canonical age for a bishop. We are told, admittedly by the great scandalmonger Liutprand of Cremona, that he died a few years later of a heart attack induced by his exertions in bed with a married woman.

The great revolution of the eleventh century associated particularly with Gregory VII (1073–85), although not initiated by him, helped to transform the papacy into an effective international authority. Those seeking reform saw as the root of the church's weakness the involvement of laymen in spiritual affairs. From this followed major corrupting abuses like simony – the buying and selling of spiritual office, nepotism – the appointment of a relation to a spiritual position, pluralism – the holding of more than one spiritual appointment at the same time, and clerical marriage or concubinage. The role of laymen in the reform movement must not be underrated. The initial fervour for reform came from the monks of Cluny. In William of Aquitaine's foundation charter he stated: 'Desiring to provide for my own salvation while I am still able, I have considered it advisable, indeed most necessary, that from the temporal goods conferred upon me I should give some little portion for the gain of my soul.' He demurred at Abbot Berno's recommendation for the ideal site, as that was actually his favourite hunting ground. The abbot persuaded the Duke with the words, 'which will serve you better at the Judgement, O Duke, the prayers of monks or the baying of hounds?'[6] An essential feature of the foundation charter was that it stated that after the death of William the monastery would come under the direct control of the papacy.

The fervour for reform was taken up in the eleventh century by the Emperor Henry III. It was he, a layman, who was responsible for nominating as pope Leo IX, whose Council of Rheims in 1049 had a tumultuous impact on Christendom. Its story has been brilliantly told by R.W. Southern in his *Making of the Middle Ages*.[7] Leo's work was passionately and energetically continued by Gregory VII, and although Gregory's life and career ended bleakly he was, as David Douglas wrote, one of the great constructive statesmen of the age along with William the Conqueror and, with him, one of the makers of medieval Europe.[8]

Gregory believed that he was the agent chosen by Peter and Paul responsible for restoring the perfection, as he saw it, of the apostolic church. The root of all evil was lay control. Only those whom he judged suitable were fit to rule in Christendom, which must enjoy *justitia* and *libertas ecclesiae*. The church could fulfil its mission to convert the world only if it was free from lay control, a control that was often demonstrated by the act of investiture of bishops by laymen with the symbols of their spiritual office. *Justitia* was not merely justice but righteousness, the power to establish that right order on earth which was essential if freedom were to be achieved. There must be a right relationship between the secular and spiritual authorities, priests must be free from secular duties and secular authorities must be subordinate to them. The world must be led by those ordained to spiritual office, and it could only be fully and truly Christian if its supreme ruler was the head of the church on earth.[9]

No pope before Gregory had made this claim in such uncompromising terms nor acted with such zeal to implement it. The implication of his thesis was that an ordained man, however lowly, by the act of laying-on of hands became superior to all laymen, however great. Theoretically this had difficult implications for a king. Consecration conferred on him a special spiritual status; nevertheless he remained a layman, subordinate to all who had been ordained. In reality no king was going to be involved in confrontation with a humble village priest, but this Gregorian view of the right order in society ensured that there was potential for friction between those who were at the peak of the secular and spiritual hierarchies. This was particularly so when the spiritual leaders, the bishops and abbots, were among the greatest of the king's tenants and indispensable to him in matters of government, politics and administration. Lest anyone should be in doubt, early in his reign Gregory VII caused to be inserted in his register a series of uncompromising statements known as the *Dictatus Papae*.[10]

The reformed papacy took the initiative in extending the frontiers of Christendom through missionary work and the crusading movement. All metropolitan bishops throughout western Christendom were required to receive the symbol of their office, the pallium, from the pope directly. The papacy imposed taxes on different countries, like Peter's Pence on England. Councils attended by senior clergy, secular and monastic, from all Christendom met periodically to determine matters of doctrine, discipline and procedures. Legates were sent out as papal representatives and permanent resident legates were appointed. Popes exercised their authority through the imposition of ecclesiastical sanctions like interdict and excommunication.

Interdict was an ecclesiastical sanction imposed upon a community. Even if it was primarily directed at an individual the whole community had to bear its effect. Like sanctions today it could impose far greater hardship on the blameless than on the person whose action had brought it about. It was hoped that interdicts would not be in force for long. The terms of interdict could vary, but essentially it meant that all ecclesiastical rites were suspended. Divine offices could not be performed, the sacraments were suspended, burials could not be held in consecrated ground – the dead were buried in woods or ditches by the roadside. Sermons could be preached on Sundays but only in the churchyard.

Interdicts were not necessarily imposed with all their rigours. The precise terms of the interdict imposed on England by Pope Innocent III in 1208 are not known, as different versions exist. In a letter to the bishops of London, Ely and Worcester sent on 14 June 1208 Innocent III wrote: 'Since on account of the Interdict new chrism could not be consecrated on Maundy Thursday, the old chrism should be used in the baptism of infants, and if need require it, to prevent a shortage of chrism, oil should be mixed with it by the hand of a bishop or even a priest.' This suggests that infant baptism was not suspended, although it may have had to take place behind closed doors. Innocent then wrote: 'although the last communion (the viaticum) seems essential to the confession of the dying, yet if it cannot be held we believe that in this case the famous saying applies – "only believe and thou hast eaten" – for it is the contempt of religion, not the co-incidence of the Interdict, that debars from the sacrament, and it is hoped that the Interdict will shortly be removed'.[11]

Excommunication could affect an individual far more seriously than interdict. The soul of the person excommunicated was put in peril, as he was barred from participation in any of the sacraments. Even the most worldly and cynical could be troubled by this. More than that, it had implications for life in this world. No one could have any contact with an excommunicated person without facing the risk of their own excommunication. If a king were excommunicated, as John was, it could lead to his effective isolation and provide potential rebels with the opportunity to withdraw their allegiance to him, for they could claim that their consciences did not permit them to follow a king so anathematised.

In the twelfth century canon law became coherent and systematic and was enforced in the church courts. A landmark in the development of canon law was the publication in 1140 of Gratian's *Concordance of Discordant Canons*, generally known as the *Decretum*. In a Christian society canon law permeated the entire social order and no one was untouched by it. It claimed full and exclusive jurisdiction over all crimes and offences committed by clerics, but no layman could avoid its reach. Blasphemy and sacrilege fell under canonical jurisdiction, as did matters of morality, including all manner of extramarital sexual misconduct. Many disputes over landholding were drawn into church courts, as were issues about wills and testaments and the rightful burial place of the dead.[12] Litigants turned more and more to the papal court. It became the final court of appeal for matters spiritual, and in the course of the twelfth century increasing numbers of appeals were made directly to the pope. These dealt with all manner of issues, some trivial. The papal chancery was developed and increasing numbers of letters, decrees and decretals were despatched with copies retained.

While the bishops in England largely retained their independence of the papacy and the Norman kings were active in attempting to maintain barriers against undue papal influence in England, the English bishops, many of whom were not, after all, Englishmen, were members of the whole community of Christian bishops. They were expected to attend councils and the English metropolitans, the archbishops of Canterbury and York, were required to receive the pallium from the pope. Popes before Innocent III (1198–1216) rarely took much interest in the election of English bishops, although they did expect to be consulted before a bishop could be translated to another diocese. They were drawn into the dispute between the archbishops of Canterbury and York over the primacy (see below), but unless invited, which was rarely, they did not become involved in English secular politics. Nevertheless their ultimate authority was recognised by the bishops and kings of England. It is to these English bishops and their kings that we must now turn.

Kings

Most societies at all times and in all parts of the world have had kings. The Saxon and Norman kings of England had their roots in the Germanic kingdoms which themselves looked back to Roman and Byzantine practices. The ceremony of king making was derived from the Old Testament, particularly 1 Samuel 16 and 1 Kings 1. It could be said that a king is a man who has been crowned and anointed by a bishop; this double act validated the title and office of a potential king. The rules of succession to the English throne were far less precise than they eventually became. Primogeniture was not an unchallenged factor, but a link with the distant past was very important. The Anglo-Saxon kings traced their ancestry back to the line of Cerdic (d. 534) and through him even to Woden. William the Conqueror, like the Danish kings before him, could not claim this descent, but although he became king by conquest he stressed the legitimacy of his claim to be the successor of King Edward, for which he had papal support, whereas Harold was a perjured usurper. The Norman line resumed its link with Cerdic when William's son Henry married the English Edith, otherwise known as Matilda.

Suitability for office, the concept of *idoneitas*, was strongly advocated by the reform papacy.[13] William the Conqueror showed himself to be more laudable and worthier of honour than other kings, and although Stephen had ignored an oath taken by the leading bishops and barons to support Henry I's daughter Matilda, his Oxford *Charter of Liberties* persuaded Pope Innocent II of his suitability for kingship. After Stephen had seized the throne various excuses were found to justify reneging on Henry's wish. Important, too, was election of the most appropriate person by the leading men of the realm. Harold was elected by the Witan. This was in no way an election in the modern sense but approval, often of what was in effect a *fait accompli*. Also important was designation by the living king. William claimed that he had been designated by Edward, but so did Harold's supporters, who took the view that the incoherent ramblings of Edward on his deathbed were not the mutterings of one out of touch with reality but were especially valid because they were the inspired utterances of one very near to meeting God.

Few successions in the period 1042–1216 were clear-cut. The accession of Matilda's son Henry as Stephen's heir went unchallenged (but see below), as did that of Richard I, but the deaths of Edward the Confessor, William I, William II, Henry I and Richard I all led to uncertainty. Speedy action as shown by Henry I and, somewhat uncharacteristically, by Stephen, was very important.[14] It gave the prospective king the chance to seize control but was no guarantee that his claim would be generally acceptable. Certainty was conferred by coronation and unction. Once the prospective king had undergone these ceremonies his position was difficult to challenge. The Capetian kings of France had their eldest sons crowned in their own lifetimes to ensure a smooth succession; Henry II did too, but he outlived his oldest son Henry. Coronation and unction made a secular lord not just a king but a king by grace of God.

Coronation and unction had an ancient history. In Christian times even that notorious reprobate Clovis, the Frankish king, had been anointed at the end of the fifth century when, so the story went, the Holy Spirit in the form of a dove delivered holy oil to him. The Carolingian successors to the Merovingians developed unction as a king-making ritual. While it is likely that English kings before Edgar had been anointed, the coronation of Edgar at Bath by Dunstan of Canterbury and Oswald of York on Whitsunday 973 was momentous for the history of the English coronation and the theory and practice of English kingship. Edgar was already a king but at the age of 30, the age at which a man might be consecrated bishop, he decided that it was appropriate for his position as a Christian king to be publicly, and with great ceremony, confirmed.

A coronation was a ceremony of great pomp and formality. It was an exclusively male occasion; women were not admitted. The chronicler Roger of Howden gives an idea of its grandeur in his account of the coronation of Richard I.[15] Those present at Westminster Abbey included 19 archbishops, bishops and bishops elect, 13 abbots, 11 earls, among whom was his younger brother John, and 17 great barons and officials. The clergy, with candles and incense, led the procession, followed by the earls and barons with the regalia. Richard, walking under a silk canopy, was accompanied by two bishops. The usual sequence of events in the abbey was that first the king was formally elected and he made a series of promises to his people, then he was consecrated and anointed, and thirdly he was dressed in ceremonial robes, crowned and enthroned.

The most sacred part of the coronation service, the part that transformed a lord into a king and made him different from other men, was the anointing. It was significant that that was the one part of the coronation of Elizabeth II in 1953 not permitted to be seen by television viewers. After the anointing the outward and visible sign of kingship, the crown, was placed on the king's head. The communion service followed and the king received communion in both kinds, unlike ordinary laymen. After the formalities and ceremonial there was doubtless much feasting and drinking. According to the royal financial records, 'the pipe rolls', for Richard I's coronation 1770 pitchers, 900 cups and 5050 dishes were specially ordered for the feast.[16]

Kings were anointed not just on the head but on the hands, breast, shoulders and arms. Before the period of papal reform the oil used was the specially sacred chrism, a mixture of oil and balsam. Only a bishop could consecrate it and it was used for the consecration of bishops and ordination of priests. The reforming papacy required that a lesser oil should be used. Henry II was certainly anointed with the inferior oil, but at the coronation of his son in 1170, the coronation that drove Becket to fury because it was conducted in his absence, full chrism was probably used. The apparel of the anointed and crowned king had a special significance. He was dressed in splendour, was girded with a sword to defend the church and protect the weak, received the orb and sceptre and was invested with a ring. On his head was placed the crown. The awesome spectacle of William I robed and crowned provoked one of his jesters to cry out, 'I see God, I see God', an extravagant piece of sycophancy that was rewarded with a whipping.

Visual display and public manifestations of royal grandeur and dignity were essential to a king wishing to impress the special nature of his position on his great subjects, lay and ecclesiastical, and to emphasise that, however grand, they were his subordinates. For this reason William Rufus built a great hall at Westminster where he held his court for the first time in 1099. According to Henry of Huntingdon:[17] 'When he first entered, to view it, some said that it was a good size, and others said that it was too large. The king said that it was only half large enough.'[18]

Perhaps the most familiar symbol of kingship is the crown. Those whose only impression of medieval history is from illustrated fairy stories will imagine that kings permanently wore their crowns. This was not so at all; they rarely did. Crowns were worn only on solemn and formal occasions. Only an archbishop, and usually the archbishop of Canterbury, could put the crown on a king's head. Eadmer tells us that when Henry I's second wife, Adeliza, was about to be consecrated queen in 1121 Archbishop Ralph was displeased to discover that Henry was already wearing his crown. So he risked the king's wrath by removing it and putting it back on himself.[19] The Anglo-Saxon chronicler and William of Malmesbury were both struck by the occasions when William I wore his crown. In his *Life of Wulfstan* Malmesbury wrote: 'King William brought in a custom which the kings after him followed for a while, and suffered to fall into disuse: to wit that thrice in the year all the great men of the realm should meet at the King's court, to take counsel on the affairs of the kingdom, and to behold the king in his majesty wearing his crown set with precious stones.'[20] It was said at the time that in the interests of economy Henry I gave up these formal occasions, but Henry Mayr-Harting points out that he continued to wear his crown on important occasions as an affirmation of his link to divinity through his kingship.[21]

It is significant that both Stephen and Richard I were each publicly re-crowned after they had suffered spells of ignominious captivity. But they were not anointed again, for the original anointing bestowed on a king the very essence of kingship of which he could not subsequently be deprived. As Shakespeare put into the mouth of Richard II: 'Not all the water in the rough, rude sea / Can wash the balm from an anointed king.' Anointing set a king apart from other laymen. It did not make him a priest – there was no way that he could fulfil priestly functions – but it gave kingship a sacred quality.

At his coronation the crowned king acknowledged that he had obligations and responsibilities. Edgar and his successors took a threefold oath. Thereby they undertook to guarantee that the church of God and the whole Christian people should have true peace at all time, to forbid extortion and all kinds of wrongdoing to all orders of men and to enjoin equity and mercy in all judgements. The coronation oath became an integral part of the coronation rite. Henry I supplemented it with a charter of promises produced with remarkable speed after the death of his brother, as did Stephen, although their motives may be seen as cynical bids for the political support which they so badly needed. In any case the Norman and Angevin kings were not absolute monarchs or despots. As *Magna Carta* made clear, the king was under the law. Later, in the thirteenth century, the king was described as a debtor to do justice to his people.

Kings of England had a dual role. They were sacerdotal monarchs and they were also feudal lords in England and France. This duality is represented by the seal of William the Conqueror. One side of it shows the king in splendour, crowned, enthroned, holding the orb and sceptre. On the reverse he is represented as a fully accoutred knight in armour on horseback. He was also a member of a family with a dynasty to foster and favour. Clearly no medieval king was a constitutional monarch. As Douglas pointed out, kings were not motivated by notions of national patriotism, to which they were probably strangers, nor by constitutional arguments derived from later Whig doctrine. The nation as an abstract concept meant nothing. William the Conqueror did not call himself king of England but duke of the Normans and king of the English. The seal of William Rufus was innovatory. His is the first surviving English seal to incorporate the phrase that he was king of the English 'by the grace of God', that is, not simply by the designation of his father, but by the designation of God.[22]

A king certainly had public obligations, or put another way, members of the community with power like the lay magnates and the leaders of the church looked to him to safeguard their interests. Above all he was expected to maintain law and order and to do justice. He was not primarily expected to be a great warrior, although he could not escape his military responsibilities and it helped if he could carry them out effectively. He was certainly looked to keep the peace and maintain law and order and, when necessary, 'put down the mighty from their seats'. He was expected to protect the church. He was turned to as an arbitrator, one who could make binding judgements to settle matters of dispute. He did not seek to be liked or popular. His people might groan under the severity of excessive taxation, but in an age accustomed to harshness and brutality a king who could maintain the full rigour of the law, however cruelly, was preferred to one who was soft and good and *'na justise ne dide'* ('did not enact the full penalties of the law').[23]

Bishops

The king was the ultimate authority in his kingdom; the bishop in his diocese. A purpose of this book is to examine the validity of that generalisation. There were three stages in making a man a bishop. He had to be an ordained priest and was meant to be aged at least 30. First he had to be canonically elected. There were no unchallengeable rules as to who could participate in an election and different interested parties might intervene to try to ensure the election of their favourite. There was nothing laid down that a king of England had a right to elect his bishops but as they were so important, spiritually and politically, it was unlikely that a bishop could be imposed on the king without his approval. Such attempts led to crises. Indeed, when the king had a particular man in mind he was not deterred by his lack of canonical status. Becket was elevated from deacon to bishop with remarkable speed.

The formal language of the twelfth century used at a bishop's consecration stated that he was elected by our pious lord the king of the English, with the consent of the clergy and people. Most of the time the king's idea of a free election was epitomised in the famous writ of Henry II to the monks of Winchester: 'I order you to hold a free election, but, nevertheless, I forbid you to elect anyone except Richard my clerk, the archdeacon of Poitiers.' Even so it seems that occasionally kings took account of local feelings and conditions and did not always get their way. After the death of Anselm in 1109 Canterbury was vacant for a number of years. In 1114 Henry I proposed that Faritius, abbot of Abingdon, should fill the vacancy. He was Italian, a distinguished scholar, an able administrator and physician to Henry and his wife. But there was considerable opposition to the appointment (see Chapter 3 below). Henry, who may not have had particularly strong feelings, decided it would be judicious not to make a stand and he agreed to the appointment of the Norman bishop of Rochester, Ralph d'Escures.

Once a bishop was elected he appeared before the king. He was now one of the king's greatest tenants and had to perform homage to the king in the same way as any great lay magnate. He was then invested with the ring and staff, the symbols of his spiritual office. Until it became one of the issues seized upon for attack by the papal reformers it was the practice for investiture to be performed by the lay ruler. At this stage he was an incomplete bishop for he had no authority to perform his spiritual functions – he could not do so until he had been consecrated. Consecrations took place on Sundays or other holy days. A prospective bishop was required to take an oath of obedience to his metropolitan bishop. This might be a matter of controversy, but once the oath had been taken he was anointed and received the laying-on of hands from the bishops present. There was a curious sequel to this: the bishop's 'prognostic' was read. The Bible was opened at random and a verse picked out. It was believed that it would foretell the nature of the new bishop's episcopate. Verses could, of course, be ambiguous and open to interpretation but one wonders what Herfast, bishop of Elmham and Thetford, made of his prognostic in 1072: 'Not this man but Barabas' (John 18:40). That of his successor Herbert Losinga was more encouraging: 'Friend, do what you have come here for' (Matthew 26:50).

On formal occasions bishops wore their formal dress. A bishop's regalia was as significant as that of a king. The basic garment was the 'rochet', a white, full-length garment like a surplice but with gathered sleeves at the wrist. As an alternative he might wear a 'chimera', a loose sleeveless robe. He might also wear a cope or chasuble, but these were not exclusive to bishops. The regalia distinctive to the episcopal order were the pectoral cross and the ring, mitre and staff. The mitre, the obvious outward symbol of a bishop's authority, had a curious history in the twelfth century following a misunderstanding of the Old Testament. Mitres originally were worn so that the two parts faced inwards, simulating the horns which, bizarrely, Moses was believed to have been blessed with. In the course of the twelfth century the 'horns' were turned round to face the back and front.[24] Archbishops wore the pallium, the woollen vestment placed over the shoulders. It was exclusive to them and conferred by the pope in person or occasionally by one of his representatives as a concession if it were impossible for the recipient to visit the pope.

Although no man was fully a bishop before consecration there were notorious instances of considerable delay between election and consecration. A number of invested bishops remained unconsecrated during Anselm's periods of exile. The career of Thurstan, who actually proved to be a distinguished archbishop of York, illustrates real irregularities. Unusually he was not already a suffragan bishop before his election to York and, remarkably, not even a deacon. He was not ordained deacon until December 1114, having been elected to York on 15 August. Shortly after his ordination as deacon he was formally enthroned at York but he was not ordained priest until the following Whitsun. A major stumbling block remained. He refused to take the oath of obedience to Canterbury and on 19 March 1116 he tried unavailingly to resign the office to which he was not yet consecrated. He was finally consecrated by Pope Calixtus II on 19 October 1119, the day before the opening of the Council of Rheims, but even then did not return to England until the end of January 1121 and did not arrive in York before February.

Most, but not all, bishops came from the higher echelons of society, and once bishops they certainly joined the very greatest of the aristocracy. Very bright young men of modest circumstances who had had the opportunity to attend one of the schools that began to flourish in the late eleventh century might find employment in a bishop's household. For all his faults, Odo, bishop of Bayeux, was a generous patron of such intelligent young men. Ranulf Flambard was one. The highly intelligent son of a village priest in the diocese of Bayeux, with Odo's support he was educated and became a clerk in the service of Odo's brother William the Conqueror. He rose to become William Rufus's bishop of Durham. But many bishops were related to the royal family, to noble families or to other bishops. Very few native Englishmen became bishops in the Anglo-Norman period.

Episcopal elections were not frequent; about one a year. Between 1066 and 1216 there were 123, fewer than one a year.[25] Bishops were often long-lived and kings preferred to leave sees vacant and enjoy the revenues on the many occasions that they were out of the country. A not insignificant number of bishops were monks but most had been royal or episcopal chaplains. This was not a precise term to mean that they had specifically sacerdotal or confessional responsibilities; a chaplain was simply one who had been active in royal or episcopal service. In the reign of Stephen, when royal control of the church was weak, only one royal clerk was appointed compared with eight monks and ten ecclesiastical clerks. By contrast, his predecessor Henry I appointed more royal clerks to bishoprics than any other king in this period. Very few bishops bought their offices, so could not be accused of simony. Herbert Losinga, bishop of Norwich, was one notorious exception, but he subsequently repented. Another was Theulf, bishop of Worcester (1115–25), who made a deathbed confession of the sin.[26] As bishops were tenants-in-chief they incurred financial obligations when they took over their estates. Tough-minded reformers might regard this as simony, but it was not the same as buying office. This does not mean that the bench of bishops was untainted by worldliness. Many owed their position to nepotism. The Salisbury dynasty was outstanding in that respect but unique only in the extent of their family ambitions. M. Brett, a historian of the English church under Henry I, wrote of a group of men with a near-stranglehold on royal patronage, the group loosely described as chaplains, who gain bishoprics, the patronage of which they distribute to their relations, whom they also no doubt recommend to the king's service and favour.[27]

Bishops had a huge range of responsibilities and duties, secular, spiritual and pastoral. Many bishops held high secular office before their election. It was usual but not obligatory to surrender this. All bishops had obligations to the king akin to those of a secular tenant-in-chief, including the military obligation of providing quotas of knights equipped and trained to fight. They did not participate actively in battle like Odo of Bayeux at Hastings, but even Anselm, despite a previous dispute about the poor quality of the Canterbury knights, acted as military commander in the south while Rufus was dealing with a baronial revolt in Northumberland, a responsibility he accepted with equanimity.[28] Archbishop Thurstan of York, despite considerable ill health, played a prominent part leading the troops in the Scottish campaign, culminating in the Battle of the Standard.[29] Although not well enough to be present in person at the battle, his spiritual and moral leadership was very important for the victory.

Before the 1070s the bishop shared the presidency of the shire court. Like kings, bishops spent a great deal of time on horseback accompanied by a considerable entourage. They had to travel to all parts of the diocese, to visit their estates to ensure that they were efficiently managed and to defend their rights against depredations by laymen. These estates could well be in several other dioceses scattered around the country. As one of the greatest tenants-in-chief in the kingdom a bishop had secular responsibilities and commitments at least comparable to the most powerful lay tenants-in-chief, with estates concentrated in the diocese but in other parts of the kingdom as well. While the majority of the estates of Canterbury, for instance, were in Kent, nearly a third were outside the diocese and accounted for as much as a third of Middlesex. At the time of the Domesday Inquest the revenues of Canterbury were assessed at £1750.[30] As great landholders they had to maintain not just ecclesiastical buildings but also secular ones: castles, palaces and in Durham, a prison. Their responsibilities could take them far beyond their diocese. They had to attend councils, royal and ecclesiastical; they had to go to other dioceses to assist in consecrations; some had to visit Rome or other foreign cities to attend papal councils.

A bishop's spiritual and pastoral responsibilities went beyond those of a priest. He confirmed the baptised, gave blessings, absolved people from venial sins on Ash Wednesday and deadly sins on Maundy Thursday. He could be called upon to assist in the consecration of other bishops. He examined candidates for the priesthood and, if they were suitable, ordained them. Although we have few surviving sermons, the remarkable collection of 14 sermons of Bishop Herbert of Norwich is exceptional: he preached and instructed in the faith and supervised others who did so.[31] He held diocesan synods for the instruction of the clergy and settlement of disputes. He dedicated churches, altars and other fixtures and consecrated chrism and utensils and vessels, as well as the iron used in trial by ordeal. He administered spiritual justice and enforced discipline, imposing penances when appropriate and in extreme cases excommunicating. Conversely he could absolve people from their sins. He presided over courts on his estates; secular courts which dealt with earthly matters on the estates, and ecclesiastical courts which dealt with moral issues and offences of the laity and handled disputes over the property and rights of churches in the diocese. He was responsible for everything, unlike today, when the bishop is in charge of the diocese and the dean is in charge of the cathedral. As tenants-in-chief bishops were required to attend the king's court and crown-wearings, along with his lay tenants. They were frequent witnesses to royal charters. If contentious matters were under discussion they could find themselves in dispute with the laymen and even with fellow bishops. They did not always present a united front. As one of the king's most important and influential political as well as spiritual advisers it is hardly surprising that any archbishop with a shred of independent spirit was at times in disagreement with his king, but they sought to work together. The intensity of Henry II's conflict with Becket and their failure to achieve reconciliation was exceptional.

In order to live in a style appropriate to his office and to fulfil his responsibilities a bishop needed the support of many. Moreover, when a bishop or archbishop was absent from his diocese for a long period it was essential that the spiritual wellbeing of the inhabitants was not neglected and administration did not break down. Like the king and the greatest lay magnates the bishop had his own household, the men who lived in his hall and formed his domestic circle.[32] Among them were both clergy and laymen. We read of chamberlains and stewards, treasurers and chancellors. Bishops had their chaplains, some of whom were well connected and wealthy and used their position on their way to something grander, like the very important office of archdeacon.[33] Archdeacons were authoritarian figures charged with collecting money and imposing discipline, but there was little evidence of their being concerned with pastoral care. Trollope's Archdeacon Grantley had many antecedents.

Henry, son of Nicholas archdeacon of Huntingdon and himself archdeacon after his father, gave a brilliant description of the household of Robert Bloet, bishop of Lincoln from 1094 to 1123.[34] He writes of handsome knights, noble young men, costly horses, golden and gilded vessels, dinners of many courses, and the splendour of those who waited on him in their garments of purple and satin. Henry's story has a moral purpose, to show how insubstantial is worldly magnificence, and he tells how this great bishop, one of the most powerful men in the land, was reduced to relative poverty when he incurred the disfavour of the king.

A good and conscientious bishop like Robert of Bethune of Hereford was well aware of his spiritual and pastoral responsibilities. Pope Gregory the Great had written *Pastoral Care* as a guidebook for bishops. Gregory was a man of essential humility and he sought that humility in all who would minister to others. A good bishop was to be a teacher and director of souls, a man of meditation, self-searching and not puffed up. Bishops must devote themselves to preaching, teaching and admonition, but unless they had learnt to perfect their own characters they were not fit to direct others. Another vital source of guidance and instruction was Wulfstan's *Institutes of Polity*. Wulfstan was well qualified to write such a tract, as he was first bishop of London then archbishop of York and bishop of Worcester at the same time in the early part of the eleventh century. His theme was that the essential responsibility of a bishop was to play a leading and dignified part in establishing an ordered and peaceful community.

To be effective and to earn respect a bishop needed to be well educated. He had to be fluent in Latin and have a grasp of music and arithmetic. A thorough knowledge and understanding of doctrine and a more than basic competence in theology and canon law were desirable. Not all bishops met these standards and William of Malmesbury, essentially a kind and generous-spirited man, wrote scathingly of Edward the Confessor's English appointments. The period covered by this book is the period of the so-called 'Twelfth Century Renaissance' which saw the rise of schools that were not the exclusive preserve of monks and were open to the public. From the schools evolved the first great universities of Europe; canon law and theology became academic disciplines of immense stature providing opportunities for scholars to advance to positions of great importance and influence.

Oxford became a university town towards the end of the twelfth century but Paris was pre-eminent for the study of arts and theology, the goal of many ambitious men, regardless of their native land, even from as far afield as Denmark and Norway. The world of learning was truly cosmopolitan, for just as Englishmen studied and taught at Paris, foreigners taught at the nascent Oxford University. The universities emerged in response to social and economic developments in the twelfth and thirteenth centuries which saw considerable economic expansion accompanied by significant population growth, circumstances which also favoured the emergence of the friars. Towns grew richer and attracted increasing numbers of entrepreneurs and artisans. Money, commercial profit, capital and credit became increasingly important. A new urban aristocracy came into existence, like the London commune, whose favour was so important to the security of the monarchy. Beneath them were professional men, lawyers, physicians, craftsmen and shopkeepers. In this environment lay literacy spread. In a more sophisticated world commercially there were increasing numbers of transactions which required at least some formal literacy. The growth of towns and cities provided the accommodation to house large numbers of students. Cash flow and credit enabled students to change and borrow money. The twelfth century has been called the golden age of the schoolmaster, and for a brief period in the history of education teachers were highly paid celebrities.[35]

Increasing numbers of bishops came to be university graduates with the title Master. Many of Becket's ideas were drawn from the Paris masters and he built up a library of their works. However he was not a trained theologian, and although he may have spent a short time at Paris he was not a Paris master. The theology of his time was different from earlier in the century when the brilliant but highly controversial and overweeningly arrogant Peter Abelard was a dominant figure. He was excited by speculative thought and his use of logic to probe ideas about the nature of God, sin and redemption led him into conflict with the champions of orthodoxy like St Bernard. In the course of the twelfth century the study of theology became more about practical issues and doctrine; the nature of authority, for instance. The standing of Paris as a university was recognised by Pope Innocent III who became well known as a friend and champion. One of his contemporaries and friends at Paris was Stephen Langton, the Englishman from Lincolnshire, whom he imposed as archbishop of Canterbury on King John.

It is clear that in terms of character and their approach to their responsibilities the English bishops of this period represented 'all sorts and conditions of men'. There were certainly genuinely saintly bishops like Wulfstan II of Worcester and Hugh of Lincoln, pastoral and spiritual bishops like Thurstan and Gilbert Foliot, Becket's great adversary, and scholarly bishops like Lanfranc, Anselm, Robert of Hereford with special interests in the abacus, the moon and the stars, Gilbert the Universal of London, so called because it was believed he knew everything, Robert Pullen and Stephen Langton. In the latter part of his reign Henry I showed a respect for men of intellectual distinction and appreciated the value of bishops who were well versed in canon law.[36] There were grand princely bishops like Henry of Blois, the brother of King Stephen, and Hugh Puiset of Durham. Some were loyal but, in the eyes of their critics, unprincipled – such as royal ministers like Ranulf Flambard and William Warelwast; others were organisers, administrators and civil servants of whom the Salisbury family, William Longchamp and Hubert Walter, were outstanding. There were unashamedly warrior bishops, Leofgar, the Anglo-Saxon bishop of Hereford, for instance, who abandoned his chrism and cross and took up his spear and sword to fight the Welsh, and Odo of Bayeux, the Conqueror's brother, shown in the Bayeux Tapestry wielding a club rather than a sword. Some were well known for their affability, like Ralph d'Escures and Thurstan. And there were bishops with gross carnal appetites like Maurice of London, who justified his sexual promiscuity on medical grounds, and Thomas II of York, whose gluttony was his downfall. To categorise in this way is to oversimplify; bishops were complex men, fulfilling a variety of roles and demonstrating a range of virtues and vices. We shall be meeting many of them.

1

The Norman Conquest and the Church in England

William the Conqueror and the church

On 25 December 1066 William, Duke of Normandy, was crowned king of the English in Westminster Abbey. The service had some novel features. Music played a significant part in the coronation ceremony. From the time of Edgar the *Te Deum* had been sung, William the Conqueror introduced the liturgical acclamations known as the *Laudes Regiae*. They had been sung at the coronation of Charlemagne in 800 and during festivals in Normandy, but not in England before 1066. As another innovation imported from France and to become an integral part of the coronation service, Geoffrey, the Norman bishop of Coutances, speaking French, and Archbishop Aldred of York, speaking English, asked the assembled congregation whether they would accept the new king. Unfortunately the cries of acclamation were misunderstood by the guards outside the abbey. The atmosphere was tense and they misinterpreted the positive support for the king as sounds of a rebellion. They panicked and set fire to the surrounding buildings.

Despite that setback a Norman duke was now also a crowned and anointed English king. One man henceforth had authority over three metropolitan provinces, Canterbury, York and Rouen. As Duke of Normandy William saw himself as master of the Norman church; in England he had no doubt of the special rights and responsibilities conferred on him by consecration. William was no intellectual and he was not profoundly spiritual. He had no concept of theocratic kingship whereby the king was the embodiment of God on earth, but he was deeply concerned for the wellbeing of his soul. His God was a jealous God who must be propitiated. This propitiation was to be achieved partly by actions that today would be seen as highly superstitious and by enforcing his authority on the church through the control of appointments that would maintain order and discipline.

The Norman church

It is important to have some understanding of the church in Normandy at this time, for as a result of the Conquest the English church was much affected by Norman practices and personalities. Norman monasticism in the period before the Conquest was greatly influenced by Cluny, thanks to William of Volpiano or Dijon. He had joined Cluny Abbey when Maieul was abbot, and in 989 he was sent by him with a small group to reform St Benigne at Dijon. William was one of the outstanding figures of his age. He was a man of great spirituality; he had considerable intellectual gifts, being a musician, physician and geometrician with an interest in architecture and the arts, and he had administrative skills. He was also a great educator who founded a number of monastic schools which were not attended exclusively by oblates but open to all who wished to benefit, regardless of background or wealth.

In 1001 Duke Richard II had invited William to establish a new community at Fécamp. This he did while remaining abbot of Dijon. His influence was felt in nearly all the monasteries of Normandy, but this influence was not exclusively French or Cluniac, for from William's roots in Italy, like those later of Lanfranc and Anselm, came the stimulus to encourage an approach to education that was open and wide-ranging, extending far beyond the cloister. The relationship between the duke and the monasteries was positive and harmonious, and of the 28 or so monastic houses in the Normandy of Duke William, 21 owed a direct debt to William of Dijon.

This reflected Duke William's policy of collaboration with the Norman church generally, a collaboration based on the assumption that as protector and governor he was the man firmly in charge. The structure of the church in Normandy, derived from Roman administrative arrangements, was that there was one metropolitan bishop, the archbishop of Rouen, and six suffragans, Coutances, Bayeux, Avranches, Sées, Evreux and Lisieux. William controlled appointments to high office, favouring members of the ducal family when he had the opportunity. He invested bishops and endowed abbeys, expecting military service in return. He presided over church councils, at Lisieux in 1054, at Rouen in 1063 and at Lisieux again in 1064.

There was much about William's control of the church that would have been blatantly objectionable to the reformers. The appointment of bishops in his minority had left something to be desired. For instance, Archbishop Mauger, the son of Duke Richard II, was probably still a teenager when appointed. William's half-brother, Odo, was well below the canonical age when he became bishop of Bayeux in 1049–50. Little good has been said of Mauger, but that may be due to attempts to discredit him by William's propagandist William of Poitiers. He had never received the pallium and he was deposed at the first synod of Lisieux, under the presidency of the papal legate Ermenfrid, bishop of Sitten. This was apparently on account of his disreputable private life – an excessive enthusiasm for hunting and cockfights, inappropriate for a bishop – but he may also have incurred the displeasure of William for opposing his marriage. William of Poitiers's description of him as lazy, self-indulgent and disobedient to the papacy[1] may be unduly harsh, and fanciful was the supposition of the poet Wace that he had his own personal devil called Toret. Mauger had actually held a synod at Rouen early in his career which denounced simony before Leo IX was to do so at the Council of Rheims in 1049. But he was married, at a time when clerical celibacy was coming to be required, and he retired to Jersey with his wife and child, where he subsequently drowned in the Channel.

Far more highly regarded was Mauger's successor, Maurilius. As David Douglas wrote of him,[2] he had experienced the learning of Liège, the spiritual fervour of Vallombrosa and the Cluniac monasticism of William of Dijon. Unlike most Norman bishops he had no links at all with the Norman aristocracy. He was respected for his saintly character and was regarded as a supporter of the papal reform movement. At his council held at Lisieux in 1064 clerical celibacy was strongly affirmed. Other men of distinction in Normandy before the Conquest were John of Avranches and Hugh of Lisieux. The greatest of all Norman ecclesiastics, Lanfranc and Anselm, will be considered later.

The consequences of the Conquest

The principal changes brought about by the Conquest can be summarised as follows. It secured a breach with the English past. In the course of the reign almost all the sees and abbeys came to be controlled by Normans. The bishops and abbots became as fully part of the 'feudal' structure of England as were the great laymen. Spiritual and ecclesiastical jurisdiction were to be separated from that dealt with in secular courts. Following Anglo-Saxon precedent a number of sees were transferred to great towns. In 1050 Leofric had transferred Crediton to Exeter, in 1075 Herfast moved Elmham to Thetford and subsequently in 1091 it was moved to Norwich. In 1075 also, Remigius transferred Dorchester to Lincoln. In 1078 Selsey was transferred to Chichester and Sherborne, which had earlier absorbed Ramsbury, was transferred to Salisbury.

The relationship of Lichfield, Coventry and Chester needs special mention. Peter, bishop of Lichfield, in 1072 removed his see to Chester. In 1086 Robert moved the see to Coventry and 'bishop of Coventry' became the normal style after 1102. The Anglo-Saxon practice of running some cathedrals by monastic chapters rather than by secular clergy was extended. Canterbury, Winchester, Worcester, Sherborne, Norwich, Rochester and Durham were run by communities of regulars, monks or canons; York, Salisbury, London, Lincoln, Exeter, Hereford, Lichfield, Chichester and Wells were secular cathedrals. As in Normandy, church councils were held regularly with a view to implementing reform and enforcing discipline. Nine were held in England in William's reign from 1070, while provincial councils continued to meet in Normandy.

Post-Conquest bishops

William did not immediately embark on a purge of English bishops. In reality he needed the assistance of the leaders of the church to help him settle. Particularly valuable to him was the support of Bishop Wulfstan of Worcester and Aethelwig, abbot of Evesham. Although Stigand, archbishop of Canterbury, did not crown William, William did not isolate him. He took him with him on his triumphant return to Normandy, perhaps because he considered it safer not to leave him in England, and Stigand actually consecrated William's first appointment, Remigius of Dorchester. The death of Aldred on 11 September 1069 provided the opportunity for some reorganisation. Aldred had served William loyally for three years but was not afraid to stand up to him.[3] Both Aldred and Stigand enjoyed lifestyles fitting for the grandest of prince bishops, and while it would be wrong to condemn Stigand unreservedly, William could not be confident of his loyalty.

Both Aldred and Stigand represented a past age that was no longer acceptable to advocates of church reform, and in 1070 action was taken to purify the leadership of the English church. With William's approval, and perhaps at his request, Pope Alexander sent a legation from Rome headed by Ermenfrid of Sitten. All the abbots and bishops were summoned to Winchester for Easter 'to cut down those things which wax evilly in the vineyard of the lord of Sabaoth and plant those that will be beneficial to the health of both souls and bodies'. Seven bishops were untainted by impropriety: William of London, Herman of Sherborne, Giso of Wells, Walter of Hereford, Leofric of Exeter, Wulfstan of Worcester and Siward of Rochester. Remigius of Dorchester's consecration by Stigand made him vulnerable, but he had the firm support of the king. The legates were ordered to depose Stigand and all bishops who had been consecrated by him. Remigius was spared; Aegelric of Selsey had been consecrated by Stigand in 1058 but not immediately deposed. Leofwine of Lichfield had been a monk, was married and resigned to return to his old monastery. Stigand did not accept his deposition with good grace. According to William of Malmesbury he sulked in prison in Winchester, where he spent an unedifying two years, even going on hunger strike until persuaded to look after himself better by the Confessor's widow Edith.[4] Stenton cast some doubt on this story when he pointed out that according to *Domesday Book* Stigand continued to hold the wealthy manor of East Meon until his death.[5]

William I required loyal service from his bishops. While they were independent-minded, determined to maintain the interests and wellbeing of their dioceses and their authority in them, they were all royal appointments, a word usually disguised as election, and William was to be their unchallenged master. He looked for loyal men who would behave with propriety and were sympathetic towards reform, so preferably celibate. They were expected to show the administrative skills which those who had been royal clerks had demonstrated.

Most of his bishops could be described as respectable and efficient rather than as men of deep spirituality or outstanding pastoral gifts. There were exceptions. Osmund, bishop of Salisbury, was called saintly by William of Malmesbury and of pre-eminent purity. 'Even fickle fame would blush to tell lies about his goodness.'[6] He was also a scholar who attracted to Salisbury a group of canons equally adept in music and literature. Other distinguished scholars were Robert Losinga, appointed to Hereford,[7] and William of St Calais.[8] A few were less worthy holders of office. The former chancellor and able administrator Maurice, bishop of London, had grandiose ideas for the building of St Paul's Cathedral[9] and, far from celibate, he justified his sexual proclivities on the grounds that they were essential for his health. In taking that line he may have been reacting to the unfortunate fate of his predecessor Hugh d'Orival. Hugh suffered from a hideously disfiguring skin disease for which castration was recommended as the cure. It had no beneficial effect at all and the poor man had the double indignity of enduring his condition and suffering the shame of being a eunuch.[10]

There is some doubt, to say the least, about the worthiness of Herfast, bishop of Elmham. Curiously for one who was perhaps the first-ever chancellor, he was described by William of Malmesbury[11] as a man of little intelligence whose knowledge, in Lanfranc's eyes, was practically nil. Moreover a letter from Lanfranc to Herfast criticises him for making a coarse joke about a serious matter and making cheap and unworthy remarks about Lanfranc in public. Lanfranc then orders him to give up dicing (to mention nothing worse) and the world's amusements in which he was said to idle away the entire day. He was also told to banish completely from his society and household a monk called Hermann, whose life was notorious for its many faults.[12] Herfast was probably exceptional. However Robert of Limesey, who moved the see of Chester to Coventry, was censured by William of Malmesbury for his rapacity and negligence towards his monks, although the kindly chronicler also describes him as amusing and generous.[13]

Clearly William did not consider any of his diocesan bishops worthy of promotion to either of the metropolitan sees. Stigand was replaced with Lanfranc and Aldred with Thomas, a protégé of Bishop Odo and a canon of Bayeux. Bayeux, like Bec, produced some very distinguished alumni, including Thomas's nephew, who also became Archbishop of York; his brother Samson, who succeeded Wulfstan in the diocese of Worcester; the bishops of Durham, William of St Calais and Ranulf Flambard; Thurstan, a later archbishop of York; and his brother Arduen, who had a long pontificate at Evreux. Thomas himself was a scholar and musician of distinction and was positively eulogised by William of Malmesbury.[14]

In the course of his reign William made 16 appointments to 12 sees. No Englishman was promoted and only one English bishop, Wulfstan of Worcester, outlived him. The episcopal bench was dominated by royal clerks, significantly outnumbering the monastic bishops, who made up only about a third of the total. Most of William's promotions were Normans, but Walcher of Durham and Robert Losinga of Hereford were Lotharingian, and when Walcher was murdered in 1080[15] he was succeeded by William, abbot of St Calais in the diocese of Le Mans. In 1072, at the time of the council of Winchester, there were eight Normans, four Lotharingians, two Englishmen and the Italian Lanfranc. Six years later there were ten Normans, and when William died, eleven. By then only two Lotharingians remained and the one Englishman. Three of the bishops at this time had been consecrated in Edward's reign.

William was conscientious in his appointments. Some of his successors were inclined deliberately to leave sees vacant for an inordinate length of time so that they could enjoy the income due to the see. William was not guilty of this practice. He was blameless of the sin of simony, so commending him to the reformers who regarded that as the paramount abuse. But there was no question of his abandoning his right to invest bishops with ring and staff. Indeed this did not become an issue in England until Anselm's pontificate. It would have been inconceivable for William to contemplate surrendering investiture or receiving homage from his bishops, for they were as much part of that order which some historians have called 'feudal' as any lay tenant-in-chief. The Norman Conquest saw a wholesale transfer of landownership and among the beneficiaries were the great churchmen. *Domesday Book* showed that the royal family possessed about a fifth of the land, the church about a quarter and a dozen or so lay magnates another quarter. The conquered country was controlled by about 250 people, of whom perhaps forty were prelates. This great wealth was not intended to make bishops and abbots fat and to enable them to live in grandiose luxury. They received it on account of their office, not as a reward for personal service. While some bishops like Wulfstan of Worcester eschewed a grand or ostentatious lifestyle,[16] others believed it was appropriate to the dignity of their office. In any case episcopal income was not spent just on themselves. They had households to maintain and servants to support. There were buildings to be replaced, restored, extended, modernised and equipped and the fabric had continually to be kept in good order. A number of bishops undertook formidable building projects. No sooner was Lanfranc installed in Canterbury than he had to embark on building a new cathedral to replace the Anglo-Saxon one which had been badly damaged by fire in 1067. Perhaps the greatest of all the Norman ecclesiastical building works is Durham cathedral.

Bishops were also expected to found, build and endow various charitable institutions and spend on pastoral care and works of charity. In Canterbury, for instance, were the leper hospital of St Nicholas and the hospital of St John the Baptist, which provided a home, food and clothing for old and infirm men and women.

The Conquest did not turn bishops into great landlords, for they were that before 1066. The redistribution of lands after 1066 was often chaotic and disorderly. In the process estates long held by a see or an abbey might be lost. Perhaps the most famous instance of an attempt to maintain the rights and possessions of Canterbury was the meeting of the shire court of Kent on Penenden Heath. It was presided over by Geoffrey, bishop of Coutances. The plaintiff Lanfranc claimed that the defendant Odo, bishop of Bayeux and earl of Kent, had, along with other magnates, wrongfully taken possession of lands belonging to the archbishopric of Canterbury and other Kentish churches.[17] Recourse was made to Old

English law and the ancient and wise Aegelric, bishop of Chichester, was brought to the trial in a wagon to declare and expound the ancient practice of the laws. The court met for three whole days, so many and complex were the issues, and Lanfranc's claims were upheld.

Ownership of lands and estates brought with it not merely spiritual and pastoral obligations but obligations to the king as ultimate lord. It was incumbent upon a bishop to attend the king's great council, not just because of his spiritual importance, but because he was a leading tenant. He was also obliged to make his contribution to the military organisation of the country. Bishops had had military responsibilities before 1066. As early as the eighth century the Mercian kings and later the kings of Wessex imposed military responsibilities among other secular duties on their bishops, and no less than the thegns[18] they had to build fortresses and bridges. Bishops whose dioceses were near the sea had to equip a ship to guard the coast. We know of several Anglo-Saxon bishops who took part in military action with enthusiasm. After the Conquest they were required to maintain and contribute knights like any lay magnate. One of the most important pieces of evidence that we have for the introduction of knight service into England is a writ addressed to the abbot of Evesham in which he is ordered to attend the king with the five knights, fully equipped, that he owes in respect of his abbacy. Calculations made in the nineteenth century by the historian and antiquarian J.H. Round state that Canterbury, Winchester, Lincoln and Worcester were obliged to have ready for the king 60 knights fully prepared and equipped, while at the other extreme Chichester's obligation was only two. The total obligation of the bishops was 471½! How they fulfilled this obligation was up to them. They could have maintained the men in their own households had they wished. According to *Vita Wulfstani* Lanfranc actually advised the king that the households of great men should be strengthened with knights as a safeguard against Danish invasion.[19] But the prospect of housing, feeding and entertaining too many testosterone-charged and physically very fit young men was not entirely welcome and a considerable part of the obligation was passed to others in return for grants of land. As an example a document exists[20] which shows that Robert, bishop of Hereford, granted land to one Roger, son of Walter, at Holme Lacy in return for the service of two knights whenever the need arose. Some tenants-in-chief actually enfeoffed knights beyond the number owed to the king. Lanfranc created one hundred knights' fees to ensure that he retained formal control of land that might otherwise have been lost.

William and the papacy

When Pope Alexander II, supported by Hildebrand – the future great Pope Gregory VII – gave his support to William's invasion he was aware of William's attitude to the church in Normandy and his uncompromising mastery of it.

He saw William as a king who would be strong in his support of reform and severe in his wish to remove moral laxity from the church. At the same time he had the experience to appreciate that while William would have a strong sense of his duties and responsibilities towards the church he would be equally assertive of his royal rights.

This stance did not fit well with the vision of his successor Gregory VII. Yet there was no open breach between Gregory and William. The story of the tension between them can be read in their correspondence.[21] Gregory's first letter to William dated 4 April 1074 is cordial but it leaves William in little doubt as to what Gregory expected their respective roles to be. William is also reminded about the time-honoured duty of the king of the English to ensure that Peter's Pence, a tax paid to Rome since the reign of Offa in the eighth century, is collected and paid. Three years later Gregory wrote to William to say that he could not support his intercession on behalf of the deposed bishop of Dol. While recognising that William loved and approved justice and was quick to execute it he was nevertheless proposing to send the legate Hubert to England.

However, in the period between these two letters momentous events had taken place concerning papal/German politics. On 15 February 1076 Gregory excommunicated the German king, Henry IV and deposed him. Early the following year, on 25 January, Henry met Gregory at the Apennine castle of Canossa where he did penance and was subsequently absolved from excommunication.

Further letters written by Gregory to William throw light on their relationship. In a letter of 4 April 1078 written in response to the reported indisposition of John, archbishop of Rouen and his alleged inability to fulfil his episcopal functions, Gregory greeted William with affection, commending him for his moral probity and liberal foresight. The legate Hubert was to look into the matter. On 25 March 1079 he wrote to Lanfranc rebuking him for his failure to go to Rome but suggesting that he may have been prevented by a proud, wilful or insolent king. On 23 September 1079 Gregory wrote to Hubert on the matter of William's refusal to allow his bishops freedom of action to go to Rome. However, he made it clear that he did not wish to create a crisis with William and is concerned that another legate, Teuzo, has been too high-handed towards the king. In his letter of 24 April 1080 Gregory was moving towards his requirement that his supremacy over the secular kingdoms of the west should be recognised and his demand that William should pay him fealty. But he is careful not to blunder in and appeals to William's sense of gratitude for past favours. We have no letter from Gregory formally demanding fealty but there exists a letter to Gregory from William, dating possibly from some time in 1080, in which he agrees to the payment of Peter's Pence but categorically refuses to pay fealty. Despite the rebuff Gregory shows that he still holds William in high regard because he is active in enforcing the reforms so important to him and he subsequently writes to show his regard for William.

Gregory's temperate approach to William was clearly judicious in the light of developments in Europe. In March 1080 Henry IV and the German nobles and bishops reacted to a second excommunication and deposition of Henry by declaring Gregory deposed. Henry then elected his own anti-pope, 'Clement III', and the following year crossed the Alps and embarked upon a long siege of Rome. Gregory had no wish to make an enemy of William, just as he needed the military support of the Sicilian Norman, Robert Guiscard, but he also respected William for the genuine reformer that he was.

For Gregory personally his pontificate ended in failure. On Palm Sunday 1084 Clement III was enthroned in St Peter's, and when in return he crowned King Henry IV Emperor on Easter Sunday, Gregory was in the secure retreat of Castel Sant'Angelo. Two months later Robert Guiscard's Normans rescued Gregory and sacked Rome. Political adroitness was not one of Gregory's skills and in his 12-year pontificate he had alienated potential supporters who shared his vision of a reformed church. Lanfranc was one whose relationship with Gregory became increasingly cool. The pope had aggravated civil war in Germany to the detriment of German churches. He failed to defeat Henry, destroyed the chance of co-operation between empire and papacy and left Western Christendom in schism. He died in exile in Salerno on 25 May 1085 apparently uttering the celebrated words: 'I have loved righteousness and hated iniquity – therefore I die in exile.'

Beyond stating that by making his impact felt throughout the European kingdoms in a way achieved by none of his predecessors, so laying the foundation for the concept of a papal monarchy, our concern here is not to examine the effectiveness of Gregory's pontificate but to consider how far William I's policy towards the church was determined by Gregory's claims. As Duke of Normandy William had insisted that he was the master of the church and that the initiative towards any reform came from him. This policy he adhered to as king of England. He could not tolerate any form of papal interference without his sanction. But he was no Henry VIII. He had no vision of an English church independent of the papacy. He fully recognised that the church in England was inseparable from the rest of Western Christendom and he held the papal office in great regard. Although he controlled the appointment of bishops and abbots he did not challenge the papal view that his archbishops should go to Rome to receive their pallia from the pope and that they should make their professions of faith to him. He recognised that disputes over spiritual and ecclesiastical matters that could not be settled locally should be referred to Rome. He looked to papal authority to sanction the changes he wished to achieve in the structure of the English church. But there was no way that he would surrender the initiative.

Eadmer tells us[22] that all things, spiritual and temporal alike, waited upon the nod of the king. No one was to be recognised as pope without his approval. No letter from the pope was to be received by anyone in England unless it had first been submitted to him. No ecclesiastical council was to issue an ordinance or prohibition without his prior sanction. No bishop was to excommunicate anyone or impose any other ecclesiastical penalty without his approval. Bishops were not to go to Rome without his permission. Papal legates would be admitted to England only if he allowed it. William's relationship with his bishops is to be considered in this light.

At the same time it must be remembered that Eadmer was perhaps oversimplifying the situation. Two dates in the 1040s were of great significance in determining the nature of William's mastery of Normandy and subsequently England. His victory at Val-ès-Dunes, with the support of his overlord King Henry I, over Count Guy of Brionne in 1047 established him as unchallenged lord of Normandy. In 1049 the Council of Rheims transformed the nature of the relationship of the papacy with the secular rulers of Western Christendom. From the mid-1040s the papacy, with imperial support, began effectively to assert its independence of the Italian aristocracy. The real drive for reform came from Leo IX (1049–54). He held perhaps as many as twelve synods which reasserted the authority of canon law, attacked simony and clerical marriage and stressed the importance of the election of bishops according to correct canonical procedures. The Council of Rheims was of particular importance for Normandy and England. It was many years since a pope had crossed the Alps. It came as a considerable shock not just to the French clergy but to laymen as well to feel the impact of a pope who was determined to impose moral reform upon their lives. The legality of William's proposed marriage to Matilda of Flanders was discussed and actually condemned, and although despite this the two were subsequently married, after the Council of Rheims William had to recognise that papal authority had become 'a powerful and intrusive presence which needed to be handled carefully in a way which had not previously been necessary'.[23]

Lanfranc

The deposition of Stigand gave William the opportunity to fill the vacant metropolitan see with a man of his choice. With the appointment of Lanfranc a partnership was formed of king and archbishop of a quality unknown since Dunstan and Edgar and probably not matched subsequently. In some respects it was a surprising appointment. Lanfranc did not covet high office and he had already rejected the offer of Rouen. He was elderly, around 60, and was happy as a monk, abbot of St Stephen's Caen. Odo of Bayeux may well have had his eyes on the post. A man of no mean ambition, the see of Canterbury would have sat well on his shoulders alongside the earldom of Kent. But he would have been quite unacceptable to Pope Alexander, who may have commended Lanfranc to William. Indeed Lanfranc himself wrote that he had been appointed on Alexander's insistence. Daunted as Lanfranc was by his ignorance of the barbarous English and their language, he pleaded failing strength and unworthiness, but saw he had no alternative but to accept the office.

Lanfranc arrived in England in the summer of 1070 and was invested as archbishop by King William on 15 August. On 29 August he was consecrated in Canterbury cathedral by William of London, Walchelin of Winchester, Remigius of Dorchester, Siward of Rochester, Herfast of Elmham, Stigand of Selsey, Herman of Sherborne and Giso of Wells. The absent bishops, Leofric of Exeter, Walter of Hereford and Wulfstan of Worcester, made their apologies. The following year, in October, Lanfranc went to Rome with Thomas of York to receive their pallia, accompanied by Remigius of Dorchester. Such was Alexander's regard for Lanfranc that he received him honourably and gave him two pallia, one which had been placed upon the altar of St Peter's as was the custom, the other which he used to celebrate mass. Although urged to do so on a number of occasions by Gregory VII, Lanfranc never visited Rome again.

Lanfranc has been well served by modern historians. His surviving letters are available in translation, as are his *Monastic Constitutions*. Today we might find much about Lanfranc's character that was harsh and severe. He was a firm advocate of moral reform and was keen to recommend corporal punishment for errant monks. The monastic community of St Augustine's Canterbury had come to be at odds with the cathedral community of Christ Church. One Columbanus led a rebellion when St Augustine's objected to the imposition on them of a monk from Christ Church. He was ordered by Lanfranc to be tied naked in front of the great door of St Augustine's, flogged in view of all the people, subjected to having his hair shaved and driven from the city.[24] However to those of his monks who acted properly he showed kindness, if not closeness, and his monks looked to him with affection. His handling of the monk Egelward[25] shows his sensitivity in a critical situation and casts a favourable light on his relationship with his prior Henry. Henry, from Bec, was a man who could be difficult but was what was needed at Christ Church at the time. Lanfranc's diocesan and national responsibilities were so considerable that the day-to-day running of the monastery was in the hands of the prior. Lanfranc found himself abbot of a far from settled and orderly community which needed to be sorted out. Henry was no intellectual but an administrator and disciplinarian. He did such effective work at Bec that William appointed him abbot of his new foundation at Battle. While in England Lanfranc continued to recognise the importance of monks from Bec and other parts of Normandy. With the support of Anselm he encouraged a number from Bec to visit England, some for a short while, others permanently, and he was also prepared to send English monks to Bec if he felt that they would benefit from some time with Anselm.

Lanfranc's attitude to English saints may have provoked ill feeling and has been seen as evidence of his insensitivity to English traditions. The long-held view that Lanfranc and other Normans were hostile to English saints has been challenged by H.E.J. Cowdrey. It is true that some of the relics of English saints were put to the test of ordeal, and it is also true that Lanfranc questioned the sanctity of one of his predecessors, the murdered Aelfheah, who had been canonised by local acclamation alone. Nothing is known about the location of the body of St Dunstan after the rebuilding of the fire-damaged cathedral. The point is made by Cowdrey that none of this shows hostility to the English past, rather that in the period of uncertainty after the Conquest Lanfranc wanted to establish incontestable proof not to discredit those who were held dear, but to accredit them.

However it is inevitable that at a time of such major upheaval, tension and stress the best intentions could be misinterpreted.

For many years there had been a feeling of mutual respect and co-operation between Lanfranc and William. The story of their early rift is well known.[26] A jest by Lanfranc soon healed the breach. This incident is associated with the church's criticism of William's marriage to Matilda of Flanders on the grounds of consanguinity but it should be put in its political context. At the time of Lanfranc's arrival at Bec his immediate secular lord was Guy of Burgundy. Circumstances were changed after William's victory at Val-es-Dunes when he ravaged some of Bec's lands and demanded that Lanfranc should leave Normandy. After the reconciliation Lanfranc won the trust of William who sought his advice on ecclesiastical matters. In 1056 Lanfranc assisted Maurilius, archbishop of Rouen, when he visited St Évroult. In 1063 William appointed him abbot of St Stephen's Caen. Four years later he resisted pressure on him to succeed Maurilius as archbishop. Such resistance was of no avail in 1070.

In some of his letters Lanfranc made clear his view of kingship. In about 1074 he wrote to the king of Munster on the matter of uncanonical divorce. Before getting down to the specific issue he wrote: 'God grants the earth no greater mercy than when he promotes to the rule of souls or bodies men who love peace and justice, above all when he commits the kingdoms of this world to the rule of good kings. Then peace dawns, discord is hushed and the practice of Christianity is firmly established.'[27] In William he found such a king. Even so he was in no doubt about the special nature of the priesthood and its superiority to the laity. In the 1050s he had been involved in an intellectual confrontation with Berengar of Tours about the Eucharist and whether the bread and wine actually became Christ's body and blood. He stressed that only through the special agency of a consecrating priest could that happen.[28] While he had not challenged William's right to invest him with ring and staff and to receive his homage he had no doubt that William was his spiritual son. As Eadmer relates, he was prepared to admonish William on spiritual matters and William was prepared to accept his admonitions.[29] He showed his regard for Lanfranc at a personal level by entrusting his son William to his care in his household and by asking him to invest both William and Henry as knights.[30]

Judging by the infrequency of his name on witness lists, Lanfranc's closeness to William was not that of a bishop working regularly at the king's court. He had no official office. Although as archbishop and a major tenant-in-chief he must have been present at the famous Christmas council of 1085, he was not a Domesday commissioner and his part in the survey did not extend beyond submitting his returns for Christ Church. He was certainly not a chancellor, an office that in any case was often regarded as a stepping stone to the bench of bishops, nor could he be regarded as an early justiciar. The statement in the *Vita Lanfranci* that when William was staying in Normandy he was chief and guardian of England is something of an exaggeration. If anyone anticipated the role of justiciar it was Odo of Bayeux or Geoffrey of Coutances rather than Lanfranc.

Lanfranc did play a prominent part in 1075 when William was in Normandy, where he had been since 1073. In 1075 the daughter of William fitz Osbern was given in marriage to Earl Ralph of East Anglia. Ralph was a Breton on his father's side, and according to William of Malmesbury of a disposition foreign to everything good. At the wedding feast a brother of the bride, Roger earl of Hereford, conspired with Ralph and Waltheof the earl of Huntingdon to overthrow the king.[31] This was a manifest act of folly for which there was no clearly obvious reason. Lanfranc felt that he had a special responsibility to Roger as his father was a patron of Bec. He therefore wrote a series of letters of advice to him once he was aware of what was afoot. The letters are warm, affectionate even, expressing concern and distress at the folly of a younger man whom he tries, unsuccessfully, to divert from his misguided actions. When the rebellion failed Lanfranc counselled him about the course of action he should take with the king. Lanfranc also wrote to William to assure him that he was quite capable of handling the situation without royal intervention. 'We would welcome seeing you as we would God's angel, yet we do not want you to cross the sea at this moment; for you would be offering us a grave insult were you to come to our assistance in subduing such perjured brigands.' Lanfranc's confidence was justified. The rebellion, which he saw as a Breton conspiracy, was put down, and he wrote: 'Glory be to God on high, [by whose] mercy your kingdom has been purged of its Breton dung.' When William returned to England and held his Christmas court at Westminster he judged Ralph and Roger according to Norman law and Waltheof according to English. Ralph was condemned to perpetual disinheritance and Roger to disinheritance and imprisonment. The Breton prisoners were banished or mutilated despite the fact that Lanfranc, perhaps in response to a recent agreement that churchmen should not be parties to capital punishment or mutilation, had previously spared them. Waltheof was the least culpable, indeed according to 'Florence' of Worcester Lanfranc judged him to be innocent, but William was merciless and Waltheof was beheaded on 31 May 1076.[32]

The attitude of Lanfranc and William to church reform may be seen from the decrees of the councils presided over by Lanfranc, but only with the approval of the king. As Margaret Gibson wrote: 'Lanfranc's control of the English Church can never quite be detached from the King's control of England as a whole.'[33] The ecclesiastical councils were held at the same time as the royal courts held by William when he was in England at Christmas, Easter and Whitsun. The two assemblies were not actually merged, but the bishops and abbots who were present at the Magnum Concilium as tenants-in-chief would also attend their own council. Business could be initiated in the royal court and confirmed in the church council. Lanfranc himself complained that the custom of holding councils had been in abeyance in England for many years. Two had been held in 1070 but that was before his installation. He built on them by holding seven councils, in1072 at Easter in the castle chapel at Winchester and the following Whitsun at Windsor; in1075 at St Paul's; 1076 at Winchester; 1077–78 in London; New Year 1081 at Gloucester and 1085–86 at Gloucester. The evidence for what was decided at these councils is limited. The *Acta Lanfranci* record that councils were held and make brief and limited references to what happened.[34] There is the evidence of the canons that were decreed or believed to be decreed and there are a few references in the chronicles. There is a detailed account of the London Council of 1075 in Lanfranc's letters. It was held in the company of Thomas, archbishop of York and the bishops of Winchester, Sherborne, Worcester, Hereford, Wells, Dorchester/Lincoln, Elmham/Norwich, Selsey, Exeter and Lichfield. Geoffrey, bishop of Coutances, was also present in his capacity as a great magnate in England. The delicate matter of who should sit next to whom was settled on the advice of some elderly men. They declared to a man that the archbishop of York should sit on the right of Canterbury, London on his left and Winchester next to York. In the absence of York the right-hand seat should go to London and Winchester should sit on the left.

Some reminders about correct procedure in monasteries followed, particularly with reference to the ban on property. In accord with early decrees that episcopal sees should be held not in villages or small towns but in cities, Sherborne was moved to Salisbury, Selsey to Chichester and Lichfield to Chester. The sin of simony was roundly condemned. Acts that might be considered as relating to witchcraft or magic were banned. So bones of dead animals were not to be hung up to ward off cattle disease and casting lots, telling fortunes and prophesying the future were utterly forbidden. No one in holy orders was to be in any way involved with a sentence of death or mutilation.

In his younger days Lanfranc had been close to Pope Leo IX. Possibly he was present at the Council of Rheims in 1049. Certainly Lanfranc was with Leo in late 1049 and early 1050. He therefore had the opportunity to see Leo at work, to get to know him personally and to become acquainted with the leading reformers like Humbert, Hugh Candidus and Hildebrand. Consequently he became aware of and sympathised with their principles and objectives. These experiences clearly influenced his views as archbishop. The condemnation of simony in 1075 has been mentioned. The other major issue was that of clerical celibacy. This was a sensitive matter indeed, as many clergy were married. John, archbishop of Rouen, had actually been stoned by the canons of Rouen when he ordered them to give up married life. The council of Winchester in 1076 issued decrees on the matter. Lanfranc was realistic and prepared to make concessions. It was determined that canons and higher clergy must put aside their wives and that in future no priest could be ordained without a declaration of celibacy. Parish priests who were already married could keep their wives. Not all bishops were as flexible as Lanfranc, Bishop Wulfstan for one. As his biographer wrote: 'The sin of incontinence he abhorred, and approved continence in all men, and especially in clerks in holy orders. Wedded priests he brought under one edict, commanding them to renounce their fleshly desires or their churches.'[35]

Lanfranc's loyalty to William persisted throughout the troubled later years of his reign. Difficulties on the Continent took William increasingly away from England. Philip, king of France, welcomed events that made life difficult for William who had problems in Brittany and with Anjou. In 1078 his son Robert turned against him and remained disaffected to the end of his father's life, much to the satisfaction of Philip. In 1085 the king of Denmark planned to invade England with the support of the count of Flanders. In autumn 1086 William crossed to Normandy for what turned out to be the last time. He campaigned vigorously against Philip and sacked Mantes, only 30 miles from Paris. But in the course of the operation William's horse stumbled on some burning cinders, William was thrown onto the pommel of the saddle and suffered internal injuries from which he died. The unsatisfactory Robert had been designated William's successor in Normandy and his middle son, William Rufus, was to become king of England. There was plenty of opportunity for trouble. Those who held lands in England and Normandy now had two masters. Odo of Bayeux had been imprisoned by William in 1082 and with great reluctance William was persuaded on his deathbed to release him but warned that a free Odo could be a focus of trouble. William had informed Lanfranc that Rufus was to be his heir and Lanfranc, loyal to William's wishes and in the interests of good order, gave Rufus his firm backing. It did not take long for peace to be disrupted, but that is a story for later.

Gundulf of Rochester

Loyal to Lanfranc and his three successive kings was Gundulf, bishop of Rochester. Since the consecration of its first bishop, Justus, in 604, Rochester had had a special relationship with Canterbury. After the Conquest the bishop was not only the archbishop's suffragan, but he was also his feudal tenant. The last Anglo-Saxon bishop, Siward, had passed on a dismal inheritance to his successors. According to William of Malmesbury[36] he left the church poor and empty, lacking everything inside and out. There were barely four canons. They eked out an existence, wearing the cheapest clothes and living poorly from hand to mouth. Lanfranc's first appointment was a monk from Bec, Arnost, but he did not live long enough to achieve anything, dying shortly after his consecration. Lanfranc appointed as his successor Gundulf, then a monk at Christ Church. Like Lanfranc and Anselm his origins were probably Italian, and it is possible that he may have been in some way related to Anselm, whose father was also called Gundulf. He had been a monk at Bec in the 1050s and became sacrist. When Lanfranc moved to Caen Gundulf went with him to be his prior at St Stephen's. He followed Lanfranc to Christ Church where he gave Lanfranc much-needed support in his difficult early years. Their friendship persisted after he became bishop. Arnost and he were the only bishops not to be invested with ring and staff by William I but William approved of Gundulf's appointment. Indeed he must have known him and his qualities when Gundulf was prior of William's foundation at Caen. Lanfranc repaid Gundulf's loyalty with generosity. He spoke for Rochester as well as Canterbury at Penenden Heath and gave to the recovering cathedral of

St Andrew twenty-five copes, two gilt candelabra and a silver shrine for the relics of Paulinus of York.

Loyn wrote of Gundulf: 'He was the archetypal useful man of his age, his saintly qualities matched by practical sense and business acumen.'[37] Early in the twelfth century the *Vita Gundulfi* was written which shows he combined the asceticism and sensitivity of a monk – he was easily moved to tears – with the ability and experience to be a practical and effective man of the world. As a spiritual leader he preached eloquently to his flock, although it is doubtful whether many could understand him, for his command of English was limited. But so moved were they by his tendency to burst into tears when preaching on the theme of Mary Magdalen that they wept and wailed in harmony with his sobs.

He was committed to the monastic life. There were at most five monks at Rochester when he arrived, but William of Malmesbury says that under him the monks grew to more than fifty: 'They were lovers of the rule and had abundance of all essentials.'[38] He ensured that there were sufficient resources to support a community of that size. He was among the first to establish the practice of separating the monks' property from his own. He gave the monks one of his own manors near the cathedral in return for one of theirs in distant Cambridgeshire to save them travelling a great distance to obtain their corn. The *Vita* tells of his business acumen in acquiring an estate in Gloucestershire. He also set up the eleventh-century equivalent of 'Friends of Rochester Cathedral'; to boost the monastery's income he established a confraternity at Rochester, probably based on Cluniac practices. Wealthy laymen and women were invited to make substantial gifts to the monastery in return for becoming members of the confraternity. Their names were written in a 'Book of Life' which was placed on the high altar during the celebration of mass. The benefactors' names might be read out individually or, if there were too many of them, they could be remembered collectively. Some of the members actually adopted the monastic habit when death was near.

Gundulf was a remarkable builder. Soon after becoming bishop he set about rebuilding the cathedral. He also built a convent at Malling and a church dedicated to the Virgin Mary. His work clearly impressed William, who engaged him to supervise the building of the White Tower. His experience in castle building was used again when Rufus had him replace the wooden castle at Rochester with one of stone, at the bishop's expense.

William I and Henry I valued him as a diplomat and adviser and we learn from the *Vita* that he was called upon whenever there were dedications of importance to be performed or holy relics were to be translated. In the absence of an archbishop of Canterbury in 1092 he was present at the ceremony of translation of the body of St Augustine and two years later at the dedication of Battle Abbey. Judged to be the most suitable bishop to take part in the rite, he was present in 1102 when Edward the Confessor's grave was opened. Gundulf released the head and beard from the covering pall and was about to pull a hair from the beard when he was reprimanded by Abbot Gilbert Crispin of Westminster.

Remigius of Lincoln

William the Conqueror's first episcopal appointment was that of Remigius to Lincoln.[39] He had been a monk at Fécamp where he was possibly the almoner. He may have been distantly related to William, perhaps from a casual relationship enjoyed by one of William's predecessors. Henry of Huntingdon, who describes him as short of stature but great in heart; dark in complexion but fair in deeds,[40] said that he was actually present at the Battle of Hastings.[41] The following year he was appointed to the bishopric of Dorchester and consecrated by Stigand, to whom he made a profession of obedience. He was present at Queen Matilda's coronation in 1068. However in 1070 the papal legates who deposed Stigand suspended him from office and in the following year he went with his two metropolitans to Rome to defend himself against a charge of simony. According to William of Malmesbury[42] he gave much help to William in the invasion of England, having bargained with him for a bishopric if he was successful. William was no slower to grant him the bishopric of Dorchester than he was to accept it. According to Eadmer, he had in effect bought his bishopric by the service which he rendered William by the outlay of much effort and lavish expenditure on his behalf when he was setting out to subdue England.[43] He may have contributed 20 knights and a ship, an action which ruled him out canonically from episcopal office. Only the personal intervention of Lanfranc saved him from deposition on the grounds that he and Thomas of York, also threatened with deposition on the grounds that he was disqualified by the circumstances of his birth, were very necessary to the new king in making the new dispositions of his kingdom. In this Remigius had the support of the Anglo-Norman élite. Even so he continued to feel insecure and felt it necessary to write to Gregory VII in December 1073 to seek his advice.

The diocese of Dorchester was huge, an amalgamation of the earlier bishoprics of Dorchester, Leicester and Lindsey. It was far larger than any diocese that the Normans would have been familiar with and it is not surprising that the new Norman incumbent should wish to transfer his see from the far south.[44] A writ of the king from about 1072 gave notice of the see's transfer to Lincoln, one of the largest towns in England and a centre of trade. Even so the establishment of the diocesan see in the northern part required astute estate management and skilled defence of its claims to property in disputes with the great abbeys and powerful lay landholders. To assist him Remigius encouraged sympathetic laymen into the diocese. Nevertheless the move created an upheaval and it seems that in the time of Remigius the well-established estates in Oxfordshire financed the whole diocese more successfully than the bishopric's new estates in Lincolnshire, Nottinghamshire and Northamptonshire. The bishopric had a 90-hide manor in Dorchester, one of 60 in Thame, 50 in Banbury and 50 in Cropredy. *Domesday Book* shows that these estates rose considerably in value between 1066 and 1086. Inevitably, as a great landholder, the bishop of Lincoln had military obligations to the king. He had a *servitium debitum* of 60 knights plus an obligation to provide 45 knights for the guard at Lincoln castle.

There is no doubt that Remigius remained a firm royal favourite who attested royal charters. Having arrived in England he did not return to Normandy, looking forward rather than back. His interests came to be English and he saw England as the place where he lived and worked. He was with William every time he visited England after 1075–76, except for William's brief visit in 1082–83 when he came to deal with brother Odo. He was a Domesday commissioner with responsibility for the counties of Gloucestershire, Worcestershire, Herefordshire, Shropshire, Staffordshire and Cheshire. He was not a landholder in those counties and he seems to have been charged with checking the findings originally returned.

The see of Lincoln was drawn into the great primacy dispute (see later). Thomas of York claimed that Dorchester, Lichfield and Worcester belonged to his province rather than to Canterbury. Alexander II, feeling that he was not in a position to judge, referred the matter to William's court. At Easter 1072, in the presence of the legate Hubert and all the interested parties, it was decided that the three dioceses should remain within the Canterbury province, a judgement that Remigius was determined to uphold. He also resisted attempts by York to transfer Lindsey to that diocese, understandably so since Lincoln Cathedral was situated in Lindsey. This new foundation was run by a secular chapter,[45] and both Henry of Huntingdon and William of Malmesbury[47] were impressed by the quality of Remigius's appointments, all of whom seem to have come from Normandy and other parts of France.

As David Bates has shown, William's debt to Remigius was considerable, and as Bates wrote: 'given Remigius' enormous diocese, it surely cannot be wrong to elevate him to the level of one of the most important makers of the Norman Conquest of England'.[46]

Wulfstan of Worcester

Wulfstan of Worcester was consecrated bishop in the reign of Edward the Confessor and was the only English bishop to outlive William the Conqueror. In considering Wulfstan we look less to his saintly attributes and his pastoral concerns than the part he played in helping to ensure that the Norman settlement went as smoothly as possible. He recognised that the Norman victory at Hastings meant the end of the old order, Norman rule had arrived to stay and it was in the interests of all to work to achieve a new order as painlessly as possible. He had become bishop of Worcester in 1062 and remained in office until his death in 1095. As H.R. Loyn wrote: 'Throughout the reign of William I, and well into that of William II, Wulfstan stood out as one toiling to keep the peace, and so supporting the legitimacy of the new Norman ruler.'[47] The quality of the relationship of Wulfstan and William is apparent from a court case held in Somerset in 1070 or 1071. Wulfstan was the plaintiff, the defendant Thomas archbishop of York. For many years the diocese of Worcester had been subordinate to York, partly because York badly needed another diocese buttressed to it, and Worcester and York were often held by the same man. Aldred was forbidden to continue the practice but even so tried to keep a hold on some of the estates claimed by Worcester. Wulfstan sought the recovery of 12 villages which Aldred had retained after his promotion from Worcester to York.[48] It is significant that the Norman William found in favour of the English Wulfstan against the Norman Thomas.

Wulfstan also found himself having to defend his interests in conflicts with the abbey of Evesham. In doing so we have the situation whereby an English bishop appeals to a Norman king to be allowed to hold a lawsuit according to English procedures in the presence of Norman judges. The abbot of Evesham, Aethelwig, was another English prelate who co-operated closely with the Normans and in whom William placed considerable trust. William made him governor of the counties of Worcestershire, Gloucestershire, Oxfordshire, Warwickshire, Herefordshire, Staffordshire and Shropshire. He was held in great regard by all who knew him both for his work in secular affairs and as a fine Christian pastor. Nevertheless there was tension between the diocese, sometimes in association with the abbeys of Worcester and Evesham. This came to a head in a great lawsuit between the bishop of Worcester and the abbot of Evesham. Wulfstan claimed that one of the Worcester estates, Bengeworth, had been held from him by a tenant Aerngrim. However, without his knowledge or approval Aerngrim had commended himself to Aethelwig, who had invested Aerngrim with the land as if the bishop had no rights to it. Wulfstan was anxious to obtain a royal writ to set an enquiry in motion. He even gave the king a valuable silver chalice to obtain the writ. This was not bribery. The gift was not to obtain a judgement in his favour but to secure a form of procedure that was normally used by the king for his own purposes. The process was in its infancy and at this stage there were no fees established.

Wulfstan received his writ from the king. It was directed from Normandy to Geoffrey of Coutances, Urse d'Abitot – the sheriff who had been cursed by Archbishop Aldred and not immune from rebuke by Wulfstan, and a tenant-in-chief, Osbern fitz Scrob. Before the case was considered Aethelwig died, so it was his successor, Walter, who was the defendant. Wulfstan claimed that he had witnesses who would swear to the situation as it was before the Conquest. The abbot could produce no witnesses so he was granted the right to swear to the truth of his claim on the abbey's relics. A trial followed. Walter appeared with his relics; Wulfstan did so with his witnesses. Confronted by powerful opposition, the abbot accepted that it would be prudent to yield. He recognised Wulfstan's claim and received Bedgeworth as a tenancy from him in return for service.

Wulfstan accepted the necessity of change even at the expense of his beloved Anglo-Saxon church of St Oswald. Reluctantly he recognised that the small Anglo-Saxon church needed to be replaced by a bigger building in the Norman style. Although reduced to tears by the change and despite his insistence that only proud men could consider the new bigger church to be better, he went along with the development.[49] Wulfstan was prepared to become involved in secular matters when loyalty to William required. When William was in England

Wulfstan fulfilled his obligation of attending the meetings of the Great Council held at Christmas, Easter and Whitsun. He owed the service of 60 knights. In the course of the rebellion of 1075 he joined forces with Aethelwig abbot of Evesham, the sheriff of Worcester Urse and Walter de Lassy, a local baron, isolating Roger of Hereford behind the Severn. As we shall see, he also became involved in military activity in support of William Rufus.

Like Aethelwig, Wulfstan was able to combine sanctity with involvement in affairs of the world. He was an ascetic and disciplinarian, but except in the matter of chastity he did not require others to abide by all the standards that he imposed upon himself. He wished for order and peace and recognised that there was nothing to be achieved by resistance to the Norman conquerors. He combined this with a belief in the authority of the crowned and anointed king. He had gone to the support of Harold when he was faced with hostility in the north, just as he had subsequently supported William I and Rufus when they were faced with rebellion.

Lanfranc and William Rufus

When William died in 1087 Wulfstan was the last surviving English bishop. The church in England in 1087 was very different from that which he had known in his younger days. The basic institutions of diocese and parish were well established in 1066, but the English sees had lost their rusticity and become urbanised. William and Lanfranc, in a harmonious partnership probably never to be matched again, had brought the English church into line with the reformed Roman church while resisting the more extreme demands of the papacy. With three surviving sons in possible contention for the English throne William was well aware that his death could lead to a crisis, and he had prepared for the eventuality by enjoining Lanfranc to give his support to his middle son Rufus. Eadmer told of Lanfranc's great distress at William's death and went on to say that Rufus would have had no chance of becoming king without Lanfranc's support. William I died on 9 September and Rufus was crowned King William II on 26 September. William was well aware of his considerable debt to Lanfranc and made him all kind of promises. When Lanfranc chided him for breaking them he retorted, 'Who is there who can fulfil everything that he promises?'[50] It was not long before William was faced with a crisis and the support of Lanfranc and that of Gundulf of Rochester and Wulfstan of Worcester was vital in helping him to surmount it.

The Conqueror had not been mistaken when he had foreseen that his release of Odo of Bayeux from prison would cause trouble. Within a few months of Rufus's coronation his leading vassals, doubtless led by Odo, were preparing to transfer their allegiance to his brother Robert, duke of Normandy. The main supporters of Odo were his brother Robert of Mortain, Roger of Montgomery the earl of Shrewsbury, and Geoffrey bishop of Coutances. There was specific animosity between Odo and Lanfranc, for Lanfranc's position in Kent threatened Odo as earl. Moreover Odo suspected that Lanfranc had been instrumental in having him imprisoned in 1082.[51] The details of the rebellion need not concern us. Readily available contemporary accounts can be read in *The Anglo-Saxon Chronicle* for 1088 and William of Malmesbury. Frank Barlow discusses it at length.[52] The rebellion ultimately failed for several reasons. First, it was not a united Norman rebellion but that of a few disaffected magnates who had personal motives and who thought they might gain more if England and Normandy were united under the potentially ineffective rule of Robert. But Robert did not show enough interest in the rebellion to take part himself or provide much support. William acquitted himself well and rallied the loyalty of a considerable number of native English who had no reason to identify themselves with the rebels. Fearful of being dismissed contemptuously as 'nithing' and lured by William's promises, they rallied to his cause.

William was also well supported by the church. Of the bishops only William of Durham proved unreliable. Wulfstan of Worcester, showing the same reverence for anointed kingship as he had shown Harold, defended Worcester like a second Moses rebuking the children of Israel. He himself took command of the royal castle while a field army consisting of the garrison, the bishop's household troops and local folk crossed the bridge over the Severn and advanced to meet the enemy. Inspired by the presence and thought of Wulfstan they made a surprise attack on those intent on destroying the bishop's estates, drove them off, killed 500 infantrymen and took captive some knights.[53] Rufus was thus able to concentrate on the south-east. Odo had established his quarters at Rochester which Rufus besieged successfully, causing Odo to leave the country in some ignominy. The cathedral was treated with respect throughout the siege, as was Bishop Gundulf, who was allowed freedom of passage by both sides.

Lanfranc lived for a year or so longer after the suppression of the rebellion. Aged around 80, he caught a fever from which he died. According to William of Malmesbury his wish had been fulfilled. Fearful of suffering impairment of speech or dementia, he hoped that he would die of a fever or dysentery.[54] He died at Canterbury on 28 May 1089 and was buried in the nave of the cathedral to the west of the choir screen. Four years were to pass before England was again to have an archbishop of Canterbury.

2

The Sons of the Conqueror and their Bishops

The ecclesiastical policies of William Rufus and Henry I

Of William the Conqueror's four sons two, William and Henry, became kings of England. One, Richard, had a fatal hunting accident when still a teenager; Robert succeeded to Normandy. Under pressure from some of his barons he showed some aspirations to the English throne, but these were hardly realistic. He could not maintain authority in Normandy, and although he distinguished himself on Crusade it was said that he declined the offer to make him king of Jerusalem on the grounds that it would involve too much hard work. He remained an irritant to his brothers until his defeat at Tinchebrai in 1106 and subsequent lifelong imprisonment, when his son William Clito became a focus of hostility to Henry.

In the days when historians made moral judgements and England was said to be ruled by good and bad kings, William Rufus was regarded as one of the worst. Frank Barlow has taught us to look differently at him. More than fifty years ago in his book *The Feudal Kingdom of England* he wrote that Rufus confirmed the royal power in England and restored ducal rights in Normandy.[1] In his full-scale biography written nearly thirty years later he suggested that the importance of his reign is that he ensured that Robert of Normandy would never become king of England and gave Henry I a strong inheritance. In Barlow's words, 'the rule of William Rufus ensured the continuity of the type of government that his father had established, namely the Old-English polity, modified and stiffened by French practices and ruthless direction'.[2] The view that William Rufus was an effective and constructive king has been developed by Emma Mason in her book *William II: Rufus, the Red King*.

William Rufus was no paragon of virtue, but he has suffered from failing to meet the exacting criteria of the chroniclers and annalists who wrote about him with prejudiced views of what was proper in a lay ruler. All the chroniclers accused him of ill-treating the church, and the author of *The Anglo-Saxon Chronicle*, writing Rufus's obituary notice in 1100, was unremittingly severe in his condemnation. Eadmer could heap only loathing and contempt upon him.[3] One of Rufus's faults, according to Eadmer, would be regarded today as a quality far in advance of his time, a tolerant attitude towards Jews. An equally critical judgement of William is given by Henry, the archdeacon of Huntingdon, who primly wrote of the king and his companions 'practising unspeakable debauchery openly and unashamedly'.[4] Eadmer was no dispassionate assessor of William's character. He had little understanding of the world beyond the cloister, as was clear when he briefly found himself bishop of St Andrews, and no sympathy for a court like William's, which lacked any feminine influence to modify its boisterous and at times loutish tendencies. His devotion to Anselm distorted his judgements. At a time when he suggests that William's relationship with Anselm was at breaking point, Anselm's letters to William give no indication of this.

Equally certainly, Rufus was no champion of moral reform and, as we shall see, was fully supported by Ranulf Flambard in exploiting the church financially whenever the opportunity arose. He was ruthless in taking advantage of bishops and abbots as great tenants-in-chief. Bishops elect were required to pay what were in effect feudal reliefs before assuming control of their estates, thereby opening them up to the charge of simony, however involuntary. Vacant sees and abbeys were treated like lay estates, and he was unscrupulous in prolonging vacancies and enjoying the income that accrued. At the time of his death eleven wealthy abbeys and three bishoprics were being administered by his men. But his reign was not one of unrelieved hostility towards the church, and the view that he was unscrupulous in his exploitation of the church has been questioned by Mason.[5] He supported his father's abbey at Battle and a recently founded Cluniac priory at Bermondsey. He did indeed keep sees vacant, and some quite improperly, but others were filled within a reasonable time. His appointments were not generally scandalous; Flambard is possibly exceptional, and most of his bishops were royal clerks, worldly men perhaps who put service to the king above moral principle, but educated with talent as administrators.

Henry I's record of appointments is not noticeably different from William's. During his reign he made or influenced 30 episcopal appointments. Some vacancies were certainly prolonged. Canterbury was vacant for five years after the death of Anselm and York for five years and eight months after the death of Thomas II. Generally he did not appoint men of distinction, but Henry of Huntingdon's acerbic comment that few of his bishops were actually remembered for anything is contradicted by the remarks he makes about some of them individually. Henry I was not keen on appointing monks and only three, including his nephew Henry of Blois, were promoted. He favoured Augustinian canons, archdeacons and clerks who had been educated abroad in a cathedral school. Only one, Gilbert bishop of London, known as Gilbert the Universal, had a reputation as a real scholar. Henry of Huntingdon wrote very warmly of his intellectual stature, but was scathing in his assessment of him as a bishop.[6]

Martin Brett discerns a change in the type of man appointed after about 1125 when Gilbert was appointed to London.[7] Until then many bishoprics were held by a reactionary group of men with a stranglehold on royal patronage, a self-perpetuating oligarchy immune to the demands of the reformers and heed-less of developments in canon law. The classic example of this is the Salisbury dynasty (see below). But as we shall see, the bishops did not give unanimous support to Henry's opposition to Anselm. The appointment of the abbot of Glastonbury, Seffrid d'Escures, to Chichester was seen by Brett as a different sort of appointment. He was the first monk to become a bishop outside Kent since Herbert Losinga went to Thetford/Norwich in 1091. Another monk, Robert of Béthune, became bishop of Hereford. He was well regarded, but there were those who claimed that Henry appointed him only so that when he died it could be said that he left one godly bishop behind. Perhaps in the aftermath of *The White Ship* tragedy[8] he appointed some men who were more spiritual, more in sym-pathy with the reform movement and more responsive to changes in canon law. Moreover, he was prepared to yield to opposition. His favoured successor to Canterbury was the Italian abbot of Abingdon, Faritius. But there was consider-able opposition to him. The English bishops, magnates and monks had had two Italian archbishops and did not want another. Nor were they comfortable with Faritius's reputation for being a stern disciplinarian. In opposing him they used the strange argument that Faritius was unsuitable as in his role as a doctor he had come in contact with female urine. Henry, who may not have had particularly strong feelings, decided it would be judicious not to make a stand, and Ralph d'Escures was translated from Rochester to Canterbury. Henry also created two new dioceses, Ely in 1109, formed from the diocese of Lincoln, and Carlisle in 1133. They were the last to be founded before the sixteenth century.

Somehow Henry I managed to escape the scathing criticism experienced by William Rufus, despite his fathering a remarkable number of illegitimate chil-dren, but few have ever found much in him that was attractive. He was certainly capable of great savagery and cruelty, but his harsh penalties were often justified. Warren Hollister, in his study of the reign, took a generous view. He judged his administrative sophistication to be unmatched in early twelfth-century Europe and he believed him to be capable of warmth, generosity and considerable loy-alty to those who were loyal to him. Two contemporaries, the poet Gaimar and the perhaps ingratiating Walter Map, wrote of the gallantry and love shown by the best king that ever was and of the woodland sports and jests, feasts, splendour and lavish gifts he bestowed on the members of his court. According to Map, once the morning's work had been done the rest of the day could be given over to sports, hilarity and decent mirth.[9]

William of Malmesbury penned a word-portrait of Henry I, writing of the king's laudable piety towards God.[10] In Henry's mind this piety demanded that he should control the church, which he saw as coterminous with his kingdom. When he approved of the appointment of a new abbot of Bec, Boso, in 1124, he wrote to him: 'You must be abbot within your order, and I shall be abbot in external affairs.' He saw it as his right and indeed his duty to appoint bishops and abbots; to control church property during vacancies; to deal with church problems in his great councils in the presence of the aristocracy, lay as well as ecclesiastical; to approve appeals to Rome; and to keep close watch on attempts by the pope or his legates to exercise authority in his realm. Whereas Rufus seems to have had no interest in reform or reformers, Henry shared his father's willing-ness to hold church councils. Rufus obstructed Anselm's ambitions to hold a council;[11] under Henry he held two, and Eadmer gives the full text of the reforms agreed to at Westminster in 1102.[12]

One of Henry's first acts after he had rushed to take the throne was to issue – with such remarkable speed that it must have been planned in advance – a Coronation Charter.[13] In its first clause he promised to make free the Church of God; 'so that I will neither sell nor lease its property; nor on the death of an archbishop, bishop or abbot will I take anything from the demesne of the church or from its vassals during the period which elapses before a successor is installed'. We know that this was a bid for support in uncertain times and there is little in the charter to commit Henry to anything very specific; some years later he wrote to Paschal II: 'so long as I live, the dignities and usages of the English realm shall not be diminished'. These included the regalian right to enjoy income from the church during vacancies. This was time-honoured and it is highly unlikely that Henry ever had any intention of abandoning it. His concern was to prevent the abuses of royal rights of the sort that had earned Rufus such censure.

It is actually possible to see Henry as benevolent towards the church. He was a friend of the Augustinian, or Austin, canons supporting or founding many new houses, the greatest being at Cirencester. Several canons became bishops; William of Corbeil, prior of St Osyth, became archbishop of Canterbury. He was generous to Benedictine abbeys, and following the tragic death of his son, he founded the great abbey at Reading and generously endowed it.[14] Its position between the rivers Kennet and Thames gave it easy access to the many visitors who were attracted by the impressive collection of relics housed there. They may also have enjoyed the hospitality of the Cluniac monks, who kept their visitors well supplied with food and drink. Peter the Venerable himself paid a fulsome tribute to Henry who, he said, 'exceeded all Christian princes of his time in prudence, in good works, and in generosity'. He was known to have made gifts to hermits, the weak and the poor, even society's outcasts, founding leper hospitals at Oxford, Shrewsbury and possibly Lincoln. Female religious also benefited from his generosity. The question therefore has to be asked: why, if his conduct was such a contrast to that of Rufus, did both kings fall out with Archbishop Anselm?

The election of Anselm to Canterbury

Anselm, abbot of Bec and archbishop of Canterbury, was one of the greatest of all medieval churchmen. A protégé of Lanfranc, he shared Lanfranc's reluc-tance to leave Bec but proved to be a bishop of a very different kind. There is an abundance of readily accessible material on Anselm. Although he did not welcome it, he inspired one of his young monks at Canterbury, Eadmer, to write at length about him, but Eadmer's biographies need to be read in conjunction with Anselm's letters, some of which have been translated into English. His *Prayers and Meditations* are available in Penguin Classics. The greatest authority on the life, career and achievements of Anselm is the late R.W. Southern, whose *St Anselm and his Biographer* and *Saint Anselm: A Portrait in a Landscape* are works of great stature. Strongly recommended, too, is Sally Vaughn's *Anselm of Bec and Robert of Meulan: The Innocence of the Dove and the Wisdom of the Serpent.* Her later *Anselm of Canterbury* is also important. It is unlikely that Mason, in her *William II: Rufus, the Red King*, would agree with her judgement that 'never again was Canterbury to attain the glory and prestige it had reached under Archbishop Anselm'.

Like Lanfranc, Anselm was Italian by birth, born in 1033 in Aosta. A dispute with his father and the attraction of Bec led him there in 1059 to join those intellectual young men inspired by Lanfranc. Four years later he became prior and in 1078 abbot. There he would have been happy to remain. Bec held estates in England and his responsibility for administering them required him to pay several visits to this country, admittedly under some pressure from the monks of Bec. Among his friends in England was Hugh of Avranches, the worldly earl of Chester.[15] Perhaps to atone for his loose living, Hugh was a generous benefactor to Bec and supported the abbey's attempts to secure its rights in England. He may have thought that if the neighbouring earldom of Shrewsbury had an abbey so should Chester. In 1092 he enlisted the support of Anselm, now reluctantly on his fourth visit to England, in turning the community of canons at St Werburgh's in Chester into a monastic community with monks from Bec, including Richard, who became the first abbot.

Anselm was reluctant to return to England lest he find himself under pressure to become Lanfranc's successor as archbishop of Canterbury. Canterbury had been vacant since Lanfranc's death. There was much distress in England about the prolongation of the vacancy, but King William remained unmoved. He was enjoying the considerable revenues that accrued and had no intention of yielding to pressure. Invoking, as was his wont, the holy face at Lucca, he declared: 'neither he (Anselm) nor anyone else shall be archbishop except myself'.[16] But in 1093 William fell seriously ill, and fearing imminent death, he decided that he needed an archbishop of Canterbury to intercede for him in his final days rather than endure the pains that might await him after death.

Many judged Anselm to be the outstanding candidate. He had a reputation that went beyond England and Normandy for personal sanctity and for intellectual ability that put him among the greatest spiritual philosophers of all time. His celebrated *Proslogion*, known generally as his proof of the existence of God, dated from between 1076 and 1078. Convinced that his end on earth was near, in March 1093 William summoned Anselm to him at Gloucester where he made his confession and promised to mend his ways. Urged by the leading magnates, lay and ecclesiastical, he called Anselm to his sickbed to be invested with the symbols of episcopal office. Anselm protested in vain, and when he closed his fingers so that he could not receive the staff the bishops present tried without success to force open his hand, causing him considerable pain. So the staff was placed against his closed hand. Staff and hand were pressed together and held there by the hands of the bishops. Cries of 'Long live the bishop; long may he live' were followed by the singing of the *Te Deum*. Still protesting, Anselm was carried rather than led into the neighbouring church. Fearful that he, an old and feeble sheep, was to be harnessed under one yoke with an untamed bull, Anselm tried to argue that the procedures were invalid because he had not given his consent. He was not objecting to lay investiture as such but to the fact that it had been forced upon him. To no avail, Anselm was received in Canterbury on 25 September and consecrated archbishop on 4 December.[17]

Fundamental to every aspect of Anselm's existence was his conviction that he must achieve a complete relationship with God. The monastic life was the way to this. His closest and warmest friendships were with those with whom he saw the possibility of attaining the desired relationship with God. He wished to be able to enjoy the freedom to give himself fully to the monastic life in order to achieve this goal. Freedom did not mean the freedom to do just as one pleased. Service was perfect freedom, freedom to be totally obedient to the demands of the monastic life as the only real way of obtaining the relationship with God that he sought. The Benedictine concept of obedience to one's worldly superior was fundamental. For Anselm this superior was the pope; at the same time, once archbishop, he acknowledged that the king to whom he had paid homage and who had invested him with ring and staff was his liege lord.

As a prior, then an abbot and finally an archbishop, Anselm could not escape involvement in worldly matters. If he was a poor administrator – and historians are far from unanimous in accepting that he was – this was not because he was an absent-minded academic but because he found difficulty in being diverted by mundane affairs from what really mattered. He proved to be a staunch defender of the estates of Canterbury and he was realistic about the world of which he was part. He recognised that in an imperfect world feudal organisation was a human attempt to respond to the problems of daily existence. Dreadful though many members of the feudal aristocracy might be, he saw them as a means of ensuring some sort of stability in a disorderly society. He was no Gregorian. He acknowledged homage as part of the feudal order. He was not an opponent of lay investiture until enjoined by Pope Paschal II to resist it. It became an issue between Anselm and Henry I, but not between Anselm and William II.

Anselm was by nature mild and gentle, slow to take offence and ready to forgive, rather than aggressive and volubly assertive, but his appearance and manner belied a huge inner strength. He could be indomitable and inflexible of purpose. He was intransigent in his attempt to establish the primacy of Canterbury over York. To the disappointment of the Christ Church monks he did not succeed and the struggle for the primacy continued well into the twelfth century (see below). Although he was far from detached from the ways of the world, it is commonly held that he was no politician. His failure to exploit in the interests of the church Henry I's weakness at the beginning of his reign when the king was vulnerable is sometimes cited as an example of his lack of political astuteness. However, Vaughn has invited us to reconsider this judgement by arguing that Anselm was well aware of the motives of others, and that he was skilled at presenting an argument in court and well able to apply his intellect and 'holy guile' to the practicalities of daily life. He was in reality an exceptional politician well able to hold his own in encounters with his adversary, Robert count of Meulan.[18]

Had Anselm been asked what gave him the greatest pleasure when he had the opportunity to relax and unwind, he may well have said the company of intelligent young men and the conversations he enjoyed with them. He inspired affection and devotion from many, above all his biographer, secretary and chaplain Eadmer. His love of conversation sometimes caused him to be disobedient and continue talking when the monastic rule enjoined silence.

As Anselm had predicted, William Rufus soon recovered, and as he feared, the king soon reverted to his bad old ways. Tension between the two quickly broke out. However, it should be stressed that they were not at permanent enmity. They could work together, and Mason points out that sometimes it was Anselm who was the irritant rather than Rufus. The nature of their disagreements concerned practical matters rather than issues of principle. These came to a head in the reign of Henry I. The matters at stake between Anselm and Rufus were the contribution of the archbishopric to the royal tax of 1094, the recognition of Urban II or 'Clement III' as pope, William's refusal to hold a church council and the quality of the Canterbury knights.

The first dispute

In 1094 William was desperate for money to finance a campaign in Normandy against his brother Robert. Anselm's offer of £500 was at first gratefully accepted by the king. However he was put under pressure 'by certain ill-disposed persons'[19] to change his mind and refuse to accept the gift on the grounds that such was a shameful amount. The least that the king should accept was £1000. On hearing of this Anselm went to the king urging him to accept the original offer, with the promise that it would be the first of many gifts. He would rather make donations more often and freely than feel compelled to offer something as if he were a slave. Rufus's ungracious response was the eleventh-century equivalent of 'stuff your £500'. So Anselm gave the king nothing but undertook to give the sum in alms to the poor for the redemption of the king's soul. This was a judicious move. Had the king accepted the money Anselm could have been accused of buying the archbishopric, thereby opening himself up to the charge of simony. This was seen by some among the reformers as fundamental to the problems of the church, and one that they might well have regarded as invalidating Anselm's episcopal order.

Urban II or Clement III?

A much bigger issue then arose. Following an expensive but fruitless expedition to Normandy, William took up residence at Gillingham near Shaftesbury in Dorset. Anselm visited him there in January 1095 with a view to obtaining permission to go to Rome to receive the pallium from the pope. An archbishop was required to receive the pallium within a year of his consecration or risk deposition. By December 1094 the year was running out. When Anselm made his request to Rufus the king responded with the question, 'of which pope do you wish to ask it?'[20] The question arose because two men claimed to be the lawful pope. Odo, bishop of Ostia, had been recognised as Pope Urban II in Italy and France. Anselm, as abbot of Bec, had recognised him and corresponded with him, while the Imperial faction was giving its support to Guibert, archbishop of Ravenna, a genuine reformer and man of distinction, whom they proclaimed as 'Pope Clement III'. In reality there was no possibility that Rufus would identify himself with the Imperialists or create a situation whereby England supported one claimant to the papacy while Normandy, which William aspired to bring under his control, had given its allegiance to another. But William intended to enjoy the opportunity to assert his authority over his archbishop and for a while left open the issue of which claimant he actually intended to recognise. When Anselm informed him that he planned to visit Urban he reminded William that he had previously told him that he recognised Urban as pope. The king replied that it was the custom in England that no one should recognise a pope without the king's consent or in accordance with his choice. Anselm's strongly held view was that he would prefer to go into exile than disown Urban. As a way forward he asked that a council of bishops, abbots and lay magnates should be assembled to consider the matter.

Detailed accounts of the Council of Rockingham can be read elsewhere.[21] All modern accounts are based on Eadmer.[22] William of Malmesbury follows him but does not name the council.[23] It is not certain that Eadmer was actually present, and his version may be a literary construct. There is no mention in *The Anglo-Saxon Chronicle*. It began as an ecclesiastical council and became a trial of the archbishop. Of the bishops present only Gundulf of Rochester remained steadfastly loyal to Anselm. Most were curial bishops and were king's men. The chief opponent of Anselm was William bishop of Durham. It was suggested by Eadmer and accepted by William of Malmesbury that he had hoped to orchestrate the deposition of Anselm so that he might succeed him. Seven years before he himself had faced trial for treachery.[24] His argument that as a bishop he should be judged only in a church court had been refuted by Lanfranc on the grounds that he was being tried as a tenant-in-chief. His duplicity in challenging Anselm is apparent from the fact that in 1088 he had stressed his right to appeal to Urban II and now opposed Anselm for claiming the right to do so.

The lay magnates were far from united with the king. Robert of Mowbray, for example, was on the verge of rebellion. They argued that as they were not

Anselm's vassals they had no allegiance to renounce and on account of his office and his blameless conduct they would continue to recognise his spiritual authority. Eadmer refers to 'one Robert' who was probably Robert of Meulan, a man very close to the king and distinguished for his considerable intelligence and ability to temper force with diplomatic persuasion and subtlety. He fully recognised that by adroit argument Anselm had successfully outmanoeuvred all his opponents. When Rufus realised that he was getting nowhere he became increasingly angry. Throughout, Anselm had hoped to retain his allegiance to the king while being obedient to the Apostolic See, but made it clear that if Rufus came down on the side of Clement his only choice would be to go into exile. In reality Rufus was well aware that he would gain nothing by driving Anselm into exile in the name of a pope recognised in Normandy. As Southern wrote, the discussion of the problem at Rockingham in February 1095 was largely a display of shadow-boxing.[25]

Following the council a truce was agreed to last until Whitsuntide. Anselm was willing to accept what the king thought right after discussion with a group of magnates and bishops, subject to the reverence and obedience he owed Pope Urban. But if Anselm had any illusions about Rufus's sincerity they were quickly dispelled when the king banished three of his closest friends and advisers, arrested his chamberlain in his very presence and condemned a number of others of his men. The king then turned to subterfuge. He sent abroad 'two especially crafty operators', his chaplain Gerard, a future archbishop of York, and William Warelwast, a future bishop of Exeter.[26] Unknown to Anselm, they were to negotiate with Urban and ask him to send the pallium to England in the secret hope that it would be given into Rufus's care to bestow as he thought fit. The two returned with the pallium and the papal legate Walter, cardinal bishop of Albano. He promised Rufus that if he personally recognised Urban, English customs regarding the church would be respected. Rufus did not hesitate, and according to *The Anglo Saxon Chronicle* for 1095 he agreed to resume paying Peter's Pence, a practice which had fallen into abeyance for some years.

King William also tried to bribe Walter into deposing Anselm, but this was out of the question and Walter would have nothing to do with the idea. According to Eadmer, William was put out to find that he had not actually gained much from acknowledging Urban, but the reality is that he had surrendered very little, if anything. He cannot seriously have expected Walter to depose Anselm and he knew all along that it was inevitable for political reasons that he would recognise Urban. But he did not want this recognition to be seen as arising from pressure from his archbishop. He doubtless derived some pleasure from humiliating Anselm by presenting him at the Whitsun Court with the information, hitherto concealed, that he had formally recognised Urban and that he had obtained the pallium. According to Eadmer, whose account of the whole affair is emphatically partisan, Anselm was dismayed to realise how tangled a plot had been set against him. But he bore no grudge and he and William, facing Mowbray's conspiracy, were reconciled. The exiles were recalled. On 27 May Walter of Albano went to Canterbury with the pallium in a silver casket. The assembled crowd shouted their applause and Anselm, barefoot but in priestly robes, went to meet the legate. At the altar he received the pallium, arranged it round his shoulders as consecrated archbishop and celebrated mass.[27]

The Canterbury knights

A period of peace and reconciliation ensued. William was preoccupied with the rebellion of Robert de Mowbray and his followers and he also faced the possibility of an invasion from Normandy led by his brother Robert. Anselm may even have hoped, in vain as it proved, that he would be able to hold his longed-for reform council. Friction resumed in 1097, this time not about spiritual matters but about Anselm's military obligations as one of the greatest tenants-in-chief in the kingdom. There had been an earlier dispute about a feudal matter. In the period of the Canterbury vacancy William had given some of Canterbury's estates as fiefs to some of his knights and he wanted Anselm to confirm them in hereditary possession. Anselm was adamant in his refusal. The matter was never resolved, and to those who see Anselm as an unworldly priest of great spirituality it might seem odd that he should be concerned about so earthly a matter. That is to misunderstand Anselm's view of his responsibilities. As archbishop of Canterbury he was responsible for the health of all the souls within his charge but he also had an absolute obligation to defend the territorial possessions attached to his church. This was, above all, property specifically dedicated to God and to His saints. A 'single failure of vigilance' could cause Canterbury's possessions to be lost for ever, as would certainly have been the case had the king alienated Canterbury lands by granting them to a knight and his heirs in perpetuity. Anselm was utterly convinced that truth, justice and charity demanded that he must safeguard such property.[28] It would be well-nigh impossible for a successor to claim them back and highly unlikely that another king would restore them.

As tenants-in-chief all lords, whether laymen or churchmen, were required to provide the king with an allocation of knights. Anselm had no quarrel with this in principle. The issue at stake in 1097 was about the quality of the knights provided by Anselm for William's Welsh campaign of that year. This might not appear a great matter, but as William of Malmesbury wrote, it proved to be 'another thunderstorm and a hurricane of hatred blew up anew'.[29] Despite the success of William's first expedition in the spring he accused Anselm of providing him with poorly trained knights in numbers inadequate for a Welsh campaign. He wrote to him saying that he would have to answer in the royal court for this negligence. Anselm ignored the charge, which was probably a quite unjustified fabrication, seeing it, according to Eadmer, as just another of those vexations which the king had inflicted on him. Even so he attended the Whitsun Court on 24 May. Anselm hoped that he could persuade William to summon a church council to tackle the various abuses that were rife in the court and country, but the king clearly had no intention of doing so. So Anselm astounded William by seeking permission to go to Rome to seek the pope's advice. Not surprisingly William refused the request, but was shaken enough to drop the accusation about the Canterbury knights. Anselm persisted, and at a meeting of the king's court in August he repeated his request, which was again refused, as was a further request made in October. By then Rufus's exasperation had become so great that he first threatened the archbishop with a fine and then warned: 'If he goes he can be quite sure that I shall take back the whole of the bishopric into my own hands and will never again receive him as archbishop.'[30] When a number of magnates and bishops, led by the worthy Walchelin of Winchester, pleaded with Anselm not to risk the dignity and opportunities for good afforded by his exalted position, Anselm insisted that he was adamant. Some debate and discussion followed, with Anselm insisting that obedience to God should come before that to men. But William's confidence having been boosted by recent military successes and the absence of brother Robert on Crusade, he remained intransigent. He was supported by Robert of Meulan who, now pre-eminent as a royal adviser, spoke up on his behalf, dismissing Anselm's arguments as 'Words, words! All he is saying is only words!'[31] Eventually the king and Robert concluded that nothing was to be gained by forcing Anselm to stay and little would be lost by allowing him to depart. Indeed, in Anselm's absence the Canterbury revenues could be diverted to William to help finance his impending ventures in Maine and the Vexin. Before Anselm went on his way Rufus could not resist a further attempt at humiliating him by sending messengers with the warning: 'You must understand that our lord will not let you take with you when you go anything you have had from him.' Anselm's response caused even Rufus to feel shame: 'I have horses for riding, clothes also and chattels and perhaps someone will say that these have come from the king. If he will not let me keep even those to take with me, tell him that I will go on foot and naked rather than give up the course on which I am determined.' The king denied that that was really his intention and he and his archbishop parted amicably, Rufus bowing his head to receive Anselm's blessing. They were never to see each other again.[32]

Anselm in exile

Anselm's humiliations were not over. Before departing he went to Canterbury to bid an emotional farewell to his monks, clergy and local folk. On 25 October he left Canterbury for Dover where he was detained by unfavourable winds until 9 November. The king had already explained that he would be met at Dover by a royal agent who would tell him what possessions he could take with him. The agent proved to be William Warelwast, whose conscientious loyalty to his king may appear unattractive but which won him professional advancement. He had a distinguished career in the royal curia, was skilled in ecclesiastical diplomacy, or put another way, was a cunning manipulator of words, and became bishop of Exeter. He had been sent by Rufus to keep a close eye on Anselm. Every day he took meals with him but refused to give any indication as to why he was there. When eventually the sailors judged it safe to embark, William detained Anselm on the shore as if he had been a fugitive or guilty of some heinous crime, and in the presence of an astonished and appalled crowd systematically went through all his possessions, every bag and chest, to discover whether Anselm was taking any money with him. Finding nothing he let Anselm go, accompanied by Eadmer and the monk Baldwin, who had previously been unjustly exiled by William. Mason suggests that in reality it was not money that Warelwast was looking for but documents that might be damaging to Rufus.[33]

No sooner had Anselm departed than Rufus ordered that all the property which had been held by him on account of his office should be formally transferred to the king and all changes and ordinances which could be proved to have been made on Anselm's authority since he first came into the archbishopric should be annulled. This probably included the separation of the archbishop's estates from those of the monastic community. In a letter to the pope Anselm wrote that the king, allowing only for the bare food and clothing of the monks, seized the whole archbishopric and converted it to his own use. Although the sources do not specifically say so, the hand of Ranulf Flambard can clearly be detected here. This is how he worked and he was impervious to the proprieties due to an archbishop. On the very day of Anselm's enthronement at Canterbury, 25 September 1093, he had appeared full of insolence and self-importance and served him with a royal writ.[34] Eadmer's personal animosity towards Ranulf may have coloured his account. Warelwast, like Flambard, was a loyal servant carrying out the orders of his king and lord, although to readers who see his actions through the eyes of Eadmer and William of Malmesbury his conduct was reprehensible.

Anselm's experiences in exile ensured that the friction between him and Henry I was of a different order. He was very well received at Rome, welcomed by Urban almost as an equal and accommodated at the Lateran Palace. He was given the place of honour at the Council of Bari in October 1098, where he impressed the assembled company by the eloquence and clarity of his exposition of the Roman view of the Procession of the Holy Spirit, effectively demolishing the Greek argument.[35] He attended the Easter Council held at Rome in 1099.[36] There he heard passed strict decrees against lay investiture, simony and clerical marriage. He had not, of course, been present at the Council of Clermont in 1095 where Urban had imposed a ban on clerical homage, but he may well have heard about it from Abbot Boso of Bec. At the Rome council the pope honoured Anselm by ordering a seat to be set for him in the apse of Old St Peter's, directly behind the altar. The loud-voiced bishop of Lucca spoke first. In a frenzied outburst he inveighed against the mistreatment of the church by tyrants, and particularly the failure of the authorities to support Anselm. Urban then rose to pronounce sentence of excommunication against the enemies of the Holy Church. These included all laymen who had conferred investiture, all who had accepted investiture from laymen, all consecrated bishops invested by laymen and all churchmen who paid homage to laymen. This was an unequivocal statement anathematising lay investiture approved unanimously by the assembled company in Anselm's presence. As a good Benedictine he had no alternative but to obey. After the council he went back to Lyons and his friend Archbishop Hugh, a committed Gregorian who strengthened his convictions.

Ranulf Flambard

While Anselm was in exile William Rufus met his controversial death in the New Forest on 2 August. Three days later his brother Henry was crowned king, not by Anselm but by Bishop Maurice of London in the absence of Archbishop Thomas of York, who was too old and infirm. In a bid for popularity Henry issued a Coronation Charter, summoned Anselm from exile and imprisoned the bishop of Durham, Ranulf Flambard.

Ranulf Flambard was one of the most remarkable characters of this period. He was of humble origins, his father being a village priest in the diocese of Bayeux, and he rose in the reign of Rufus to be the most powerful man in England after the king. His ability was recognised by Bishop Odo, a generous benefactor to able youths from modest backgrounds, his most talented protégés entering his brother William's service as clerks. Flambard's rise was phenomenal. In 1099 he succeeded William of St Calais in the diocese of Durham. Doubtless he could have been elected to episcopal office before 1099 but he spurned anything but the grandest. Not only was Durham one of the richest and most extensive dioceses in the kingdom; its bishop also enjoyed the lordship of the County Palatine of Durham.

Formidably able, Ranulf combined a striking presence with a flamboyant personality which earned him his sobriquet. Outrageous stories were told about him, often scurrilous and worthy of an episode of *Blackadder*, and probably fictitious.[37] The chroniclers had little good to say of him. The normally generous William of Malmesbury called him 'that sink of iniquity',[38] Henry of Huntingdon called him the perverse bishop of Durham, of all England the judge, but the perverter of justice, and the tax collector but the despoiler.[39] The chroniclers' judgements are understandable. Priest though he was and bishop that he became, he conducted himself in ways that were in stark contrast to the ideals of the reformers. No champion of clerical celibacy, he was an unashamed nepotist, providing well for his relatives and sons. It was even said, with as much credibility perhaps as the scandalous stories of modern celebrities blazoned forth in the tabloid press, that he once tried to seduce the young woman who became the anchorite Christina of Markyate. He would have had little success, for she loathed any kind of sexual contact.

Ranulf joined William II's service shortly after his accession. The work for which he became notorious, milking the revenues of vacant abbeys and churches, began in 1088 with Ely, Ramsey and Winchester, then Canterbury after the death of Lanfranc. By 1091, although he had no official title, he was authorising royal writs, ingratiating himself with the king with whom he enjoyed an excellent relationship. Southern wrote of the range of functions he performed as reported by various chroniclers.[40] He was overseer of the business of the whole kingdom and the head of all royal officials. He was the chief manager of the king's wealth and justice and chief agent of the king's will, the tax collector of the whole of England and judge of all England after the king. Evidence of his work can be found in the increasing numbers of writs issued in Rufus's reign. Royal writs had long been used to make transfers of land. Under William II they began to be used as a means of regular communication between the king and local officials commanding them to hear pleas, assess liability, survey property, enforce judgements and maintain the king's peace. Three men in particular worked under Flambard: Urse d'Abitot, and two men with the title *dapifer* (steward), Haimo and Eudo.

Above all Flambard drove himself to exploit every potential resource for augmenting the royal income. Rufus may have drawn up to £4000, a quarter of his entire annual revenue, from the ruthless exploitation of vacancies by Flambard. He milked monasteries by providing the monks with a meagre pension and passing most of the revenue to the king. The church was not alone in suffering from novel ways of fundraising. In 1094, when Rufus's military needs in Normandy were critical, the fyrd[41] was summoned to Hastings. Flambard met the men there, took ten shillings from each of them and sent them home.[42] According to William of Malmesbury, whenever Rufus demanded money Flambard said he should double it, to which the king laughingly commented: 'That's the only fellow who knows how to make use of his abilities in this way, not worrying if others hate him, provided he pleases his master.'[43]

Within a fortnight of his coronation Henry I arrested Flambard and imprisoned him in the White Tower, its first state prisoner. The charges against him were that he had misappropriated funds while a royal official, had been guilty of misconduct inappropriate for a bishop, had been guilty of simony and had failed to clear himself before the royal court of the charges against him. Possibly Henry's real concern was not to punish Flambard but to make a gesture that would bring himself some public approval. Certainly Flambard lived in grand style in the Tower, supported by a very generous grant of two shillings a day provided by Henry himself. So well did Flambard live that he put on a great deal of weight. It is also possible that Henry connived at his escape from the Tower, by a rope smuggled into his room in a flagon of wine.[44] Flambard proved useful to Henry as an agent in Normandy, turning to the king's advantage all the knowledge he acquired there. He returned to England after Henry's decisive victory at Tinchebrai in 1106. In addition to serving the king's interests he secured the bishopric of Lisieux for his brother Fulcher and then his son Thomas.

Back in England, free from the burden of national responsibilities, he could concentrate his gifts and energies on his diocese. He established two sheriffs for the secular business and two archdeacons for the spiritual. His efficient household attracted scholars, including a student from Laon, William of Corbeil, a future archbishop of Canterbury. He looked after family interests, ensuring that sons and nephews were well provided for. He was never a model bishop or a man of deep spirituality, but he performed his episcopal duties conscientiously and cared for the Durham monks, granting them tithes and estates. He enlarged the monastery and completed the cathedral, enriching it with elaborate vestments. Lawrence, a Durham monk, told of the golden age under Ranulf. As Southern wrote: 'His earthy and tumultuous energies were dedicated to the task of making things work, and although he was guided by no ideals he did less harm than better men who set Europe in arms to create the world of their dreams.'[45]

The return of Anselm and the issue of lay investiture

On 23 September 1100, in response to Henry I's plea to return to England, Anselm landed at Dover. Six days later the two men met at Salisbury. Henry gave him a warm, friendly welcome and his apology for going ahead with his coronation in the archbishop's absence was graciously accepted. But conflict was inevitable, not because either man sought it, but because each was in a position incompatible with that of the other. Although Henry genuinely intended to correct abuses, there was no way that he was prepared to do anything that might diminish the privileges and usages of the kingdom of England, as he subsequently wrote to Pope Paschal II, who had succeeded Urban II in 1099. Accordingly he asked Anselm to perform homage in accordance with the custom of his predecessors and to receive the archbishopric from his hand. This Anselm could not in all conscience do. As he wrote: 'It is not on my authority that I forbid the king to invest churches, but I have heard the pope in a great council excommunicate laymen who grant investitures as well as churchmen who receive such investitures and those who consecrate the receivers.' Anselm would have been happy for the bans to be waived had Paschal agreed, but Paschal was inflexible and Anselm had to stand by him. Having warned Henry that he might have to resume his exile Henry could not risk the possibility, however remote, of Anselm going over to Robert's side. The king and archbishop therefore agreed to a 'truce' which would last until the following Easter, 21 April 1101.[46]

It is possible that Henry I and Anselm would have welcomed a working relationship akin to that of William I and Lanfranc, but Lanfranc had been no inflexible Gregorian and circumstances had changed. Nevertheless Anselm showed his willingness to co-operate with Henry at this time in two ways. First was the matter of Henry's marriage to Matilda, a descendant of the old Anglo-Saxon line and daughter of King Malcolm of Scotland. Matilda had spent some years in a convent and had been seen wearing the veil. Some believed this disqualified her from future marriage. Anselm did not take this view. He positively supported the marriage and conducted the wedding ceremony. Secondly, in association with Bishop Gundulf of Rochester he gave Henry stalwart support in his preparations to resist the invasion of Robert Curthose, even camping with his own men in the field near Pevensey.

Robert soon capitulated. Among the reasons may have been Anselm's threat to excommunicate him if he persisted, although it is difficult to imagine that Robert seriously wanted the responsibility of becoming king of England. It is more likely that he was under pressure from his associates keen for the rich prizes they imagined would be theirs if Robert was king. He disappointed them. By the so-called Treaty of Alton Robert renounced his claim to the English throne and recognised Henry.

Despite his clear debt to his archbishop, Henry resumed his demand for homage and insisted that Anselm should consecrate those who had been invested with bishoprics and abbeys or leave the country. Henry had meanwhile received correspondence from Paschal, who was emphatic that he would not yield ground on clerical homage and lay investiture, while ignoring Anselm, whose obedience to him had never faltered. Not until late spring 1102 did Anselm receive a letter from Paschal dated 15 April which did nothing to help his relationship with Henry. Not only did it repeat the earlier bans, but it stated that the venerable majesty of the earlier holy councils had decreed that the power of secular princes must be altogether excluded from ecclesiastical elections.

Well before this letter reached Anselm he and Henry had parted, unable to reconcile their differences. Inevitable though the rift became, neither side wanted or sought it. Although Eadmer suggests rather improbably that Henry threatened Anselm with mutilation, there were no angry outbursts or attempts to vilify either party. Dignity and courtesy prevailed. The problem lay with Paschal. After the death of 'Clement III' he was not seriously challenged by an anti-pope so found it unnecessary to act with political circumspection. Three embassies were sent to Rome to try to win greater flexibility from Paschal but he was adamant that he could not sanction any form of lay investiture. Even so, the legation headed by Gerard, archbishop of York, Robert of Chester and Herbert Losinga of Norwich appeared, in a rather curious way, to have achieved some success. When they returned they testified that they had been instructed verbally and confidentially by Paschal to indicate to Henry that in matters of investment he would be lenient and refrain from imposing ecclesiastical sanctions if in other respects Henry conducted himself like a virtuous Christian. He was not prepared to put this concession in writing lest other lay rulers should get wind of it and take advantage.

The monk Baldwin who, with the monk Alexander, had accompanied the three bishops, denied that anything of the kind had been said, to which the bishops responded by saying that the concession had been made to them in private. The atmosphere became charged and a verbal battle ensued between Baldwin and spokesmen of the king. Baldwin claimed that his words and those of his fellow monk Alexander matched a written document authenticated by the papal bull or seal. They were more credible than the conversation reported by the bishops. The bishops, for their part, dismissed what they described as a sheepskin marked with black ink and weighted with a little lump of lead and asserted that their testimony was worth far more than that of mere 'monklings'. 'We do not accept the evidence of monks against bishops, Eadmer reported, and should we then accept that of a sheepskin? Anselm's monks cried in response: Alas then! Are not the very Gospels written upon sheepskins? What deceitful quibbling is shewn in this!'[47]

The papal curia was quite capable of saying one thing to one group and something different to the other as political expediency required, but it is most improbable in these particular circumstances. Had Paschal really been willing to relax lay investiture in England to support Anselm, he would surely have informed Anselm through Baldwin and Alexander. Moreover, in December 1102 Paschal wrote to England denying everything that the three bishops had reported and excommunicated them. In reality it is all very murky and made even more confusing by the fact that on 11 December a papal letter was despatched to Anselm from Benevento affirming opposition to lay investiture, although allowing Anselm to use his discretion in the matter of a Welsh bishop on the grounds that the Welsh were uncivilised people who acted in a barbarous and stupid way. While the duplicity of the three bishops cannot be proved, their careers show them to be opportunist royal servants not known for their spirituality. Henry and Anselm had received verbal reports of the contents of the papal letters of excommunication and evaded the matter by not opening them.

The bishops were not unanimous in support of Henry. The king insisted that if Anselm would not consecrate bishops and abbots whom he had invested he would require others to do so. Robert Bloet of Lincoln and John of Bath acquiesced and invested some abbots. When Anselm refused to consecrate William Giffard of Winchester, Roger of Salisbury and Reinhelm of Hereford, the king tried to get Archbishop Gerard to do so. This would have been a grave affront to Anselm. Showing considerable courage and moral strength, William and Reinhelm refused to be consecrated by anyone else. Reinhelm returned his ring and staff to Henry and William returned his staff. They both incurred the king's considerable displeasure. Roger, too, was not consecrated at this time but, in the words of William of Malmesbury: 'with admirable good sense he kept the matter so well balanced that he did not annoy the king or wrong the archbishop'.[48]

In one major respect Henry had shown his willingness to support Anselm. In September 1102 he allowed him to hold his longed-for council, the Council of Westminster. Henry summoned the council, Anselm presided, and it was well attended by bishops and abbots and a number of leading lay magnates. The decrees of the council can be read in full in the *History of Recent Events*[49] and are summarised by William of Malmesbury.[50] They were very wide-ranging, condemning simony and sodomy, tightening monastic discipline and regulating the relationship between parish churches and unscrupulous laymen. Clergy were expected to conduct themselves in a manner appropriate to their order. They were not to go to drinking parties or over-indulge and were forbidden to wear fashionable clothes and shoes. Men generally were told to have their hair cut so as to leave part of their ears visible and their eyes not covered. Clergy were to be tonsured. Clerical celibacy was a big issue: the idea that clergy should not marry had no long history and Lanfranc had been flexible. Anselm insisted that henceforth married clerics would have to choose between keeping their wives or surrendering their orders. Not surprisingly, this canon proved to be virtually unenforceable. Nine abbots and abbots-elect were deposed, six for simony and three for unspecified improper conduct.

Although king and archbishop were apparently in accord over the council, their views on homage and investiture remained irreconcilable. In 1103 Anselm was persuaded to go to Rome with some royal envoys to try to obtain Paschal's sanction for a more flexible attitude. In April he embarked on the voyage, and so began what proved to be his second exile. He was unlikely to have been very pleased when he subsequently discovered that William Warelwast had been sent ahead to present the king's case. Southern described Warelwast as the first clear example of a professional civil servant in English history. Those less charitable might, following Eadmer, see him as a royal toady. Anselm travelled to Rome via Bec, where he was rapturously received, and there he opened the hitherto sealed papal letter excommunicating the three bishops and affirming Paschal's opposition to lay investiture. This in effect doomed him to remain abroad. From Bec he went to Chartres where his friend Ivo, the great canon lawyer, advised him to delay going into Italy as he would find the exceptional summer heat too much for him. He returned to Bec, eventually setting off for Rome in August, apparently being joyfully received at every stage of his journey. There he found Paschal prepared to take some action to support his claim to the primacy of Canterbury (see below), but intransigent on the matter of lay investiture. However, it did appear that the pope was beginning to adopt a more moderate stance on the matter of whether or not a man in orders could perform homage to a layman. Urban II's conviction had been that at the Eucharist the bread had become Christ's body only in the hands of a priest. Such hands should not be enclosed in the blood-stained hands of laymen; Paschal seemed willing to be less rigid.

After the meeting with the pope in autumn 1103 Warelwast remained in Rome for a while. He rejoined Anselm at Piacenza and from there they travelled towards Lyons. They then went their separate ways. Warelwast was clearly frustrated by his failure to secure any concession on lay investiture from Paschal, and before he left Anselm he assured him that Henry would welcome his return to England on the understanding that he would treat him in all respects as the archbishop's predecessors had treated the king's.[51] Anselm could not accept this and realised that there could be no prospect of reconciliation so long as Henry stood firm. He therefore sought the company of his old friend Archbishop Hugh, who was delighted to welcome him back. Canterbury lacked an archbishop again. At once Henry seized the land and revenues of the diocese.

Anselm's decision to remain in Lyons did not pass uncriticised. Even some of his friends felt that he was too resolute in adhering to a principle that did not really justify abandoning his flock. The abbot of Westminster, his old pupil and friend Gilbert Crispin, actually wrote a poem lamenting the absence of the shepherd from his fold.[51] But the dispute dragged on. Now an old man of around 70,

Anselm doubtless found it more agreeable to be with congenial company away from political pressures. He remained at Lyons until late May 1105. In the meantime, in line with established procedure, he warned Henry three times that he faced excommunication if the Canterbury lands and revenues were not restored. In March 1105 Paschal actually excommunicated Robert of Meulan and the bishops who had been invested by Henry. Henry became persuaded of the wisdom of trying to resolve the conflict. On 22 July he and Anselm met at l'Aigle, where they were reconciled. In return for the restoration of the Canterbury revenues Anselm dropped the threat of excommunication. Henry asked Anselm to return and recognise the bishops of Winchester, Hereford and Salisbury whom he had invested. But Anselm continued to insist that he could do nothing without papal approval. By now even Paschal was beginning to realise the need to achieve a compromise, and with less than full enthusiasm gave his consent to the so-called Compromise of Bec of 15 August 1106. The Compromise established four principles. Elections were to be free, but in practice Henry continued to control episcopal elections, which took place in the royal court under his influence. Bishops and abbots, as great landholders and tenants of the king, were to do homage to him for their territorial possessions. The king was to renounce investiture with ring and staff. Homage was to precede investiture.

An important mediator in the preliminary negotiations was Henry's sister Adela, daughter of William the Conqueror and mother of the future King Stephen. She had a good relationship with Ivo of Chartres, who favoured a compromise and saw a way to it. The solution was to recognise that just as a king after coronation and unction had a sacred as well as secular character, a bishop or abbot had two capacities. His spiritual status was essential to his functioning as an abbot or bishop, but he was also a great landholder with associated privileges, duties and obligations. In recognition of this he could first do homage to the king for his fiefs and so become his vassal, then, as a consequence of participating in religious ceremonies, he could assume the spiritual office. Only a fully ordained priest could become a bishop. If he was judged to be a suitable person for elevation to the episcopal order he would be elected or appointed to it. He would do homage for his estates and swear fealty to his lord in the same way as a lay lord. He could then have the title of bishop. Next he would be invested with ring and staff. Mere symbols, they conveyed no particular spiritual authority on the recipient. Until he had been consecrated by a fellow bishop in the presence of other bishops, he was not fully a bishop and could not perform those functions exclusive to a bishop. While this distinction was not acceptable to rigid Gregorians, it did not trouble those who were more pragmatic and acknowledged the need to recognise the realities of the world in which they lived. Lanfranc had used that very distinction against Odo of Bayeux and William of Durham. Ivo of Chartres found no problem with it and the concept was expressed by Hugh of Fleury, who dedicated his *Treatise concerning royal power and priestly dignity* to Henry.[52]

In the same year as the Compromise of Bec Henry found himself once more in conflict with his brother Robert. He defeated him at Tinchebrai on 28 September

1106 and Anselm sent him a letter of congratulation. The following spring Anselm returned to England. A great council of magnates and prelates was summoned for 1 August and it duly met at Westminster. For the first three days it met without Anselm. The king discussed the issue of investiture with the bishops, some of whom misguidedly urged him to stand fast and continue to invest as his father and brother had. Their lack of judgement was tempered by the wise advice of Robert of Meulan and Richard de Redvers. When Anselm joined the assembled company he was given a standing ovation. He and Henry announced the terms of the settlement. Lay investiture was forbidden, but no prelate would be denied consecration because he had paid homage to the king.

Work could begin to fill vacancies and consecrate elected bishops. Sunday 11 August 1107 saw a veritable festival of consecrations. At Canterbury, in the presence of Archbishop Gerard of York, Bishop Robert Bloet of Lincoln, Bishop John of Bath, Bishop Herbert of Norwich, Bishop Robert of Chester, Bishop Radulf of Chichester and Bishop Ranulf of Durham, Anselm consecrated William Giffard of Winchester, Roger of Salisbury, Reinhelm of Hereford, the zealous royal envoy William Warelwast of Exeter and Urban of Glamorgan. Anselm lived for another 18 months. The final period of his life was not free from controversy, for the primacy dispute between Canterbury and York (to be discussed later) continued to be an issue. But the archbishop and king were at peace with each other and Anselm could resume his regular duties. He was an old man wearied by the persistent quarrelling so alien to his nature and such a diversion from what he considered his real work and purpose. In July 1108 he fell ill at Bosham but recovered. The following January he fell ill again at Canterbury. This proved to be his final illness and he died on 21 April. The next day, Maundy Thursday, he was buried in state in Canterbury cathedral at the head of his predecessor Lanfranc.

Anselm's quarrels with his two kings must be kept in perspective. They appear to dominate his career as archbishop, but that is partly because the decidedly partisan Eadmer wrote so fully and eloquently about them. He would have considered them irritating diversions from far more important matters. He continued to exercise pastoral care when not in exile, and write important works of theology. The defence of the rights of Canterbury was more important than the relatively unimportant investiture dispute. Blame for the way it was conducted and protracted must lie more with Pope Paschal than Henry or Anselm. The settlement was in line with what Anselm had been content with all along. It was his sense of his obligation to obey his superior, the pope, that caused him to take his line against the king. Paschal did little to recognise Anselm's loyalty in this matter but was more supportive in his dispute with York.

Henry lost little by the settlement. He continued to control episcopal elections which took place in his court under his influence. He kept bishoprics vacant for long periods; he appropriated the revenues and exercised his right to the personal belongings of a dead bishop. However, he had had to recognise papal authority in an unprecedented way. For all his political strength Henry was not immune from the papacy's attempts to assert its authority in England.

Paschal II had been reluctant to recognise the translation of Ralph from Rochester to Canterbury in 1114 as he had not sanctioned it in accordance with canon law. Despite Henry's attempted resistance, in 1125 Honorius II sent the legate John of Crema to England and he held a legatine council at Westminster. A mere priest, he asserted his authority over the two English archbishops. The position with regard to legates was settled satisfactorily when Archbishop William was granted legatine authority in 1126. However, as we shall see in the next chapter, the struggle between the archbishops of Canterbury and York for the primacy drew the papacy further into English affairs.

3

The Struggle for the Primacy

The primacy

A feature of the history of the church in England in the half-century or so following Lanfranc's becoming archbishop of Canterbury was the struggle between the archbishops of Canterbury and York to determine which of the two had ultimate authority over all the bishops in the country, that is, which bishop was to be regarded and respected as primate of all England. The struggle for power was prolonged and at times unedifying, and this chapter will discuss why archbishops of Canterbury were so determined to assert their primacy and why archbishops of York were equally determined to resist them. We shall examine how far this was a matter of concern to their kings and the extent to which the papacy was drawn into what was an essentially insular matter. For kings and popes the prolonged dispute was irksome and time-consuming, but it could not be ignored, for it had implications for the king's authority over two of his greatest subjects and for the nature of his relationship with the papacy. It was a dispute during which tempers were lost in public and subterfuges of questionable honesty resorted to. Behind each archbishop was his respective cathedral chapter, the monks of Christ Church, Canterbury and the canons of York. The chapters expected their archbishops to fight their corner with all possible determination and vigour and were reluctant to concede defeat. Each chapter had its own publicist whose writing provides the principal sources for following the struggle (see Further Reading).

It is important to distinguish between a metropolitan and a primate. The metropolitan was the senior bishop presiding over a number of subordinate dioceses and their suffragan bishops in his province. As we have seen, the outward and visible symbol of a metropolitan's office was the pallium. A metropolitan had no authority over another metropolitan unless he had the status of primate. The fact that the Canterbury province was far more extensive than York with 13 English dioceses under its authority did not deter York, with only Durham and later Carlisle, from claiming the right to primacy. A problem for York was that canon law required the presence of at least three bishops at the consecration of a new bishop, which made York beholden to Canterbury. The relationship of the English archbishops with the bishops of Wales, Ireland and Scotland will be considered later in the chapter.

The primate had authority over the whole English church and might even claim that it extended over the whole of Britain. With it went the right to convene councils which all bishops were required to attend. There was an expectation that the primacy gave the archbishop the right to claim superiority over visiting papal legates, or that if they were present at an English synod they were subordinate to the primate. This view did not go unchallenged by the legates. The archbishop of Canterbury expected the archbishop of York to make a profession of obedience to him in writing and to take an oath of loyalty. For their kings this might be a matter of some contention, as the kings of England required their subjects to be 'loyal to them against all other men'. Other issues concerned seating arrangements and whether the archbishop of York was entitled to have the cross carried before him in the Canterbury province.

The archbishop of Canterbury claimed the right to crown kings and future kings, not only at the coronation but on subsequent occasions when the king wore his crown, and conduct royal wedding ceremonies. This was not always possible. Stigand was deemed unsuitable to crown William I; Anselm was in exile for Henry I's coronation. There is a well-known story of Archbishop Ralph taking offence at the wedding of Henry to his second wife Adeliza of Lorraine at Windsor on 29 January 1121.[1] Ralph had enjoyed the reputation of being good-natured and genial, but his health had declined seriously, he had difficulty speaking and he was decidedly touchy. He was not well enough actually to conduct the marriage ceremony and insisted that William Giffard of Winchester should act for him rather than the diocesan bishop, Roger of Salisbury. The following day, when he was about to celebrate mass for Henry and Adeliza, he was much put out to see that the king was already wearing his crown. He demanded that Henry should remove it and give it to him, maintaining that only the archbishop of Canterbury could place the crown on the king's head. He then grudgingly crowned Henry and consecrated and crowned Adeliza. This uncharacteristic show of bad temper is usually attributed to Ralph's poor health. Jean Truax interprets it differently.[2] She sees it as a well-orchestrated and powerful statement of the rights of Canterbury that he had devoted his life to upholding. Indeed there may have been a conflict of views, Henry demonstrating that as king it was proper to crown himself but yielding on this occasion to avoid an embarrassing scene. Nearly fifty years later the coronation of Henry II's son Henry by the archbishop of York set in motion the train of events culminating in Becket's murder.

The origins

To support his claim to the primacy Lanfranc and the monks of Canterbury drew upon history, or their assertion as to what was historical truth. The primacy of Canterbury was traced to a letter from Pope Gregory the Great written to St Augustine in 601, quoted by Bede in chapter 29 of the first book of his

Ecclesiastical History of the English People.[3] With the letter Gregory sent the pallium, which was to be worn only during the performance of the solemn rites of the mass. Understandably ignorant of the political situation in England, Gregory had assumed that the Roman Imperial organisation still survived and that London would be the seat of a southern archbishopric, and in due course York the seat of a northern one. The archbishop of London was to ordain 12 bishops subject to his jurisdiction. In future the archbishop would be consecrated by his suffragans and receive the pallium from the hands of the pope. In due course a bishop consecrated by Augustine would become archbishop of York. He would be styled a metropolitan, would receive the pallium from the pope, and when the time was right he too would consecrate 12 bishops. During Augustine's lifetime the archbishop of York was to be subject to his authority; subsequently the archbishop consecrated first was to be regarded as the senior. Augustine was to have ultimate authority over not just the bishops of the southern province but also over those of the northern province and those of Britain. Events did not turn out like this. The archbishops did not move from Canterbury to London. There was no archbishop of York until 735 and there were nowhere near 12 sees in the province.

William of Malmesbury quoted a series of letters produced by Lanfranc and the Canterbury monks[4] purporting to be written by nine popes between 610 and 960 sent variously to archbishops of Canterbury, kings of England and bishops of England. The authenticity of these has been questioned.[5] The fabrication of documents to support a cause was far from unknown in the Middle Ages, not like a modern forgery, but usually to put in writing assumptions believed to be true and widely accepted but for which no written evidence actually existed. The classic example was *The Donation of Constantine* allegedly written by the Emperor Constantine to Pope Sylvester I in 315 but actually composed around 750.[6]. It has not been suggested that the letters were inventions in their entirety, but that some key sentences in support of the claim to primacy had been inserted by the monks of Christ Church, Canterbury or even Lanfranc himself. The essence of the interpolations is that the primacy had been granted in perpetuity to the successors of Augustine, the first archbishop.

Lanfranc v. Thomas

The primacy was no great issue before the pontificate of Lanfranc, but Stigand's career and reputation had diminished the status of the archbishop of Canterbury and William I had been crowned by the archbishop of York. Lanfranc had to assert his authority. If he were effectively to put the English church in order and to undertake the necessary task of moral correction he had to establish Canterbury's primacy over the whole of the English church and, indeed, beyond (see below). For William a united church under one primate was a necessary condition for a united kingdom under one king. Moreover, according to Hugh the Chantor,[7] he was easily convinced by Lanfranc's argument that unless his primacy was everywhere recognised, invading Scandinavians or even Scots might exploit the situation and have one of their number crowned by the archbishop of York.

It has also been suggested that there may have been a political factor which added to the tension between Canterbury and York. Following Odo of Bayeux's quarrel with the archbishop of Canterbury and his monks he may have set his protégés against them. Bayeux men were prominent in York. Odo's brother Robert of Mortain was the greatest Yorkshire tenant-in-chief and the powerful Lascy family held considerable land from Odo. Clergy from Bayeux were the most powerful ecclesiastical influence in York itself.[8]

The issue arose very soon after Lanfranc's consecration at Canterbury on 29 August 1070. William's choice to succeed Archbishop Aldred was Thomas of Bayeux, a royal chaplain, well educated, a former pupil of Lanfranc and a man of good repute, hardworking and intelligent. William of Malmesbury paid a very generous tribute to him.[9] Thomas was not yet a bishop and his consecration was to be carried out by Lanfranc. Although the two men always remained on good terms with each other personally, friction between them at an official level became immediately apparent when Lanfranc demanded that before the consecration Thomas should make him a full profession of obedience and take an oath of loyalty. Wulfstan of Worcester had had no problem with doing so,[10] but Thomas saw the demand differently. He was a fellow metropolitan and refused both demands. Only if written evidence of a precedent were produced would he consider it. Malmesbury says that Lanfranc produced witnesses who vouched for such evidence, although it is difficult to know what this evidence was or whether it really existed. At any rate Thomas refused to accept it and left without being consecrated.

At first Thomas was supported by King William, who thought that Lanfranc was being unreasonable. When Lanfranc subsequently presented his case before William the king was persuaded of its justice and ordered Thomas to return to Canterbury and write a profession that could be read out before the other bishops. Nothing was said of the oath, and in any case William would not have welcomed tenants-in-chief taking oaths of loyalty to others than himself. When the profession of obedience was made it was far from binding for all eternity. Thomas professed obedience for himself personally, but insisting that this was only between himself and Lanfranc he conceded nothing that would commit his successors in any way. He was then duly consecrated.

In the autumn of the following year both archbishops went to Rome to receive their pallia. At the papal court Thomas raised the issue of the primacy and he went further by claiming that the dioceses of Worcester, Lichfield and Dorchester rightfully belonged to the northern province. There was no justification for the claim, but York needed more sees and there had been times when Worcester and York had been held in plurality, with York enjoying the revenues of both. Pope Alexander considered that these matters did not fall within his competence and referred them to an English council to be presided over by a legate, the cardinal deacon Hubert.

At the Easter council at Winchester in 1072 Lanfranc made his case based on a variety of sources, including Bede and the series of letters already referred to. Other important material was claimed to have been destroyed in the fire which had recently engulfed the cathedral at Canterbury. It is possible that at this stage the papal letters contained the forged interpolations, but historians today absolve Lanfranc from guilt in the matter, putting the responsibility on the Christ Church monks who had prepared the case for him. Indeed, R.W. Southern argues that the additions to the papal letters were not made until 1120. On the face of it Lanfranc secured a convincing victory at Winchester, confirmed at the subsequent Whitsun Council at Windsor. The church of York was to be subject to Canterbury and its archbishop as primate of all England. The archbishop of York and his suffragans were to attend councils summoned by the archbishop of Canterbury. Lichfield, Worcester and Dorchester belonged to Canterbury; York was to have only Durham and such dioceses as existed in Scotland. York was to make the profession of obedience to Canterbury. Lanfranc 'out of love of the king' withdrew his insistence that Thomas should take an oath to him, but the concession was not to be taken as a precedent. Victory for Lanfranc this may have been, but developing papal policy did not favour primacies and Alexander II refused to confirm it. Future archbishops of York consequently did not feel obliged to be bound by the decision. The conflict persisted whenever there was a new archbishop in either province.

Anselm

It may come as a surprise that Anselm championed the cause of Canterbury's primacy with tenacity and vigour until the end of his life. He was certainly not interested in the exercise of worldly power for its own sake but the primacy of Canterbury was fundamental to Anselm's whole vision of his role as archbishop. He believed strongly that the see of Canterbury and all that pertained to it was granted to him in trust by God and His saints and that any diminution or alienation of its rights would be a betrayal of that trust. More than that, he saw it as fundamental to his vision – a vision that by 1109 had become anachronistic – of a monastic cathedral of Canterbury with primatial authority over the 'whole of the British Isles'.[11] He 'believed in a monastically orientated Church, in which monastic communities served as centres of devotion and offered the hope of Redemption to a surrounding population of benefactors, friends and well-wishers of all ranks of society. He believed also that the monastic community of Canterbury with a primatial authority was the source of order throughout the whole huge area of the archbishop's primatial authority. This was part of an unchanging order of things.'[12]

The history of Anselm's struggle for the primacy is the history of his failure to secure this vision, despite a letter which he wrote near the end of his life to archbishop-elect Thomas II of York: 'You can be very certain that I shall exert myself in every possible way to see that the church of Canterbury does not lose one scrap of her prestige in my time.'[13] A few years before, in 1101, he had written to Pope Paschal II: 'Your Holiness should be aware that as long as I live, with God's help, the privileges and usages of the kingdom of England shall not be diminished.' This demonstrated an attitude to the papacy which he extended to an insistence that the archbishop of Canterbury should be a papal legate, *ex officio*, and any other legate should be excluded from the kingdom. The presence of papal legates at the Windsor Council of 1100 was far from welcome to him, and in a charter issued at that council he styled himself 'archbishop of Canterbury, primate of Great Britain and Ireland, and vicar of the supreme pontiff Paschal'.[14]

As has been shown above, however, Lanfranc's success in asserting his authority over York had been illusory and Anselm's attempts to do so were therefore ultimately doomed. At his consecration by the archbishop of York a dispute broke out over whether he should be consecrated as 'metropolitan' or 'primate'. The two sources, Eadmer and Hugh the Chantor, in describing this demonstrated their partisanship. According to Eadmer, the phrase that Thomas objected to was 'of the whole of Britain metropolitan' and the phrase he approved of was 'of the whole of Britain primate'.[15] In Hugh's version the word objected to was 'primate' and he reported that Anselm was consecrated metropolitan.[16]

When Archbishop Thomas died he was succeeded by Gerard, who was translated from the see of Hereford. As a suffragan he had already taken an oath of obedience to Anselm and it could be argued that this remained valid when he moved to York. Even so, Anselm was determined to secure papal confirmation of his claim to supremacy. Paschal II had no wish to be committed to this for it ran contrary to post-Gregorian principles. The notion of episcopal hierarchies was alien. Metropolitans were part of the accepted order provided that their only superior was the pope, who had personally confirmed their suitability for office by bestowing the pallium on them. Whenever a messenger went from Anselm to Rome he sought confirmation of the primacy of Canterbury, and every time Paschal sought to avoid yielding anything significant. Anselm found himself faced with an equivocal pope, an increasingly hostile king, a difficult archbishop of York supported by a determined chapter and a Canterbury chapter that gave the impression that he was not fighting his cause as effectively as he should have been.

Perhaps to offset his lack of wholehearted appreciation of Anselm's attempt to remain loyal against his own judgement to the papal line on investiture and homage, Paschal made some piecemeal concessions regarding the primacy.[17] In April 1102 he confirmed Anselm as primate as his predecessors had held it. The following November he ordered Gerard to swear obedience to Anselm and a year later he extended this obedience to all future archbishops, but only so far as it had been enjoyed by Anselm's predecessors. In reality Paschal had granted nothing substantial for Canterbury, or that might embarrass future popes. Eventually, at the settlement of the investiture dispute in England in 1107, Archbishop Gerard promised to show Anselm the same obedience as he had shown when bishop of Hereford, but nothing was done to bind his successors. Hugh gives a colourful example of the basic emotions that the issue could provoke in men who should have known better.[18] At the Westminster Council held at the end of September 1102 (see Chapter 3) a seat for Anselm had been placed by some of his monks in a superior position to that for Gerard. Gerard felt himself insulted, and openly cursing the man who had done this, kicked over the seat. He refused to sit down until his seat was placed on an equal level to Anselm's. Not surprisingly, Eadmer says nothing of the incident, making it quite clear that Anselm presided while Gerard took his place with 12 others.[19]

Gerard died on 21 May 1108. Thomas, nephew of Thomas I, son of Bishop Samson of Worcester (1096–1112) and a member of one of the greatest families of royal administrators, was nominated Gerard's successor. Anselm was not unfavourably disposed to Thomas personally but he remained intransigent in his determination to obtain Thomas's submission. It was an issue that loomed large in the final year of Anselm's life. He wrote to Paschal urging him to withhold the pallium until Thomas had professed obedience to him, for he feared that once Thomas had received this symbol of his metropolitan office he would never submit. Anselm wrote: 'If this should happen, you may know that the Church in England will be torn asunder and brought to desolation. I could on no account remain in England for I neither ought to, nor can suffer the primacy of our Church to be destroyed in our lifetime.'[20] We do not know whether it troubled Anselm that if he once again abandoned Canterbury for exile he might be doing even more damage. He was an old man approaching the end of his life and one wonders whether he had become afflicted by an obsession, as can happen with old people. His final letter to Thomas[21] was written in uncompromising language and he suspended Thomas from his priestly office until he should become more submissive. Every bishop was sent a copy.

Many readers today would probably agree with Bishop Samson that Anselm had got the matter out of perspective. William of Malmesbury describes Samson as belonging to the old school.[22] He was far removed from the Gregorian reformers, no champion of clerical celibacy and a scholarly administrator who enjoyed a comfortable lifestyle. Like his friend Ivo of Chartres he favoured workable compromises. He was the very antithesis of Anselm but he was a loyal suffragan of Canterbury and Anselm trusted him. When Anselm sought his advice he diplomatically replied: 'If I truly knew what would be best for you and for us, I should not hesitate to tell you. But this I may say, that it seems unworthy of you that you should be too angry over this affair.'[23]

It must be remembered that the canons of York were remorseless in their determination not to allow their archbishop to do anything that might lead to a diminution of his and so their status. They were able but difficult men. Their influence extended beyond the cathedral. Along with the archbishop they played an important part in the community's legal and commercial transactions. The archbishop owned one of the six wards. His land was 'as free from all customs as the king's is to the king', and he derived considerable income from commercial tolls and customs duties, as his ward was based on the River Ouse. The archbishop and canons also enjoyed immediate supervision of the frithstol, or chair of peace, which gave them great influence in the administration of criminal justice and provided the canons with a substantial income. In their houses and lands the canons enjoyed the same customs as the king and archbishop did in theirs and all under the protection of St Peter.[24]

Thomas II had grown up with the canons and must have been well aware of the sort of men they were. When his predecessor Gerard died they opposed with the greatest stubbornness his burial in the church.[25] William of Malmesbury does not explain why, but presumably it was because they believed he had dishonoured the province by what they saw as a failure to stand up to Anselm. They were in no way reluctant to throw back any mud that the monks of Christ Church slung at them. Two quotations will suffice to illustrate the point. According to Eadmer,[26] when the canons refused to sanction Thomas visiting Canterbury and he sought Anselm's advice as to what he should do, 'These Canons, knowing that Anselm was worn by ill-health as well as by advancing years, reckoned that he would very soon depart this life and so they raised a fictitious claim that the Church of York was on a level with the Church of Canterbury', and wrote to Anselm to that effect. The Canons had no reservations about challenging in graphic language any claims they believed to be wrongly made by Canterbury: 'The monks of Canterbury do not cease to aim at and shamelessly demand what is unjust; they think on it while awake and dream of it in their sleep, and pine away for grief; nor do they mind by what means they recover it, as long as they succeed.'[27] Both writers could be economical with the truth. When Eadmer quoted documents from York he had no compunction about dropping phrases that did not help the Canterbury cause, and Hugh was ready to distort the truth if it suited.

Anselm died with the primacy issue unresolved, but soon after his death the king and the bishops combined to put pressure on Thomas. They were doubtless weary of the whole business. Henry's main concern was to secure a unified church rather than canonical niceties and supported Anselm as a way to achieve that goal. He and the bishops combined to put pressure on Thomas, who yielded and made a profession of obedience to the church of Canterbury through Richard, bishop of London.[28] Canterbury's victory was brief. Archbishop Thomas was grossly overweight. 'He was full-bodied and fatter than he should have been', wrote Hugh, and he died prematurely on 24 February 1114 after less than five years in office and just two months before Ralph d'Escures, bishop of Rochester, was translated to Canterbury. Thomas's successor Thurstan, urged on by his chapter, was even more intransigent than his predecessors. What had been an irritation was turned into a crisis.

Thurstan of York

This crisis must be put in its broader context. Henry was determined to maintain established customs and judgements regarding the church. He wished to support Canterbury against York and he wished to maintain the barriers to papal influence in England. He had problems with the king of France. The dispute was an irritating diversion but more threatening than that papal politics might be used against him in France. It had been royal policy since the Conquest to restrict the entry of papal legates into England without the king's consent. Nor did Henry want them interfering in Normandy. The legate Cuno, for instance, was a militant and inflexible reformer. According to William of Malmesbury,[29] he was an intransigent supporter of the pope and was quite impervious to the bribes used by Henry I to discourage other legates from meddling in his affairs. He had no qualms about suspending all the Norman abbots and bishops when they refused to attend a council at Châlons-sur-Marne in July 1115. Moreover he supported the French King Louis VI in excommunicating Henry's nephew Theobald count of Blois and Chartres and laying his lands under an interdict.[30] The papacy, for its part, had problems of its own. Paschal's relationship with Emperor Henry V was not easy and he had a series of anti-popes to contend with. The situation was made more complicated when, following his marriage to King Henry's 8-year-old daughter Matilda in 1110, Emperor Henry became King Henry's son-in-law.

This was the setting when Thurstan was appointed to York on 15 August 1114 without any reference to the chapter. Clearly Henry thought he was the right man despite the fact that at the time he was a mere sub-deacon. Before he could function as an archbishop he had to be ordained deacon and then priest, installed in York Minster and finally consecrated bishop. His parents came from Bayeux, as did his archiepiscopal predecessors the two Thomases. He may well have been educated at Caen, with its recently founded abbey of St Stephen quite a nursery for bright young men and potential leaders of the Anglo-Norman church. Maurice, bishop of London, had granted Thurstan's father Auger a prebend in St Paul's which passed to his brother Arduen, later to be bishop of Évreux, when Auger died in 1104. Thurstan also received a prebend in St Paul's. This was worth very little as most of the land assigned to it was under the sea. Such was Thurstan's ability that he soon became a chaplain to William Rufus and then Henry I, and in time he succeeded Anselm as spiritual adviser to Henry's sister Adela of Blois. Further evidence of his intellectual ability is the fact that among his friends and supporters was the great Ivo, bishop of Chartres.

In December 1114 Thurstan was ordained deacon by William Giffard, bishop of Winchester and he was enthroned in York while still a mere deacon by Robert de Limesy, originally bishop of Chester but subsequently of Lichfield and Coventry. His intellectual ability, administrative skills and warm and generous personality quickly won over the canons as, no doubt, did his friendship with some of the rich and powerful. They looked to him to withstand with full vigour the claims of Canterbury, and he did not disappoint them. His first step was to delay ordination. Although this was a severe limitation on his spiritual functions and a necessary prerequisite for consecration, it meant that he had done nothing to put himself in a position of obligation to Canterbury. He and the chapter had time to work out their policy towards Canterbury while he attended to pastoral and administrative duties.

The archbishop of Canterbury was the former bishop of Rochester Ralf d'Escures, sometime abbot of Sées. As we have seen, he was not actually Henry's choice. Despite the pope's anger at his being translated from Rochester to Canterbury without his approval, Ralph received the pallium from the papal legate Anselm of St Saba, the great Anselm's nephew. Until his temper was soured by the very unpleasant and dangerous illness which killed him in 1122, he had a reputation for being a witty and genial man who enjoyed a joke and was known for his generosity, although he perhaps lacked the gravitas expected of an archbishop.[31]

For all Ralph's good nature he was not prepared to yield to Thurstan on the matter of the primacy. Thurstan was equally resolute. He pointed out to King Henry that nowhere else did one metropolitan make a profession of obedience to another. He also made the shrewd point that if he did make profession to Canterbury he would be obliged to side with him if he were ever to come into conflict with the king. He told his chapter that only the pope could resolve the problem and that he would go to Rome to seek his advice. Intelligence reached Henry that Thurstan and some of the canons had crossed to Normandy on Christmas Day 1114. Henry did not act unreasonably towards the man he had always held in high regard, and following the advice of legate Cuno he allowed Ranulf Flambard to ordain him priest in Bayeux at Whitsun (6 June) 1115. Thurstan continued to enjoy a positive relationship with his notorious suffragan.

Thurstan remained an unconsecrated bishop. When he and Ralph were together at the royal council at Westminster in September 1115 Canterbury demanded the oath of obedience, and not surprisingly Thurstan refused. Although Paschal was moving ever more positively to his side, Thurstan was wracked by anxiety and qualms of conscience. He believed himself to be a fraud for he had the office, title and income of an archbishop of York but was unable to fulfil his spiritual responsibilities. He accordingly took a step that caused considerable consternation. In March 1116 the king had summoned a council at Salisbury at which he required his magnates, lay and ecclesiastical, in the interests of the security of the realm to accept his son William as king in the event of his death.[32] This was uncontentious. Then the Canterbury–York issue came up. The king wanted to put an end to the whole dispute and threatened Thurstan with severe consequences if he remained obstinate. But Thurstan knew that Paschal was firmly on his side, for on his way to Salisbury he had received two letters from a papal messenger for the attention of the clergy of York and the archbishop of Canterbury. They made clear that the pope confirmed Thurstan's election and that he must be consecrated without the profession, preferably by Ralph, but failing that, another bishop. Fearful of the consequences, Thurstan had kept the letters to himself. Four of the king's leading magnates were required to deliver his ultimatum to Thurstan. His response was publicly, in the presence of king and magnates, to resign his archbishopric.

Dramatic though this gesture was – according to Hugh the Chantor it reduced the king and most of his court to tears[33] – once the initial sensation had passed little changed. Thurstan himself came to doubt whether he really could resign without papal approval, and the York chapter continued to recognise him as their archbishop-elect, as did both Henry and Paschal. Thurstan actually went with the king to Normandy in April, and although Henry denied him permission to go to Rome he remained in Normandy, where the king treated him honourably and continued to refer to him as 'archbishop'. In due course Henry restored his temporalities to him.

Meanwhile Ralph had been sent on what proved to be an abortive mission to Rome. His illness was getting a grip[34] and he was unable to reach Benevento, whence Paschal had fled in the face of hostility from Henry V and rebellion in Rome. Instead he aggravated relationships with Paschal by accepting the Emperor's invitation to visit him in his camp outside Rome, where he stayed for eight days. His attempt to negotiate with Paschal through messengers was met with a particularly unhelpful response that was symptomatic of the pope's adroitness at expressing himself in such a way that he appeared, at first reading, to be making a concession, while in reality granting nothing precise.[35] He merely assured Ralph that 'we in no way diminish any authentic privileges possessed by Canterbury'. However a subsequent letter issued on 5 April left Ralph in no doubt as to the reality of Paschal's thinking.[36] Ralph was ordered to consecrate Thurstan without any demand for submission. If he refused, York's suffragans were to perform the ceremony. To help Thurstan's cause further the papal chancellor, Cardinal John of Gaeta, came down firmly on his side. None of this was good news for Henry, for it became increasingly clear that he was completely losing a grip on the situation which could only be resolved at the papal court.

Even so, Thurstan remained unconsecrated when he returned to his diocese early in 1118. Not long before, on 18 January, Paschal had died and was succeeded by John of Gaeta as Gelasius II. The international situation was becoming increasingly complicated as Henry had to face attacks in Normandy by Louis of France and his Angevin and Flemish allies while the Emperor set up his own anti-pope. This was a year of considerable drama, as Henry also faced several assassination attempts while Thurstan's return to Normandy was real 'cloak-and-dagger' stuff. In the autumn he left England with his household, all in disguise, Thurstan as a common labouring man. Their hope was to meet Pope Gelasius, known to be travelling to France, without Henry's knowledge. Having agreed on a meeting place in Normandy they split up so that one group would go via Dover the other via Hastings. Even so Henry got wind of what was happening and they were apprehended in Dover, not, however, without their being able to send a messenger to the pope informing him of recent events. Gelasius decided firmly in favour of Thurstan and despatched three letters. One was to Henry – if Ralph persisted in refusing to consecrate Thurstan they would both have to appear before him for judgement. A second was to Ralph – he must consecrate Thurstan, as he had so often been ordered to do before, and must appear with him before the pope who would settle the dispute. A third was to Thurstan – if Ralph persisted in refusing to do what the papacy had required of him he must appear before him on his own.

Henry's predicament was delicate indeed. It was not in accord with English custom to allow an external authority to adjudicate on an English dispute. However, if he failed to co-operate with Gelasius he risked the situation being exploited by his enemies in Normandy, who were using William Clito as a focus of discontent. There were certainly precedents for papal intervention in northern France in the person of the legate Cuno, who was held in high regard by Thurstan and his canons. Even worse for Henry was the fact that Gelasius was dying in January 1119 after only a year in office and clearly he favoured Cuno as his successor. Cuno, in fact, had no ambition for the ultimate office but recommended someone of similar stamp, Guy, archbishop of Vienne, who succeeded as Calixtus II. The canons of York were not slow to offer him their congratulations on his election. He replied to them: 'I know that the see of Rome is a greater honour than any other, but its glory is misery and tribulation to me.' He was kept out of Rome by an imperial anti-pope but was welcomed into the protection of Louis VI, whose wife Adelaide was the pope's niece. This was not particularly good news for Henry, but Calixtus had announced his intention of working for peace and reconciliation and he was also a distant relative of Henry.

Calixtus summoned a great council to be held at Rheims on 18 October 1119. Henry actually granted permission to his Anglo-Norman prelates to attend the council on condition that they did not turn to the pope to adjudicate on complaints against each other. But to Henry's apparent horror and anger and despite, according to Eadmer, Thurstan's undertaking to refuse papal consecration, he was consecrated by Calixtus on the eve of the opening of the council.[37] He received the pallium on 1 November. This was a major breach in the barrier against papal interference in England set up by William I, which Henry I had been determined to maintain and which Canterbury, as keen as the king to keep legates out of England, had also defended. Henry's reaction was to prevent Thurstan from returning to York. Thurstan therefore found himself in the position of at last being endowed with the spiritual authority to function fully as a bishop, but with no diocese in which to do so.

Calixtus's desire for peace and reconciliation was confirmed when, perhaps urged to do so by Thurstan, he agreed to meet Henry in person near Gisors on 23 November 1119. This was the first occasion since the reign of Cnut that a pope and an English king had met face to face. The principal topic of the meeting was peace between the French and the Anglo-Normans but the issues of papal legates and the Canterbury–York dispute were also discussed. Although discussions were cordial, no decisions were made. Thurstan's banishment was not relaxed and he remained with the papal court as it continued to journey through France. The time was not wasted, for Thurstan had the chance to meet and get to know some of the most distinguished and influential leaders of Western Christendom. As Donald Nicholl wrote: 'Thurstan had now become a man of European status.'[38] He had gained the confidence of Henry I, Louis VI, the rather narrowly inflexible Cuno, on whom he became a moderating influence, and Calixtus. On the eve of his return to Italy the following spring,

Calixtus granted Thurstan a papal bull permanently exempting archbishops of York from the profession to Canterbury and another bull threatening an interdict on England and the suspension of the archbishop of Canterbury unless Thurstan was allowed to return to his diocese.

Not surprisingly this aggravated the position with regard Canterbury. The monks were determined not to let the matter rest. Having been defeated in open conflict they resorted to duplicity. It is possible that in 1120 they had inserted forged passages purporting to demonstrate Canterbury's supremacy into the series of papal letters already referred to (see above and R.W. Southern, *St Anselm*). They also played on Henry's sensitivities. Henry at no time seems to have shown personal animosity towards Thurstan, but he had been forced to allow him back despite having taken an oath to the effect that he would never do so. Moreover it was a group of mere cathedral canons who had been instrumental in his humiliation. Bishops of the southern province who for any reason felt grudges against York could also work to make things difficult. Among them were William Warelwast of Exeter, Ralph's brother Seffrid, bishop of Chichester and Alexander of Lincoln. Eadmer was appointed to St Andrews in an attempt to extend Canterbury's influence beyond the border, but he did not get on well with King Alexander and proved himself to be so unsuited to the office of bishop that he soon resigned (see below).

On 20 October 1122 Archbishop Ralph died, his illness perhaps made worse by what had amounted to humiliation by Pope Calixtus. Henry acted with uncharacteristic haste, another sign perhaps of the changing relationship of the king of England with the papacy. Possibly he feared criticism at the impending Lateran Council summoned for 18 March 1123 and which all the leading prelates of Christendom were expected to attend. He convened a council ordering all the leading men of the realm, lay and ecclesiastical, to meet him at Gloucester on 2 February.[39] It seems that Henry had no preconceived idea as to whom he wanted as archbishop, and according to *The Anglo-Saxon Chronicle* he asked the assembled company to choose an archbishop for themselves. This was the cue for friction. One group, which included most of the lay magnates, was led by the monks of Canterbury, who were clearly keen to reassert themselves after their defeat by the canons of York. They wanted a monk as archbishop. The other group, led by Roger of Salisbury, disliked monkish austerity and monastic practices so sought a secular archbishop. The monks argued that the right of election lay with them as the archbishop would head their monastic community; the suffragans claimed the right on the grounds that they too would be under the archbishop's authority and would be required to make a profession of obedience to him. They were strongly opposed to having a monastic archbishop. A compromise solution, which the monks resisted for two days, was that they would indeed be allowed to choose the archbishop, but from a shortlist drawn up by the bishops. The final choice was an Augustinian canon, William of Corbeil, prior of the house of Cicc in Essex, subsequently known as St Osyth. According to Malmesbury, 'He was a man of great piety, fairly friendly, but not lazy or lacking in sense.'[40]

Far from being the end, this was the start of more friction and wrangling. In accordance with ancient tradition that the consecration of an archbishop should be performed by the other, Thurstan offered to consecrate William. William agreed only on the condition that Thurstan would acknowledge him as the primate of all Britain. This was quite unlooked-for. The bishops, in nominating William, had misjudged him to be a nonentity. Thurstan had backed him for they liked each other and William had hitherto shown himself to be a supporter of York's case. The outcome was that William was consecrated in the royal chapel by Richard bishop of London, the founder of St Osyth priory.

He then had to go to Rome to receive the pallium. Thurstan also went to Rome in response to the pope's summons. That the two archbishops went separately does not imply mutual hostility. Thurstan arrived before William and was received with great cordiality by Calixtus and other old friends. When William arrived he faced a much cooler reception. There was serious doubt as to whether he had been canonically elected and consecrated, on the grounds that the Canterbury monks had been denied the decisive vote, the consecration had not taken place in Canterbury, the consecration was not performed by the archbishop of York and the monastic community was to be ruled by a canon rather than a monk. However, both Henry I and his son-in-law the Emperor wrote warmly in support of William and Thurstan argued strongly on his behalf. *The Anglo-Saxon Chronicle* reported that something else played its part, too: 'what overcame Rome was what overcomes the whole world, gold and silver'.[41]

The Canterbury party, not a faction willing to let matters rest, then brought up the issue of Canterbury's primacy. In doing so they made complete fools of themselves. The story is best told in the words of Hugh the Chantor, with the necessary caution that in reading them it must be remembered that Hugh delighted in any opportunity to discredit Canterbury. According to Hugh the Canterbury delegates were asked to produce written evidence of the formation of two metropolitan sees and the privileges they were claiming for their archbishop. They could only produce copies for, they said, they had left behind the originals with the papal bulls attached. However, copies without bulls were not acceptable as proof so the delegates were asked by members of the Roman curia to swear that the originals had bulls. This presented them with a problem, for they knew full well that the documents which they claimed to possess were without bulls, even if they existed at all. In the course of their discussions as to what to do one of their number suggested that they should make a false assertion, but the others had no wish to perjure themselves. They therefore agreed to the lesser evil of telling the papal officials that the bulls had not survived or had been lost. When they reported back to the curia with this explanation they were greeted with mirth at the risible suggestion that parchment should survive while lead should perish or be lost.[42]

Their subsequent attempt to bribe Guy, the papal chamberlain, was equally disastrous. Although he took their money he was in such poor standing with the majority of the curia that his support carried no weight. The monks tried to salvage something from this debacle by having Thurstan summoned before the curia to support the case for York. He refused to do so on the grounds that he had come to a council, not a trial, so was without the appropriate documentation and had had no opportunity to prepare the case. Calixtus decided that the way ahead was to have the matter settled finally by a papal legate going to England and holding a council there.

For Henry this was probably not an ideal solution. Normally he was far from enthusiastic at the prospect of papal legates entering England and holding councils, but he wanted to put an end to the whole tiresome issue. The urgency was greater because friendly relations with Anjou were coming to an end and Henry needed papal support against Fulk V.[43] He therefore went along with the proposal. On 14 December 1124 Calixtus II died and was succeeded by Honorius II, who dispatched as legate the very able John of Crema. That he was not welcome in England, probably because of his hostility to clerical marriage, can be gathered from the description of him as 'the interfering busybody from Rome' and the accounts, almost certainly fictitious, of the scandalous end to his time in England.[44] He was certainly very busy[45] and held a council at Westminster on 8 September 1125. Before he returned to Rome he made the following proposals to the two archbishops. He recommended that York should make a spoken, not written, profession of obedience to Canterbury, that Thurstan's successors were to place their hands in those of Canterbury and promise to obey him as primate and that Canterbury would cede the three rather undistinguished dioceses of Chester, Bangor and St Asaph to York.

While such a proposal had its merits, neither side found it wholly satisfactory and each set out once more for Rome. They went independently of each other, legate John accompanying Thurstan's party. Their journey was far from trouble-free and the York party arrived three weeks after Canterbury. This gave the Canterbury party the chance to do some effective lobbying and to win over to their side the distinguished academic Gilbert the Universal, bishop of London. Although Gilbert was a highly respected biblical scholar and dialectician, Hugh the Chantor was contemptuous of his preoccupation with acquiring worldly wealth, an opinion supported by Henry of Huntingdon.[46] At one stage it was part of Archbishop William's plan to make Thurstan submit by initiating a case against him in the curia. But this would have been folly. Henry I was resolute in his determination that cases should not be decided in a court outside England and any victory William might have won in Rome would have been wrecked by Henry's revenge.

The outcome was satisfactory for William, positively supported by Thurstan and welcomed by Henry. In return for renouncing his claims to the primacy William, as archbishop of Canterbury, would be a papal legate *ex officio*. This would make him the ultimate ecclesiastical authority in England, but the tenure of legateship would be only for the lifetime of the pope who granted it. Henry had been looking for such a solution since 1120. It appealed to him, for he was not slow to recognise the importance of legates as the striking force of the papal curia and to appreciate the advantage of having his own man in that office.

Irritations persisted. William could not be magnanimous in victory, for he informed Henry that he would not attend the 1126 Christmas court at Windsor if Thurstan had his cross carried before him or if he had any hand in the crown-wearing; Thurstan refused to attend William's legatine council in the following May. Even so, after more than fifty years of wrangling which ranged from petty backbiting to serious attempts at resolution in the theatre of international diplomacy, the struggle for the primacy was effectively over. Roger, archbishop of York attempted to revive the matter again in 1163 at the papal Council of Tours when he took up three days rehearsing the history of the dispute and arguing his claims. The reality was that no pope would grant a formal primacy, and without papal approval the cause was lost.

It is possible that the importance of the dispute has been exaggerated because each side had such eloquent propagandists. Although historians agree that Eadmer's *History* after the death of Anselm is not of the quality of the earlier part, Hugh the Chantor's *History* is an extremely vigorous, vibrant and, indeed, entertaining work. Although many aspects of the dispute may strike modern readers as petty and unworthy of two church leaders, recent times are full of disputes and actions by people of great power and influence that seem hardly creditable. The dispute certainly raised questions about the king's authority, his relationship with two of his greatest subjects and his place within Christian society, and it casts some light on the development of papal institutions at this time. The respective archbishops felt very strongly about the matter, as did their respective chapters, who were determined that their masters should not yield anything. The archbishops were not petty, small-minded people; among them were men of great distinction, most were very well-respected men of integrity.

Primacy of Britain

The primacy dispute extended beyond the issue of the nature of the authority of one English archbishop in his relationship with the other to that of the extent of the authority of York over the Scottish bishops and whether the archbishop of Canterbury was primate of all Britain. The ambitions of the English archbishops are paralleled by those of their English kings. There were dioceses in Ireland, Wales, Scotland and the Isles, but there was no established structure of a group of bishops under a metropolitan. This lack of structure reflected the fact that the Roman rather than Celtic form of ecclesiastical organisation had not become established outside England. Some of the Conqueror's Anglo-Saxon predecessors had claimed that they were kings of all Britain, and although William made no such assertion the establishment of his authority over Wales and Scotland suited his ambitions. This fitted with Lanfranc's statement that his predecessors had exercised the primacy over the church of York and the whole island called Britain and also Ireland, a claim echoed by Archbishop Ralph, when he wrote to the pope that the church of Canterbury had not ceased to provide pastoral care for the whole of Britain and Ireland, both as a benevolence and from its rights of primacy.[47] Eadmer reported that at the Council of Rockingham the bishops said to Rufus of Anselm: 'He is primate not only of this realm but also of Scotland, of Ireland and of the adjacent islands.'[48]

Ireland

The Irish church had long been dominated by great monasteries. Ireland had never been part of the Roman Empire and for centuries lacked the urban life necessary to the development of the Roman diocesan structure. As C.H. Lawrence explained: 'it was a pastoral society bound together by the ties of tribe and kindred'.[49] The mission of St Patrick may well have created an episcopal organisation, but the church in Ireland remained essentially monastic. There were no precise diocesan boundaries and a bishop's authority extended over the tribal settlements and the towns of Viking origin under the rule of Irish overlords. They coexisted with the tribal monastery, which had as its head an abbot who was an ordained priest. Some monasteries built up territorial empires of daughter houses, estates and churches, and even colonies like Iona founded across the Irish Sea. Such an empire was known as a *paruchia*, a pastoral unit under the authority of the ordained abbot of the founding house. Bishops worked alongside this structure and within it. Some actually entered a monastic community. Their monastery became their see and they fulfilled their specifically sacramental responsibilities in the *paruchia* while sharing administrative responsibilities with the abbot. In some monasteries, Armagh for example, the bishop was also the abbot.

In the late eleventh and early twelfth centuries a diocesan organisation akin to that in England slowly developed. Several Irish bishops were consecrated either in Canterbury or at Lambeth, the manor of the archbishop of Canterbury, among them four bishops of Dublin between 1074 and 1121. At their consecration they took the canonical oath of obedience to the archbishop. Around 1028 Donatus had been consecrated bishop of Dublin, probably by Aethelnoth of Canterbury.[50] Lanfranc consecrated two of his successors, Patrick and Donatus. Eadmer reported that in 1096 Murdoch (Muirchertach) the High King and Donald archbishop of Cashel wrote to Anselm, 'in right of the primacy which he held over them, and of the apostolic authority which he exercised', on behalf of the people of Waterford, stating that because of the size of its population Waterford required a bishop. The man of their choice was Malchus. The letter was signed by Murdoch and Donald along with Bishop Idunan of Meath, Bishop Samuel of Dublin and Bishop Ferdomnachus of Leinster. Having received favourable reports on Malchus and thoroughly examined him, Anselm received from him the profession of obedience. Then, supported by Bishop Radulf of Chichester and Gundulf of Rochester, Anselm consecrated Malchus on 28 December.[51]

A few months before, on the first Sunday after Easter, assisted by four of his suffragans, Anselm had consecrated Samuel, bishop of Dublin in Winchester cathedral.

He, too, had been thoroughly examined by Anselm, who received from him the profession of obedience. Irish by birth, Samuel and Malchus were no strangers in England as they had been monks in English monasteries, Samuel at St Albans and Malchus at Winchester, a cathedral monastery under Bishop Walchelin.

Lanfranc and Anselm were prepared to assert their authority over the Irish bishops. In 1074 bishop Patrick of Dublin had referred to Lanfranc as 'primate of the Britains', which Bartlett suggests probably means 'of the British Isles'. Eadmer's report that the people of Waterford approached Anselm out of respect for the primatial authority may not have been strictly accurate. Their letter to Anselm certainly made no mention of this.[52] Lanfranc and Anselm did not refrain from expressing, in trenchant terms, their concern about the weaknesses apparent in Irish ecclesiastical institutions and the need for moral reform. For example, moved by a letter from Gregory VII, Lanfranc admonished the Irish to abandon their immoral practices wherever they occurred, specifically the practice of abandoning and selling their wives.[53] At the same time they respected the Irish overlords, who in their turn acknowledged the claims of Canterbury.

Wales

The structure in Wales at the time of the Conquest was apparently more diocesan, as the Welsh princes had their own bishops largely independent of Canterbury.[54] In reality there was no true diocesan structure and in practice Lanfranc's relationship with the church in Wales fell far short of his ambitions to achieve authority over all Britain. He found the Welsh church 'archaic and disorganised', and not one Welsh bishop of his time is known by name.[55] As the Norman kings of England extended their authority in Wales they appointed their nominees to bishoprics under their control. Anselm asserted his authority on two occasions. In 1095 he suspended the bishop of Glamorgan, we do not know why,[56] and he suspended Wilfred, the bishop of St David's. Eadmer reported: 'he restored Wilfred, bishop of St David's in Wales, to the episcopal office, from which when his fault required it, he had himself formerly suspended him'.[57] We are not told the nature of the fault. Anselm later obtained professions of obedience in writing from the bishops of Llandaff, St David's and Bangor.[58]

In the first part of the twelfth century Bishop Urban of Llandaff (1107–34) and Bishop Bernard of St David's (1115–48) were in dispute about the boundaries of each bishop's jurisdiction. In 1132, following a number of appeals to the pope, Innocent II appointed judges delegate, as they were known, to hear the case back in Britain. Llandaff was defined as lying between the rivers Wye and Tywi, with 46 churches within the diocese. Urban, a Welshman, had apparently been a priest of Worcester as well as archdeacon of Llandaff. Bernard was Queen Matilda's chancellor when he was made bishop. He had been ordained by William of Winchester at Southwark, then, following a dispute about the rightful place for his ordination, he was consecrated by Archbishop Ralph in Westminster Abbey in the presence of the queen.[59]

In North Wales Gruffud ap Cynan had established his authority eastward. He died in 1137, and before his death his sons had continued to move further east to the Clwyd at the expense of the native rulers and the earl of Chester.[60] Previously Rufus had tried to assert his authority in North Wales by securing the appointment of the Breton Hervey to the diocese of Bangor in 1092. This proved to be disastrous. Hervey and the native Welsh soon proved to be incompatible. They had no intention of showing him the respect and reverence that he considered due to a bishop. He reacted by excommunicating many of them and enlisting the help of his brother in attempting to crush them by force of arms. Nothing was achieved, Hervey's brother was killed and Hervey, finding himself in mortal danger, hastily returned to England.[61] There he enjoyed the comforts and security of the royal court. After Henry I's victory at Tinchebrai he had thoughts of appointing Hervey to the see of Lisieux, but Anselm strongly advised against it. When in 1109, with the authority of Pope Paschal, Henry created the diocese of Ely with the abbey as its see, the worldly Hervey was appointed its first bishop.

Bangor remained vacant until 1120 when Gruffud, supported by 'all the clergy and people of Wales', nominated David 'Scotus'. He wrote to Archbishop Ralph asking him to consecrate David, threatening to find a bishop from Ireland if Ralph refused.[62] Gruffud had a good relationship with the Irish and David may have been of Irish origins. He had also spent some time as a student in Germany and in the service of the emperor.[63] He took the oath of obedience to Canterbury. Henry I had no problems with the appointment as he had probably been a loyal clerk. Henry's relationship with the Welsh princes was based on a combination of subtlety, diplomacy and cunning rather than aggression.[64] In the course of his reign Welsh bishops, most of whom were not actually Welshmen, showed loyalty to the king. Bernard of St David's attested at least forty-five royal charters and on three occasions acted as Henry's emissary to the pope. At the same time Canterbury had succeeded in asserting its authority over the Welsh dioceses, insisting that every new episcopal appointment should take a public and formal oath of obedience to the archbishop. Despite later attempts by Gerald of Wales to establish St David's as a metropolitan see, the Welsh dioceses remained subordinate to Canterbury until 1920.

Scotland and the Isles

Scotland, unlike Ireland and Wales, was a long-established kingdom in its own right, although the Anglo-Scottish political border was not clearly defined and changed according to the ambitions and military strength of the respective kings. In the period from the Norman Conquest to 1135 there were nine Scottish dioceses, including Orkney and the Isles. There was no metropolitan bishop of Scotland; not even St Andrews, despite its eminence, had an archbishop. The Scottish bishops had therefore to turn to England when the services of a metropolitan were needed, but not necessarily to Canterbury. When Lanfranc secured the primacy of Canterbury at the two councils of 1072 he conceded that the whole of Scotland should recognise York as the metropolitan with authority over the bishops from the Humber 'to the furthest limits of Scotland'.[65] Presumably, as primate of Britain he had ultimate authority over the Scottish dioceses, although he did not press it. A problem for the archbishop of York was that three bishops were required to officiate at a consecration and York had only one suffragan until Carlisle was formed in 1133. When, for instance, Archbishop Thomas consecrated Ralph of the Orkneys in 1073, Lanfranc ordered the bishops of Chester and Worcester to support him. When the diocese of Glasgow was revived Bishop Michael was consecrated by Thomas II of York and professed obedience to him as a metropolitan, but his successor John was far more reluctant to be compliant.

This may well have been due to pressure from David, brother of King Alexander I (1107–23) and his successor (1124–53), who, as an assertion of his independence of Henry I, insisted that John should be consecrated by Pope Calixtus II. As king of Scotland Alexander had acknowledged Henry's overlordship but became increasingly resentful of his subordinate status.[66] This explains his attempts to reduce the authority of the English metropolitans over Scotland. Lanfranc's grant of authority to York in 1072 had been made without any consultation with the Scots. At the same time Thurstan was determined to assert his metropolitan authority. In an attempt to counter this in 1120 Alexander approached Eadmer with a view to his filling the vacancy at St Andrews.[67] The choice proved disastrous. As Anselm's disciple Eadmer would not accept investiture at the king's hand. That particular issue was resolved when he was allowed to take the staff from the altar while receiving his ring from Alexander.

The problem was much greater than this. Alexander had hoped that Eadmer's well-known hostility to York would lead to a reduction of York's authority over St Andrews. He had not anticipated that Eadmer would insist that instead the authority of Canterbury over all the Scottish churches should be recognised. Eadmer's stance was intolerable to him and Alexander made it clear that he would never consent to a Scottish bishop being subject to the archbishop of Canterbury. Eadmer was not one to fight his cause and resigned the bishopric.

Henry I had responded to the Scottish challenge in a number of ways. In 1121 he approved Ranulf Flambard's plan to build a castle at Norham upon Tweed to protect the northern border while resuming control of the lordship of Carlisle. In 1122 he began work on a castle at Carlisle and 11 years later the pope sanctioned the formation of the diocese of Carlisle, thereby establishing for the area independence of the bishop of Glasgow. A consequence of the Eadmer fiasco was that Alexander and then David, as a mark of their independence of the king of England, sought the elevation of St Andrews to metropolitan status. The papacy refused to acquiesce and not until 1192 did Celestine III, while not granting St Andrews metropolitan status, state unequivocally in writing to King William (1165–1214): 'the Scottish Church shall be subject to the Apostolic See, as an especial daughter thereof, without the intervention of any person whatsoever'.[68]

4

Mitred Civil Servants: The Rise and Fall of the Salisbury Dynasty

The bishops were among the most powerful men in any kingdom. They were the dominant members of an exclusive sector within society, the clergy, and they were great lords and landowners. Some notorious exceptions apart, they were well educated and literate, with the administrative skills and experience required to run their own households and dioceses. To attain the office of bishop was the goal of many very intelligent, highly ambitious young men, some of whom owed their worldly success to their ability to make themselves indispensable to the effective working of the king's government. Of William the Conqueror's chancellors four – Herfast, Osbern, Osmund and Maurice – became bishops, of Elmham, Exeter, Salisbury and London, respectively. In twelfth-century England government and administration were becoming increasingly complex.

Medieval government was the king's government. Although at his coronation service the king made promises which recognised that he had obligations to those whom he ruled and his powerful subjects, at least, had certain expectations of him, the machinery of government, such as it was, existed primarily to serve his interests. Henry I's coronation charter included a series of promises which he hoped would be acceptable to the lay magnates. It was very much intended to secure their support and, indeed, that of a range of members of the community after his hasty seizure of the throne. Although it was probably worth about as much as an election manifesto today, it was still remembered in the period leading to *Magna Carta* (see Chapter 9). Stephen also issued a charter at the time of his coronation in which he promised to maintain all the good laws and customs which had been enjoyed in the time of Edward the Confessor and which King Henry his uncle had granted and conceded.[1]

Medieval government is often described as household government. Anglo-Norman kings and their Angevin successors were continuously on the move in their capacities as kings of England, dukes of Normandy until 1144, rulers of an Angevin 'empire' in the reigns of Henry II and Richard I, and feudal lords. Certain towns or cities were more important than others, like London, Winchester and Gloucester. The treasury had long been at Winchester and by Stephen's reign the exchequer was coming to meet regularly at Westminster. Even so, although

Rouen was regarded as the chief city of Normandy, there was no formal capital city of England. Kings enjoyed staying in their hunting lodges such as Clarendon on the Wiltshire/Hampshire border. There was no fixed point from which they governed the Anglo-Norman realm. They travelled with their household, *curia regis*, of which there were two aspects, that which was permanently with the king, and *magnum concilium*, the great council. This was a gathering with the king of the great men of the realm, lay and ecclesiastical, on grand formal occasions like those at Christmas, Easter and Whitsun when the king wore his crown and matters of moment were discussed.

Curia regis was less formal and was, in a sense, the king's extended family (the Latin for household is *familia*). An important document exists from the reign of Henry I, *Constitutio Domus Regis*. This is a handbook listing the offices of the king's household and the salaries attached to them. It has its limitations but includes not only great men like the chancellor, the master of the writing-chamber, the chaplain and the treasurer, but also those who looked after the king's daily domestic needs and those, like the keeper of the greyhounds, who ensured that the royal sport of hunting went smoothly. The chancellor was well rewarded with five shillings a day, a superior simnel loaf and two salt simnels, four gallons of dessert wine and one of *vin ordinaire*, one large wax candle and forty candle-ends. The keepers of the greyhounds each received threepence a day and twopence for their men plus a halfpenny for each greyhound.[2]

When the king was in Normandy a great deal of business followed him and we find the same names looking after English or Norman affairs in his absence. William I often left his wife Matilda in Normandy as his representative. Among the baronage were those who witnessed charters in Normandy and in England. In the king's absence England was entrusted to members of his family like Odo of Bayeux and Robert of Mortain, or great magnates like William fitz Osbern. Lanfranc, too, played a vital part in looking after England in William's absence. At the time of the rebellion of 1075 Lanfranc wrote to William to say that he had everything under control and there was no need for William to return to England.

Rufus spent most of his time in England until Robert went to the Holy Land. This provided Ranulf Flambard with his opportunity to emerge and demonstrate his 'shrewd and ruthless efficiency'.[3] He was skilled at extorting money from all available sources and consequently became very unpopular. His promotion to the see of Durham did not prevent him from fleecing the church. He had judicial responsibilities as well and Orderic gave him the title *justiciar*. One of Henry's first acts in his bid for popularity was to arrest and imprison Flambard.

After the defeat and capture of his brother Robert, Henry I spent much more time in Normandy than did Rufus. He visited Normandy on 11 different occasions, spending about 230 months out of England. His household and court went with him and some magnates and household officers were active in both England and Normandy. Others concentrated their time and work in either Normandy or England. After the death of Queen Matilda and the tragedy of 1120 the position of Bishop Roger of Salisbury as second in command was unassailable. He, and a number of his lay associates like Ralph Basset, acted as justices hearing pleas in the king's absence.

It is sometimes said that it was the effectiveness of Anglo-Saxon institutions which enabled the Norman Conquest to proceed so speedily and efficiently. The existence of shires, hundreds and vills is well known. While the earl lost his importance after the Conquest as a regional administrator his place as royal offi-cial acting in the localities was taken by the sheriff. In the sealed writ, a royal command tersely expressed in writing and sealed, the king had an effective instru-ment for asserting his authority.[4] The English coinage was the finest in northern Europe. *Domesday Book* is a remarkable and unique tribute not only to the effi-ciency of Anglo-Norman administration but to the Anglo-Saxon inheritance. The skills and methods used in the course of the Domesday inquest must have been employed in the actual implementation of the Conquest. The entry in *The Anglo-Saxon Chronicle* for 1085 is well known. Stubbs, in his *Select Charters*, also quotes an important statement by the bishop of Hereford about the Domesday inquest procedure and the reaction to it.[5] The investigation was made by a number of barons, lay and ecclesiastical, who sought answers on the oath of the sheriff of the shire and of all the barons and their Frenchmen, and of the whole hundred, of the priest, the reeve and six villani of each village.

The 'twelfth-century renaissance' and birth of the civil service

As well as being a geld book and a tribute to the legacy of the Anglo-Saxons, *Domesday Book* can be seen as an expression of the intellectual revival in Europe that was becoming apparent at this time: 'Normandy was a fertile breeding ground for clerks.'[6] Lanfranc and Anselm were pre-eminent among many. From about the middle of the twelfth century western Europe became stirred by an intellectual excitement partly stimulated by the challenges posed by the inves-titure conflict. A consequence of and a stimulus to the intellectual activity of the period were the schools. Hitherto the principal schools were those that were part of monasteries and those that were attached to cathedrals. Without literacy it was not possible to lead a full monastic life and the cathedrals needed men who could administer them, as well as meeting their liturgical demands. The main role of the monastic schools was to teach the boys who entered as child oblates. They were essentially closed institutions, although there were a few mon-asteries, as we have seen, like Bec, with schools which welcomed outsiders and attracted them by the quality of their teachers. The cathedral schools were open to a wider range of people and during the twelfth century schools came into existence that, while being subject to the control of the ecclesiastical authorities, were only loosely attached, if at all, to a specific cathedral or monastery. Instead they were focused on individual masters whose fame attracted students to them. Some of these masters moved from place to place, taking established pupils with them and inspiring new ones. The most exciting and controversial teacher of the first half of the twelfth century was Peter Abelard. His massive ego was matched by his intellectual ability – there were others less sensational and equally distinguished, although Abelard refused to acknowledge that this could possibly be so. The twelfth century was the golden age of the schoolmaster and teaching and in R.W. Southern's famous words: 'teaching – it is hard to believe it, but it seems to be true, became a road to profit as well as fame'. As Southern also wrote: 'a kind of bush-telegraph rapidly developed to signal the masters who were worth finding and places where they were to be found'.[7]

Anselm's fame drew to Bec students from Pisa, Milan and Germany and large numbers travelled from England. Another celebrated school in the early years of the twelfth century was that at Laon, which flourished under another Anselm and his brother Ralph. Links with England were strengthened when, in 1107, Henry I managed to impose his chancellor Waldric on Laon as its bishop. The demand for fine teachers grew because they could teach the skills that commanded great rewards. Their practitioners filled the highest places in the government and administration of the church, and as secular government became more sophisticated they became royal servants as well. The use of the abacus, crucial to the development of the English Exchequer, had been the subject of a treatise by the future Pope Sylvester II (999–1003) when he was the distinguished schoolmaster and tutor to the future emperor Otto III, and Ralph and Anselm wrote about the abacus and taught mathematics. Another distinguished mathematician who taught at Laon was the Englishman Adelard of Bath, who also wrote about the abacus and may later have become an exchequer official.

The election of Bishop Waldric was certainly highly controversial. Although Laon was not in Henry I's dominions it suited him to have an Englishman in a key position there, a goal achieved by paying significant sums of money, the sin of simony. Waldric was hardly a spiritual man. He had participated in the Battle of Tinchebrai and actually taken Duke Robert prisoner. He was not welcomed by the clergy of Laon cathedral. The citizens took such a great dislike to him that in an uprising in 1112 they subjected him to a violent death. Nevertheless the school attracted many Englishmen of distinction; indeed 'it became a Mecca for English scholars'.[8] They included Alexander and Nigel, the nephews of Roger of Salisbury who themselves became bishops; Gilbert the Universal, the scholarly bishop of London; Robert bishop of Exeter; Robert Bethune bishop of Hereford and an archbishop of Canterbury, William of Corbeil. In 1113 a disastrous fire broke out in Laon cathedral. The canons went on a fundraising tour of England, where they were welcomed by distinguished former students.[9] Fine schools also became established in England at the cathedrals of Salisbury, Lincoln, St Paul's and Exeter. The distinction of Salisbury was due to the fact that Guy of Étampes had studied at Laon and Ranulf, Waldric's successor as chancellor, sent his sons there also. Their tutor was William of Corbeil. Oxford and Northampton were not cathedral towns but, thanks to the Augustinian canons at Oseney and

St Frideswide's, Oxford became an important centre of teaching and learning in the reign of Henry I, and Northampton had a brief period of distinction in the latter years of the century.

These fine schools educated men of the calibre required to run the institutions of government that were emerging at this time. In 1066 and, indeed, in 1087 and 1100 there were no permanent centralised institutions of government that could run independently of the king under their own momentum. The reign of Henry I saw a great step forward with the formation of the Exchequer. We see at this time the creation of the office of Justiciar, its holder being 'second only to the king', and the regular appointment of a chancellor. The men who held key offices and those who worked with and under them enjoyed a combination of formal training in the schools and practical experience in a royal, episcopal or baronial household. There were opportunities for able and ambitious men, regardless of their background – to 'rise from the dust' in the somewhat derogatory words of Orderic Vitalis – and work with some of the greatest magnates of the realm, lay and ecclesiastical. Leading clergy like Roger of Salisbury, Henry of Blois and Gilbert Foliot, like Odo of Bayeux before them, gave opportunities not just to members of their own families, although they found nothing wrong in that, but also to poor scholars who showed promise regardless of their family circumstances. Great English civil servants were willing to learn from experts in Norman Sicily, like the Englishman Thomas Brown, who was distinguished at the court of Roger II and returned to England on Roger's death in 1154.

The birth of bureaucratic government

In the words of Judith Green: 'By 1135 it is possible to identify much more clearly than in 1100 the beginnings of a central administration in England distinct from the royal household.'[10] There is no evidence of a chancery in England or Normandy before the Conquest. The Norman chaplain Herfast, whom Lanfranc disapproved of so strongly, was the first to be designated chancellor in England. As came to be usual he was rewarded with a bishopric, that of Elmham, for which, in Lanfranc's eyes at least, he was ill-suited.[11] By the time of Henry I the chancellor was in the first rank of household officers and very highly paid. He was responsible for the king's devotional needs as well as his secretarial ones. In charge of the king's seal, he had beneath him the master of the writing office who actually had custody of the seal. He and the chancellor supervised the royal chaplains, part of whose work was to write writs and keep records.

By the end of the reign of Henry I financial administration had become more professional than ever before. Government continued to be household government, functioning wherever the king was. The chamber travelled with the king, received cash and made payments when he was on the move. It met the king's daily needs whether in his private capacity or as the chief public figure.

The earlier Anglo-Saxon kings had kept their cash and moveable wealth in their own bedchamber and wardrobe. From the reign of Cnut there are references to a store at Winchester where a permanent treasury came to be located. In the twelfth century aspects of financial management came to be detached from the royal household. The Treasury remained fixed at Winchester and became more than just a storehouse. It received much of the royal revenue and disbursed it to the king's creditors. Its officers, who lived in Winchester or had manors in Hampshire, kept elaborate accounts subject to the scrutiny of external auditors. It heard pleas as well as looking after cash. *Domesday Book* was housed there and consulted in cases of dispute. In 1111 the bishops of Salisbury, London and Lincoln were present with Queen Matilda and gave judgement in favour of the Abbot of Abingdon when he claimed that his manor of Lewknor owed nothing to Pyrton Hundred. Cases of that sort were soon to be heard by the Exchequer.

In fact, according to Roger of Salisbury's great nephew, Richard fitz Nigel, the author of *The Dialogue of the Exchequer* (*Dialogus de Scaccario*), the main task of the Exchequer was to determine court cases. The Exchequer was not at this time a place so much as an occasion when the Justiciar and other Barons of the Exchequer met to deal with financial business and hear pleas. It took its name from a rectangular table 10 feet by 5 covered with a cloth ruled in such a way that it looked like a chessboard. In reality the white columns of the abacus were painted onto a black cloth. The sheriff attended twice a year to present his accounts in the presence of the Justiciar and Treasurer who subjected him to rigorous questioning. Counters were placed on the cloth according to the system used on the abacus. The abacus came to be known in England in the reign of Rufus thanks to the Lotharingian bishop of Hereford, Robert, who demonstrated its use.[12] Using the counters it was possible to compare what the sheriff owed with what had been received. The results were then recorded on wood and parchment in the form of tally sticks and pipe rolls. A notched stick was split down its length and one half was stored in the Treasury (see the photograph in *Dialogus de Scaccario* opposite page xi). The sheriff , who might be illiterate, kept the other, which he could easily understand and produce if there was a dispute. Details were also recorded on pieces of parchment which were rolled up and known as pipe rolls and kept along with the tallies in the Treasury.

The rise of Roger of Salisbury

The greatest of all the 'mitred civil servants' in the first part of the twelfth century was Roger, bishop of Salisbury. Not only was he personally essential to the efficiency of the government of King Henry I, he created a dynasty of distinguished administrators. While Roger of Salisbury did not actually invent the Exchequer its development under him has been regarded as one of his greatest achievements. According to William of Newburgh's well-known but possibly fabricated story, Roger as a young man was a poor priest in the suburbs of Caen who commended himself to Henry on account of the speed with which he celebrated mass. According to this story, when Prince Henry was campaigning against his brother Rufus, he and his companions by chance called at a church where Roger was officiating. Apparently he rattled his way through the service, which so pleased the soldiers that they could think of no one better to be a chaplain to military men. Having been commanded by Henry to 'Follow me', he stuck as closely to him as Peter did to Jesus Christ.[13] An invention the story may well be, but it is perhaps an attempt to account for Roger's remarkable rise. He remained a loyal servant of the king until Henry's death in 1135. He was probably born some time between 1065 and 1070, and although Newburgh somewhat loftily states that he was practically unlettered, there is documentary evidence from the time of his election as bishop of Salisbury that he had been a priest of Avranches. As we know from Eadmer[14] under Lanfranc, who taught there for a while, it became a well-regarded centre of intellectual activity.

Shortly after the alleged initial meeting, probably in 1091 when Roger was in his early twenties, Prince Henry placed his new chaplain in charge of what remained of his £5000 inheritance and Roger sorted out his finances. After Henry's coronation Roger entered the royal household and witnessed a royal charter issued at Westminster during Henry's first Christmas court. The following Easter he was appointed to the highly paid office of chancellor in succession to William Giffard and kept the king's seal with a staff of two or three clerks. As Henry's chancellor he rose to be elected bishop of Salisbury in 1102. Shortly after he had been invested with the ring and staff by Henry on 29 September 1102, he resigned the chancellorship, to be succeeded by Waldric.

Throughout his career Roger usually referred to himself as bishop of Salisbury rather than any other office. He paid his first recorded visit to Salisbury after his initial investment on 13 January 1103. While it was in order that he should be referred to as bishop, and he may have accepted jurisdiction over his see, he technically remained bishop elect until his formal consecration. He was not actually consecrated until 1107, when he was one of the bishops consecrated in that year at Canterbury by Anselm. He was everything that a Gregorian bishop was not. He was a highly efficient and worldly civil servant who made a fortune from his labours. However, there is no suggestion that he was ever guilty of simony. He probably had no need to be. But at a time when clerical celibacy was being asserted as proper for a priest he was married, or at least he had a long-standing and loyal 'hearth mate', Matilda of Ramsbury. Few contemporaries wrote of her but Orderic Vitalis described her as Roger's 'concubine' rather than his wife, perhaps because canon law was asserting that no bishop should be married. He had at least one son by Matilda, Roger and possibly another, Aldelm. He was certainly guilty of the third offence so roundly condemned by the reformers, nepotism, and created an extraordinary dynasty of prince bishops and royal servants.

His son Roger, later nicknamed 'the Poor', became chancellor under Stephen and an archdeacon of the diocese of Salisbury. Aldelm, too, was an archdeacon of the diocese of Salisbury and became a royal treasurer and dean of Lincoln. Roger had two nephews, probably sons of his brother Humphrey, intelligent young men who attended the school at Laon. Both became bishops. In 1123 Alexander 'the Magnificent' succeeded Robert Bloet at Lincoln where he commissioned the archdeacon, Henry of Huntingdon, to write his *History*. Alexander's brother Nigel, who had been Henry's treasurer, became the second bishop of Ely in 1133 in succession to Hervey, who had died two years before. Nigel's son Richard (fitz Nigel or Neal) was treasurer under Henry II and became bishop of London. Their intimate knowledge of the operation of the king's household and government is apparent from the treatise *Constitutio Domus Regis*, probably written by Nigel, and his son's *Dialogus de Scaccario*. Roger of Salisbury and Alexander of Ely owned six castles between them. Sherborne, Salisbury, Malmesbury and Devizes enabled Roger to dominate Dorset and Wiltshire; Alexander had Newark in Nottinghamshire and Sleaford in Lincolnshire.

Undoubtedly Roger was a decidedly worldly bishop who was unlikely to have been a great spiritual leader, but he seems to have been conscientious and hardworking. It was said that he reserved the mornings for his secular duties so that he could fulfil his episcopal responsibilities in the afternoons. His resignation of the office of chancellor did not mean an end to his secular responsibilities for, as William of Malmesbury said, Henry 'committed to his care the administration of the whole kingdom, whether he might be himself resident in England or absent in Normandy'.[15] It seems that Roger was reluctant to shoulder so great an undertaking and would not have done so had not Anselm and two of his successors as archbishop of Canterbury, Ralph and William of Corbeil, and even the pope, assured him that it was his duty as an obedient subject to do what his king required of him.

Roger remained unconsecrated, and so unable to carry out the sacral duties that none but a consecrated bishop could perform, until 1107. Eadmer reported that on the occasion when, in the absence of Anselm in exile, Henry ordered Archbishop Gerard of York to consecrate Roger along with Reinhelm of Hereford and William Giffard of Winchester, Reinhelm gave back the ring and staff and resigned and William went into exile, having complained that such consecrations would be illegal.[16] Eadmer says nothing of Roger's conduct on this occasion. He too was not consecrated but discreetly avoided a confrontation (see above, p. 38).[17]

Clearly Roger was more adroit at man management and more skilled in the arts of diplomacy than Ranulf Flambard. However it would perhaps be wrong to suggest that he was a more creative and constructive administrator than Flambard, for Flambard had laid foundations on which he could build. As bishop he was no more canonically correct. His responsibilities were akin to those of Ranulf but greater, and he amassed far more wealth and power, but while Ranulf was reviled by the chroniclers little unfavourable was said of Roger. There were plenty of grumbles, but the target seems to have been those who worked on

Roger's behalf rather than Roger himself. For nearly forty years he was close to Henry and for nearly forty years until his dramatic downfall in 1139 he, in association with his kinsmen, had more influence in England than any other man. Of all the men whom Henry raised from the dust none was raised higher than Roger, the former priest of Avranches, and none wielded comparable power and influence for so long.

'Administration was a major part of Roger of Salisbury's lifework, and his ideas and actions reshaped the Anglo-Norman government and erected foundations for institutions and procedures which last to this very day.'[18] Evidence of the developments in administration and bureaucracy in Henry's reign is provided by a number of sources, the celebrated *Dialogus*, the pipe roll of 1130 which must surely have not been unique, the related tallies and the royal writs and charters. Five hundred writs and charters survive from the reigns of the first two Norman kings; more than three times that number survive from Henry's reign. About one in five of Henry's writs, 318 in all, involved Roger in some way. *The Anglo-Saxon Chronicle* for 1123 refers to Henry's love of the bishop of Salisbury who was 'strong and ruled all England'. Indeed, wrote the chronicler, Henry 'entrusted all England into the care and control of the bishop Roger of Salisbury'. Roger supervised existing institutions of government and created new ones to make it more efficient. When Henry was in England Roger was the chief administrator; when Henry was absent Roger effectively ran the country. In Henry's absence Queen Matilda was the formal regent, supported when he was old enough by their son William. Matilda was by no means a mere figurehead; Roger was her chief support. By the end of 1120 both Matilda and William were dead and Roger was supreme. The supervision of justice and finance, two closely related matters, dominated his time, but he dealt with anything that required his attention.

One of his first challenges was to raise the aid for the marriage of Henry's eldest daughter Matilda to the Emperor Henry V. The marriage of an eldest daughter, like the knighting of an eldest son, was one of the occasions when by tradition a lord could demand a financial contribution from all his tenants. To provide the 8-year-old Matilda with a fitting dowry in 1110 a tax of three shillings was imposed 'on every hide in England'.[19] Despite the fact that this was a colossal burden to impose upon the country in what was, according to *The Anglo-Saxon Chronicle*, a 'very disastrous year' due to 'bad weather by which the earth-crops were badly damaged and tree-crops all well-nigh ruined all over this land', the huge sum of £45,000 was raised for Matilda's dowry. Henry's confidence in Roger was fully justified.

One of Roger's most important contributions to the development of English government was his extension of the practice of sending justices to different parts of the country. Justices had been sent from the curia to arbitrate in local disputes and perform commissions before the reign of Henry I. The sworn inquest in the presence of royal justices may pre-date the Conquest. It had been used by William I and played a significant part in the compilation of *Domesday Book*.

Roger developed the practice and it is probably under him that judicial eyres, regular circuits through one or more counties, came into existence. There is certainly evidence from the 1130 pipe roll of circuit justiciars in one or more counties. Among the itinerant justices sent round the country by Roger was Ralph Basset.

Rarely, but when necessity and loyalty to the absent king dictated, Roger could be harsh and cruel. Another very bad year for England was 1124/5: 'There were many failures in grain and in all crops.'[20] This led to considerable inflation in the cost of seed, inflation made worse by the poor quality of silver coins: 'The penny was so bad that the man who had a pound at a market could not buy twelve penn'orth with it.' As we have seen, perhaps driven to theft by starvation, 44 men were hanged in Leicestershire by Ralph Basset, 'more thieves than ever were before'. At the same time Henry's mercenaries in Normandy complained that the coins with which they were paid had been so badly debased that they were almost worthless. Much displeased, Henry wrote to Roger demanding 'that all the moneyers who were in England should be deprived of their limbs, that was the right hands of each of them'. They were then to be castrated. This cruel penalty was enacted by Roger between Christmas 1124 and Twelfth Night, when 94 minters were summoned to Winchester. Clearly the punishment had its due effect, for we hear no more of bad coinage. Offensive though such a penalty might be to modern sensibilities, we must remember that those who deliberately set out to debase the coinage in their own interests, like tax evaders today, could be very damaging to the country's fragile economy. Unfortunately it is possible that all moneyers were linked together and the innocent were punished along with the guilty. Contemporaries were warm in their approval: 'It is rewarding to hear how severe the king was towards wicked men';[21] 'It was all very proper because they had done for all the land with their great fraud, which they paid for.'[22]

The succession problem

The death of Prince William in 1120 not only plunged Henry into overwhelming grief but presented him with the considerable problem of who should succeed him. The security of the kingdom depended on its solution. He had a number of surviving children, but only one was legitimate, Matilda. Married in 1114 at the age of 8 to the Emperor Henry V, in 1125 she became his widow. On 21 February 1121, aged 51, Henry took as his second wife Adeliza, daughter of the count of Lower Lorraine, but as time passed it became increasingly apparent that she would fail to produce the desired male heir.

The only legitimate representative of the Norman, and indeed English line was Matilda. Henry was therefore determined to secure the succession for her. Being a woman did not necessarily rule her out. In 1142–43, Brian fitz Count, who became one of her staunchest allies, engaged in a written intellectual exchange with the bishop of Winchester and Gilbert Foliot, abbot of Gloucester, seeking moral justification for his support of Matilda rather than Stephen.[23] Gilbert quoted Numbers 36 of the Bible where it was stated that daughters had a right to succeed where there were no sons. Queen Melisende ruled Jerusalem on her own after the death of her husband Fulk, but St Bernard advised Matilda to show the man in the woman; order all things so that those who see you will judge your works to be those of a king rather than a queen.

To achieve his end, in September 1126 Henry took Matilda away from Germany, where she was held in high regard and would have preferred to remain enjoying her 'many possessions',[24] and brought her with him to England. Matilda was a stranger both to England and Normandy and there was no great enthusiasm in England for the idea of a female ruler. It has been suggested that she and Bishop Roger were not well disposed towards each other. For many years after his defeat at Tinchebrai in 1106 Henry I's older brother, Robert Curthose sometime Duke of Normandy, had been held in captivity in Roger of Salisbury's castle of Devizes. But in 1126 *The Anglo-Saxon Chronicle* reported: 'the king had his brother Robert taken from the bishop Roger of Salisbury, and committed him to his son Robert earl of Gloucester, and had him led to Bristol and there put in the castle. This was all done through the advice of his daughter and through her uncle, David the king of Scots.'[25]

There was a possible alternative to Matilda to succeed Henry, his nephew William Clito, the legitimate son of Duke Robert, so the one surviving legitimate grandson of the Conqueror. He was the focus of political hostility to Henry on the Continent but had support from many Anglo-Normans who welcomed the possibility of his being a peaceful successor to Henry. Bishop Roger may well have supported William in preference to Matilda and the chronicler Henry of Huntingdon positively championed him. When Clito died from an infected wound to his hand in battle in 1128 Huntingdon was effusive in his praise of him.[26] He even went so far as to suggest that machinations against the king on Matilda's part contributed to Henry's death.[27] This may have reflected the views of Bishop Roger and his nephew Alexander bishop of Lincoln, for Henry was archdeacon of Huntingdon and a canon of Lincoln cathedral.

In 1126 Henry held his Christmas court at Windsor. According to Hugh the Chantor,[28] this could have been disrupted by friction between Archbishop William of Canterbury and Archbishop Thurstan of York. William warned the king that he would absent himself if the archbishop of York had his cross carried before him or if he had any hand in crowning him. To prevent a public spectacle Henry advised Thurstan that he must remain in his lodgings, which he reluctantly agreed to do. On 1 January 1127 the court moved to London where Henry planned to advance the cause of Matilda. 'He bound the nobles of all England, likewise the bishops and abbots, by the obligation of an oath that, if he himself died without a male heir, they would immediately and without hesitation accept his daughter Matilda as their lady.'[29] To this end the great men of the realm were required to undertake that they would give their support to Matilda should Henry die without a male heir.

There are several contemporary accounts of the council, each of which views it from a different perspective.[30] At Henry's request Bishop Roger, 'as a man of discretion and second only to the king', oversaw the proceedings.[31] The first to take the oath was the archbishop of Canterbury. William's election in 1123 had been controversial and it had required a good deal of pressure from Bishop Roger to secure it.[32] If he shared Roger's reservations about Matilda he did not make them known. In the absence of Thurstan of York Roger took the oath next, followed by the other bishops and abbots. The first layman to take the oath was David, king of Scotland, Henry I's brother-in-law. Stephen was certainly present. We are told by William of Malmesbury and John of Worcester that there was a dispute between Robert of Gloucester, illegitimate son of Henry I and half-brother of Matilda, and Stephen about who should take the oath first. This tale may conceal the reality that, along with other magnates, they were reluctant to take the oath and did so only under pressure from the king.[33] Matilda was not actually elected queen and none swore formal allegiance to her. There was, after all, the possibility that Queen Adeliza might bear Henry a male heir. Nevertheless Matilda's supporters were confident that her position for the future was secure. The oath was renewed on at least one occasion, notably at a great council at Northampton in 1131 when Matilda 'received an oath of fealty from those who had not given one before and a renewal of the oath from those who had'.[34] It is very likely that Stephen was not present on that occasion.[35] At this council Henry granted Roger the abbey of Malmesbury perhaps, suggests Kealey, on condition that he remained firm in his allegiance to Matilda.[36] Yet when Henry died in 1135 it was not his daughter Matilda but his nephew Stephen who succeeded.

Stephen secures the throne

Stephen acted with energy and secured the throne for himself. A grandson of the Conqueror, he had been the favourite nephew of Henry and had been treated with considerable generosity. He had estates in 20 English shires, mostly in the south-east. He was count of Mortain in western Normandy and count of Boulogne between Normandy and Flanders through his marriage to Matilda, daughter of Eustace III. Boulogne had important trading contacts with London and the Londoners were favourably disposed towards him. Stephen was strategically well placed in Boulogne to move with haste to England when Henry died. As soon as he heard of his death Stephen rushed to London, where the citizens acclaimed him as king. He then sped to Winchester where he was welcomed by brother Henry, bishop of Winchester, Roger, bishop of Salisbury and William de Pont de l'Arche, who controlled the treasury. There is little doubt of the importance of Henry of Blois, abbot of Glastonbury and bishop of Winchester, in helping to secure the throne for his brother. Henry was a Cluniac – Cluny was still in the ascendant, and Pope Innocent II was a Cluniac sympathiser and later confirmed Stephen's coronation and unction.

However, until Stephen had actually been crowned and anointed his position was not totally secure. Although there had been exceptions, it was usual for the ceremony to be conducted by the archbishop of Canterbury. But Archbishop William had a problem. He had been the first to take the oath to Matilda, along with other bishops and Stephen himself. His scruples had to be overcome. Stephen's supporters claimed that the oath had been extracted by force and so was worthless. They also claimed, with no evidence to confirm it, that on his deathbed Henry had changed his mind.[37] Hugh Bigod swore that this was true. Roger of Salisbury also produced a reason for breaking the oath. He claimed that he had taken it on the understanding that Henry would not marry Matilda to any foreigner without consulting him and the other chief men of the kingdom.[38] In June 1128 Matilda had married Geoffrey of Anjou, to whom she had been betrothed for political reasons, to counter the influence of William Clito. Although few at the time had known of the betrothal, Roger's argument was somewhat specious for everyone was well aware of the marriage at the time of the Northampton council three years later. The archbishop of Canterbury could resist no longer and on 22 December, three weeks after Henry I's death, Stephen was crowned. Unfortunately, perhaps, for Stephen, only three bishops were present, William, Henry and Roger. There was a complete absence of abbots and very few nobles. Nevertheless he was now a crowned and anointed king. At the coronation Archbishop William demanded that Stephen should publicly acknowledge his debt to the church by swearing that he would restore and maintain its freedom. This he did and his brother Henry made himself guarantor and surety of the oath.[39]

We need to consider why Archbishop William and Bishop Roger had broken their oaths to Henry I. Both may have felt personal animosity towards Matilda but that was probably not a significant reason. William of Malmesbury commented shrewdly on Roger's ability to adapt himself to any occasion according as the wheel of fortune turned, an echo of his remarks made at the time of his consecration.[40] Bishop Henry, Stephen's brother, undoubtedly played a significant part in securing Stephen's success. He doubtless argued the case for Stephen to Roger of Salisbury and William Pont de l'Arche, thereby ensuring Stephen's control of the machinery of government and the treasury. By assuring the archbishop that he would act as guarantor of Stephen's oath to safeguard the church he was able to overcome William's scruples. Perhaps William saw himself fulfilling the role of Stephen's principal spiritual adviser.[41] Such hopes as he had, probably illusory, came to nothing, for he died on 21 November 1136. Finally all those who had taken the oath to secure Matilda's succession, whether willingly or reluctantly, were aware of the possibility that if Stephen were not made king the country would face a threat from Matilda and the possibility of civil war. In March 1137 Stephen felt secure enough in England to cross to Normandy, where one of his actions was to placate his older brother Theobald with a promise of an annual payment of 2000 marks for, according to Robert of Torigny, 'he was indignant that Stephen, who was the younger, had received the crown which – he said – was rightfully his'.[42]

The fall

Despite the support given to Stephen by Roger of Salisbury, four years almost to the day after Stephen's coronation Roger died a broken man. There are five principal sources for the events which brought about the fall of Roger of Salisbury, *Gesta Stephani*, possibly written by Robert, Bishop of Bath,[43] William of Malmesbury's *Historia Novella*, Henry of Huntingdon's *History of the English People*, Orderic Vitalis's *Ecclesiastical History* and William of Newburgh's *History*. Orderic and the author of the *Gesta* were supporters of Stephen; William of Newburgh was a critic, as was William of Malmesbury, who favoured the cause of Robert of Gloucester, his patron. His monastery at Malmesbury was firmly in Salisbury territory. Henry of Huntingdon, archdeacon in Roger's nephew Alexander's diocese of Lincoln, was a severe critic of Stephen and his closest allies. However, he suggested that Roger brought about his fate as a consequence of the significant part he played in helping Stephen to take the throne: 'For this reason, by the just judgement of God, he was later arrested and tormented by the very man he had made king and pitiful ruin was his lot.'[44]

Although favourably disposed to Stephen, the author of the *Gesta Stephani* strongly defended the rights of the church and could not condone an attack upon the bishops, even though he censored their grandiose lifestyle and was not averse to their being humbled. The monk Orderic is very critical of the bishops, whom he sees as arrogant and treacherous, thoroughly deserving of their lot. Newburgh wrote of Stephen's ingratitude for Roger's great services, and William of Malmesbury of 'the poison of malice, long nurtured in Stephen's mind, which at length burst forth to be observed by all'.[45] Henry of Huntingdon had personal reasons, as we have said above, to be critical of Stephen's actions. But even Stephen's sternest critics temper their criticism. Whatever they thought of him, he was God's anointed. His actions, which were unquestionably wrong, were due not to Stephen's malign nature, but the evil counsellors who led him astray.

To understand the background to the events that were calamitous for the Salisbury dynasty, but possibly also for Stephen, we need to look at one of the most powerful Anglo-Norman secular families in England, the Beaumonts.[46] Robert of Meulan had been a trusted confidant of Henry I and, showing an ability to combine subtle diplomacy with a more forceful approach, had been the skilful adversary of Anselm in his dispute with Henry over lay investiture. Robert died in 1118 leaving twin sons, two brilliant boys, Waleran and Robert, aged 14. Waleran was the sort of young man who today would get a first at Oxford or Cambridge and a cricket or football blue while managing to be president of the

Union, and he perhaps overshadowed his brother Robert, nicknamed *le bossu* (hunchback). They had both been well educated, possibly at Abingdon at the hands of Faritius and subsequently at the king's court. At the age of 15, at the time of Pope Calixtus's meeting with Henry at Gisors, they were presented to a group of cardinals to debate theological matters with them. So skilful was their command of logic and so lively their presentation that the cardinals admitted defeat.[47] Waleran was the senior twin. He had interests in France – Meulan was in the Vexin – as well as Normandy. He was descended through his grandmother from the French royal family. However, his political judgement was not always sound and his integrity was suspect. In 1123–24 he joined a revolt against Henry, associating himself with William Clito, but was subsequently restored to favour. He became acquainted with Stephen while Henry was still alive and after 1135 he and his brother Robert, earl of Leicester, dominated the power politics of the reign. Waleran, count of Meulan, was also earl of Worcester and lord of Sturminster Royal in Dorset.

Soon after Stephen's accession the two young men were put in charge of Normandy, where they repelled Angevin attacks in 1136 and 1138. In England not only did Waleran become earl of Worcester and Robert earl of Leicester, but their half-brother, William de Warenne, was earl of Surrey and cousin Roger of Beaumont was earl of Warwick. Their younger brother Hugh became earl of Bedford. This was undoubtedly one of the greatest houses of the old Anglo-Norman baronage. But superficially charming and attractive that Waleran was, so much so that a monk of Bec wrote an extraordinary verse panegyric about him, he may well have been less distinguished than he appeared. Henry of Huntingdon was far from complimentary. He called him 'an expert in deceit, a master of trickery, who was born with wickedness in his blood, falsehood in his mouth, sloth in his deeds, a braggart by nature, stout-hearted in talk, faint-hearted in deed, the last to muster, the first to decamp, slow to attack, quick to retreat'.[48] This invective may have been earned as a consequence of Waleran's implication in the arrest of the bishops.

The power of the Beaumont family was offset by that of the Salisburys. It was not just the concentration of power in the hands of one family that stimulated hostility but the grandeur and ostentation of their lifestyles, which did not accord well with the spiritual office of bishop. Roger's extravagance may have been his reaction to his humble origins. He built castles at Salisbury, Sherborne, Malmesbury and Devizes, described by Huntingdon as the most splendid in the whole of Europe.[49] Alexander had castles at Sleaford, Newark and Banbury; Nigel had strongly fortified the Isle of Ely. Of them the author of the *Gesta Stephani* wrote: 'they were men who loved display and were rash in their reckless presumption. They devoted themselves utterly to warfare and the vanities of this world, disregarding the holy and simple manner of life that befits a Christian priest.'[50]

After Stephen's disastrous expedition in Normandy in 1137 and return to England, Roger's influence declined. The year 1138 was a difficult one for Stephen. His problems were compared with those of Hercules when facing the

Hydra.[51] In spring 1139 rumours were current that Robert of Gloucester was about to invade on behalf of Matilda. The atmosphere was tense and Stephen was ill at ease. He even arrested some knights on the mere suspicion that they were siding against him.[52] It is just possible that Bishop Roger was conspiring with the enemy, although it is unlikely. True, the author of the *Gesta Stephani* claimed that he favoured King Henry's children, but there is no evidence that he did and it is unlikely that he had anything to gain from doing so. He had been instrumental in securing the throne for Stephen and was the second to add his seal to the Oxford Charter (see below). There was no reason to be confident that Matilda would be a more effective champion of the church. However, it suited Roger's enemies at court to feed the king the idea that he was consorting with the opposition. They had to work hard. Waleran of Meulan and his friends did not refrain from 'goading him perpetually, urging him to commit a disrespectful assault on the priestly order'.[53] Malmesbury reported that the three bishops were preparing for Matilda's arrival so that they could meet her and hand over their castles to her.[54] At first Stephen, nervous of an attack on his bishops which he believed would be sacrilegious and would open him to criticism, resisted the pressure.

Waleran persisted. He used the well-known argument, applied against Odo of Bayeux and William of Durham, that a distinction could be made between the bishops in their spiritual capacity and their secular role as warlike landowners. It would not be improper to arrest and imprison Roger, Alexander and Nigel and then, 'in pious and Catholic fashion', he could restore 'what pertained to the Church and to the sacred character and rights of a bishop'.[55] But Stephen remained uncertain that it was the right course of action. What may ultimately have caused him to act was his urgent need for more funds. He had dissipated the very considerable treasure that he had inherited from Henry. Some suggested that he should look to the monasteries, but that was out of the question. However, the Salisbury family was immensely wealthy and their enemies had furnished Stephen with a justification, however baseless, for striking at them. The forthcoming Oxford Council would provide him with the opportunity to act.

Following a successful campaign against the king of Scotland Stephen returned to Oxford and summoned Roger to a council there scheduled for 24 June 1139. He was reluctant to attend: 'By my blessed lady Mary, somehow I am disinclined to this journey!'[56] He set off, accompanied by his nephew bishops, Alexander and Nigel, who had been visiting him. They arrived at Oxford with considerable ostentation. Stephen gave them no cause for concern, for they were well received. Then a brawl suddenly broke out. The three bishops had brought many knights with them who had to arrange their own accommodation. According to Malmesbury, [57] they fell into dispute with the men of Count Alan of Brittany about who was to be lodged where, and as a result the bishop of Salisbury's men, who were sitting at table, leapt up to fight before they had finished eating. Angry words gave way to armed hostility. Alan's followers were put to flight and many of the bishop's men were wounded and one killed. The author of the *Gesta Stephani* wrote that a brawl suddenly arose between the bishops' knights and the king's knights 'at the instigation of the crafty Count of Meulan and some others'.[58] The bishop's baggage was stolen by the royal knights.

Unaware what was happening, Roger was in his room when men burst in and dragged him off to the king. The bishop of Lincoln was also arrested, as was Roger the chancellor, but the bishop of Ely escaped and fled to Devizes castle. He laid waste to the surrounding countryside and prepared for a siege. Roger and Alexander were taken before Stephen, who made the outrageous claim that they had been arrested for a breach of peace. It is unlikely that any of these events had happened spontaneously. The brawl which sparked off the trouble was surely prearranged and Stephen's actions must have been premeditated.

The escape of Nigel provoked Stephen to a rage and he determined to gain possession of the castles of the bishops of Salisbury and Lincoln. He demanded the keys of their castles as pledges but they refused to surrender them. They did, however, offer to stand trial. Stephen would have none of this, and according to *Gesta Stephani* he led them to Devizes under close guard. There he treated them shamefully. He ordered that they should be kept apart from each other and lodged dishonourably on very meagre rations. Roger was apparently put in a cowshed. To aggravate their distress he threatened Roger's son Roger the chancellor, already captured and in chains, with being hanged on high at the gate of Devizes castle unless Nigel surrendered it.[59] Henry of Huntingdon's account is slightly different in that he said that Alexander was kept in prison at Oxford.[60]

The siege of Devizes lasted three days. Such was Nigel's confidence in its impregnability that he paced the battlements in full view, knowing that the royal forces could do nothing. Stephen therefore sent his favourite mercenary captain, the Flemish William of Ypres, under a flag of truce to advise Nigel to surrender. According to William of Malmesbury, Bishop Roger underwent a voluntary fast in the hope that this might encourage Bishop Nigel to surrender. Others question the extent to which the fast really was voluntary. Nigel remained obdurate, so according to Orderic,[61] uncle approached nephew in an attempt to get him to surrender. When they met Roger lost his temper, blaming Nigel for fleeing to Devizes rather than to his own diocese and for imposing grave hardship on the local people by laying waste to the surrounding area. Nigel was unmoved and Roger had to retreat to his cowshed, humiliated.

At this stage young Roger's mother, Matilda of Ramsbury, came into the story. Again according to Orderic, Stephen ordered young Roger to be dragged forth in chains and placed on a high platform with a noose around his neck. Nigel must surrender the castle at once or Roger would be hanged there and then. Matilda actually had ultimate control of the castle and so moved was she by her son's plight that she jumped up and down and cried: 'It was I that bore him and I ought not to lend a hand to his destruction. Yea, rather, I ought to lay down my life to save his.'[62] She then told Stephen that she would surrender the keys. Thereupon Nigel had little alternative but to give up. Young Roger was released and apparently banished from the realm.

Soon after Salisbury, Sherborne and Malmesbury fell to the king. The treasure that he had seized he apparently used for the betrothal of his son Eustace to Constance, the sister of the king of France. He then released Bishop Alexander and took him to Newark. Malmesbury seemed disappointed that he yielded that castle and Sleaford without putting up any resistance – he lacked 'resolution, buying his freedom with the surrender of the castles of Newark and Sleaford'.[63] Huntingdon wrote that Stephen starved him into submission. In any case there was little point in trying to prolong the resistance. Stephen kept the bishops in custody for a while before allowing them, humiliated and dejected, to return to their dioceses. While they could continue to act as diocesan bishops they were broken as royal ministers. The banished Roger the Poor was replaced as chancellor by one of Waleran's men, Philip d'Harcourt. He had no known experience of this sort of work, but that suited Stephen, who wanted a fresh start. The royal seal was changed to make it easy to tell whether grants had been made under the old regime or new. It is likely that sheriffs who had been associates of Roger were deprived of office and it is from this period that Stephen's prolific creation of earldoms can be dated.

Bishop Roger did not see the year out, dying of a quartan fever (a form of malaria) on 11 December 1139, broken and unloved. Henry of Huntingdon, with his characteristic interest in the transitory nature of worldly achievement and success, advised all who read his work 'to marvel at so great and sudden a reversal of fortune'. He suggested that the bishop's life had been one of such apparently endless achievement and success that he had been unaffected by fortune's mutability. But in the end 'he was smothered by a great landslide of troubles. Let no one trust in the continuance of happiness.'[64] William of Malmesbury wrote a long obituary.[65] He wrote of 'the abundance of wealth that followed him in every high office he held' and 'how little he boasted of the fact that he made bishops of two nephews, who thanks to the education he gave them were men of credit for learning and zeal, and not in poor dioceses but as rich perhaps as any that England holds'. In later years, however, 'fortune stung him with a scorpion's tail'. At the end he was humiliated, for in his dying days he witnessed the removal of all the money and precious vessels he had left from the altar of Salisbury cathedral. Alexander remained bishop of Lincoln until 1148, Nigel bishop of Ely until 1169.

Stephen's treatment of the three bishops was thoroughly dealt with at the Council of Winchester summoned for 29 August. It was convened by Henry, bishop of Winchester and now papal legate. Quite unmoved by any sense of fraternal loyalty he was determined to expose the error of his brother Stephen's ways. His view was that if the bishops had been in the wrong it was not for the king to judge them, but for canon law. He maintained that they should not have been deprived of any property without the consent of a church council and that the king had acted out of self-interest. He required Stephen's presence at this council.

William of Malmesbury reported on the council at some length.[66] Stephen had no intention of attending the council in person and responded to the summons to do so by asserting that the archbishop and the others must decide the action to be taken. Archbishop Theobald attended but Archbishop Thurstan excused himself on account of ill health. Several suffragans were also absent, including the bishops of Ely and Lincoln. At the beginning Henry read out the bull of Pope Innocent II appointing him legate. This bull had been despatched early in March and those assembled were impressed by Henry's restraint in delaying the announcement. Then, as he was addressing educated men, he made a speech in Latin. He spoke of the indignity that the three bishops had suffered. The king had acted criminally in following the advice of those who had encouraged him to treat his bishops so badly, especially when they were enjoying his peace at his court. To compound his offence he had robbed the bishops' churches of their property. This was an outrage upon divine law, stated Henry, charged with emotion. He would rather endure great damage to his person and possessions than allow a bishop's dignity to be affronted so.

Stephen did not lack confidence in his case and sent some earls to the council to discover why he had been summoned. Henry answered with a tone of some contempt. Stephen had been guilty of an offence such as the times had never seen; as one who owed obedience to the faith of Christ he should attend and give satisfaction. The king would be well advised to appear and either give account of what he had done or submit to judgement according to canon law. He should remember that he owed his throne to the church, and not the prowess of knights.

At this point the earls departed and returned with a shrewd and experienced advocate, Aubrey de Vere, the royal master chamberlain, to speak on Stephen's behalf. He gave the king's answer and did all the harm he could to Bishop Roger's case. Skilled and articulate advocate that he was he spoke with restraint, refraining from indulging in abuse, unlike the earls, who kept interrupting by hurling insults at Roger. He made a number of points. He claimed that Bishop Roger had inflicted many wrongs on Stephen and had rarely come to court without his men brawling. At Oxford they had attacked Count Alan of Brittany and other aristocrats. The bishop of Lincoln, bearing an old grudge, had encouraged his men to stir up trouble; the bishop of Salisbury had craftily concealed his favour for the king's enemies and had not allowed Roger de Mortimer when on king's business to stay even for one night at Malmesbury, even though he was in fear of the Bristol rebels. It was openly said that the bishop, along with his nephews, would support Matilda and hand over his castles. Finally Roger had been arrested not as a bishop but as a servant of the king, whose pay he received for managing his affairs. The bishops had freely surrendered their castles to avoid the charge regarding the brawl. Such money as the king found lawfully belonged to him and this Roger had willingly handed over.

Bishop Roger gave an angry and spirited reply. He denied that he had ever been Stephen's servant or received his pay. He threatened to appeal to Rome if he failed to find justice here. Bishop Henry now sought to act as the voice of moderation. In an echo of the trials of Odo of Bayeux and William of Durham, he pronounced: 'Let the king do what the law requires, reinstate the bishops in their property, otherwise, by natural law, if they are dispossessed they will not plead.'

Much unreported discussion then followed before the court was adjourned to the next day and then adjourned for two more days pending the arrival of the archbishop of Rouen. Archbishop Hugh was firmly of the opinion that the bishops had rightly been deprived of castles they had built in defiance of canon law. He held that they should be evangelists of peace, not builders of houses that might be used as refuges for evil men. He would allow them their castles if they could prove by canon law that they were entitled to them. Even so, in these uncertain times they should hand over the keys for the king's use in defending the realm. 'So the bishops' whole case fell to the ground.'

Aubrey de Vere then issued a warning. The king had been told that the bishops were preparing to go to Rome. They would be well advised not to, for they might not be readmitted to England. Indeed, the king felt wronged himself by the bishops and intended to appeal his own case to the pope. That was effectively the end of the council. Any thought that the bishops might have had of pronouncing excommunication on Stephen was abandoned, and that for two reasons. They thought it would be ill-advised to do so without prior papal approval; moreover they felt intimidated by some of the laymen present who were beginning to unsheathe their swords. At some point in the council it was enacted that any refuges for war and disturbance that were in the hands of the bishops should be passed to the king as his property.

After the council ended, so unsatisfactorily for Roger and his nephews, Archbishop Theobald and Bishop Henry sought Stephen, knelt before him and begged him to have pity on the church and heal the divisions that now existed between the monarchy and the clergy. William of Malmesbury stated that although he responded respectfully, 'he showed no fulfilment of righteous promises'. The *Gesta Stephani* presented things differently, stating that Stephen 'put aside his royal garb, and groaning in spirit and with a contrite heart, he humbly accepted the penance enjoined for his fault'.[67] Few would put it past Stephen to say the right thing and do little about it.

Bishop Henry had stressed the impropriety of Stephen's action on the grounds that it was contrary to canon law and in contravention of the promises made in the Oxford Charter. However, Archbishop Hugh supported Stephen. He had argued that even if they could prove by canon law that it was right for them to have the castles, at this difficult time they should hand over the keys to the king. Henry himself was in reality as guilty of uncanonical conduct as the bishops of Salisbury, Lincoln and Ely, for he had more castles than any other bishop with fortifications in Hampshire, Wiltshire and Somerset at Winchester, Merdon, Farnham, Bishop's Waltham, Downton and Taunton. Had he been challenged it is difficult to see how he could have argued his case. It was perhaps self-interest rather than the defence of church freedom that was the real reason for his support of the Salisbury family. It certainly did nothing for a harmonious relationship between the king and his brother, and Henry's failure to impose the ultimate sanction of excommunication upon Stephen may well have been less due to fraternal loyalty than his own worldliness.

Historians today argue that the consequences of this episode for Stephen were far less damaging than was once believed.[68] Few are likely to follow the great nineteenth-century historian Bishop Stubbs, who claimed that as a consequence the whole administration of the country ceased to work and the whole power of the clergy was arrayed in opposition to the king. It has been shown that government and administration did not collapse with Roger of Salisbury[69] and as we have seen, Bishop Nigel's son actually wrote the *Dialogue of the Exchequer*. However, a consequence of the episode was a demonstrable shift in the balance of power in favour of the Beaumonts. In managing the fall of the Salisburys Stephen had without question acted badly. He had abandoned many of the undertakings made in the Oxford Charter. His arrest of the bishops while apparently in his peace was a blatant disregard of what was considered proper at the time and was damaging to Stephen's moral authority and the respect others might have for him. Even so, as we shall see in the next chapter, the bishops were not turned irrevocably against Stephen by the events of 1139.

5

King Stephen and his Bishops

King Stephen initially owed his throne to the support given by great churchmen, in particular his brother Henry of Winchester, Roger of Salisbury and the archbishop of Canterbury, William of Corbeil. However, while the premature death of his son Eustace in 1153 ruled out any chance of the succession passing to him, the decision of Archbishop Theobald to back the Angevins had already made it clear that Stephen's successor would not be his younger son William, but Henry of Anjou, and this was confirmed by Stephen in the Treaty of Winchester of November 1153. Stephen did not live long enough to contest this later, and following his death on 25 October 1154 Henry succeeded unchallenged. So secure did he feel that he was not crowned until 19 December. In 1135 Stephen was supported by the senior English bishops because they saw this as the most effective way to prevent civil war. More than that, Henry of Winchester in particular was confident of his ability to ensure that, through him, his brother would protect the liberties of the church. According to William of Malmesbury,[1] when addressing the council in 1141 which confirmed Matilda as the lady of England, Bishop Henry claimed that he had made himself guarantor between Stephen and God that he would honour and exalt Holy Church, maintain good laws and repeal bad ones.

The Oxford Charter of 1136

Stephen's personal spirituality, fortified by that of his wife Matilda, compared well with that of his uncles and was different from the authoritarian and disciplinarian approach of his grandfather. He inherited more of his father's qualities than those of his mother Adela, a formidable virago who bullied her husband into joining the First Crusade, on which he acquitted himself well until his unfortunate flight from the siege of Antioch. Awesome though she may have been, Adela's friends included Ivo of Chartres, Peter the Venerable and Anselm, and she ended her life as a nun. Stephen and Matilda were conscientious in participating in acts of corporate devotion and also showed an appreciation of holy men like Wulfric of Haselbury, whom Stephen is said to have visited on more than one occasion. Both Stephen and his wife took a positive interest in the reformed monasticism of the Savignacs and they founded abbeys at Furness, Buckfast and Coggeshall, but despite the number of Cistercian houses founded in his reign Stephen seems to have shown less interest in them. However in 1147 the Orders merged and the Savignac houses became Cistercian. Stephen and his wife Matilda were generous to Cluniac foundations and Stephen was regarded by contemporaries as a patron of the order of the Temple. Inevitably Stephen saw misfortunes and disasters as omens or the consequence of sin. The *Gesta Stephani* tells how on the morning of the Battle of Lincoln, 2 February 1141, the feast of the Purification, during the celebratory mass the lighted candle which Stephen was holding went out and the candle was broken. This was interpreted as a warning that Stephen would suffer a loss that day, but the subsequent miraculous recovery of the candle and its light meant that Stephen would not abandon the kingdom or lose his royal title. It was reported that Stephen saw his defeat and capture at Lincoln as God's punishment for his sins.[2]

Stephen's first public statement of his policy towards the church was the so-called 'Oxford Charter of Liberties' issued in April 1136.[3] Stephen promised that he would forbid any actions that smacked of simony, and he undertook to recognise the right of bishops to have jurisdiction over all clergy and their property and not to interfere in the disposal of ecclesiastical estates. He would respect church immunities as laid down in their charters and their ancient customs. He promised to protect church property and the tenures that they had on the day when William I died and to exempt them from vexatious claims. He undertook to investigate cases of church lands lost before that date and to confirm all lands given since. He guaranteed that bishops and abbots could reasonably distribute their property before their death, but on the sudden death of a bishop or abbot disposal of his property should be made at the discretion of the church for the salvation of his soul. When a see became vacant he would not exploit it, but commend it to the care of appropriate clergy until a new pastor should be canonically appointed.

In addition to the promises to the church he undertook to lift the oppressive 'forest law' from those new forests created by Henry I and to annul injustices and unfair exactions for which the sheriffs were responsible. Finally, he declared that he would observe good laws and customs and maintain law and order.

The bishops who subscribed to the charter were, in order of signature: William of Canterbury, Hugh archbishop of Rouen, Henry of Winchester, Roger of Salisbury, Alexander of Lincoln, Nigel of Ely, Everard of Norwich, Simon of Worcester, Bernard of St David's, Arduen of Évreux (brother of Thurstan), Richard of Avranches, Robert of Hereford, John of Rochester and Aethelwulf of Carlisle. Thurstan of York was not present. He had attended the London council a few weeks before but had felt the need to return to his see, perhaps because King David of Scotland, uncle of Empress Matilda,[4] was not happy at Stephen's seizure of the throne.

A cursory reading of the charter suggests that Stephen had publicly renounced the policies of his grandfather and uncles towards the church, but the reality is that while he had moderated them he had not abandoned them. He had no wish to do so, and in the early part of his reign saw no need to. Two concessions in particular read like a surrender of royal authority, the clause stating that jurisdiction and authority over clergy and their property was to be in the hands of the bishops, and that which stated that when sees fell vacant they and their possessions were to be entrusted to worthy men of the church. The wording of the clauses allows flexibility of interpretation. Moreover, the apparent force of the charter is significantly modified by its final sentence: All this I truly grant and confirm, 'saving my regal and just dignity'.[5]

The Second Lateran Council

The introduction to the charter stresses the importance of the church in helping to secure the throne for Stephen. It states: 'I, Stephen, by the grace of God and, with the assent of the clergy and people, elected king of the English, and consecrated thereto by William, archbishop of Canterbury and legate of the holy Roman Church, and confirmed by Innocent, pope of the holy Roman see, out of respect and love towards God, do grant freedom to Holy Church and confirm the reverence due to her.' The importance of the support of Pope Innocent II is therefore duly recognised. This support was confirmed at the Second Lateran Council held in Rome in April 1139.

The council was convened as an occasion of celebration marking the end of the papal schism, with Innocent facing an anti-pope since 1130 in the person of Peter Pierleone, known by his supporters as Anacletus II. Although Anacletus controlled Rome and kept out Innocent, Innocent had the support of King Louis VI of France and France's spiritual leaders, Peter the Venerable, abbot of Cluny and Suger, abbot of St Denis. Emperor Lothar II and some of the senior German clergy also backed him. Henry I had given him his support, as did Stephen and his brother Henry. Although not a monk himself, Innocent had Cluniac sympathies and looked favourably on the Cluniac monk Henry. Innocent continued to face a formidable adversary in Roger II, count then king of Sicily, so had no wish to alienate the kings of France and England or Stephen's brother Theobald, count of Blois, and was not well disposed to any Angevin claim to the English throne. He accordingly responded to Stephen's request for support by recognising him as king and urging him to maintain the good order imposed by his uncle.

The Lateran Council was attended by more than five hundred bishops and abbots, among them Theobald, the new archbishop of Canterbury, Simon of Worcester, Roger of Chester, John of Rochester and Robert of Exeter. Henry of Huntingdon also attended but ignored it in his *History*, perhaps because the council did nothing for the Angevin cause. According to a letter written by Gilbert Foliot, abbot of Gloucester and later bishop of Hereford, and a passage in John of Salisbury's *Historia Pontificalis*, in the course of the council Innocent heard a challenge from Empress Matilda contesting the legitimacy of Stephen's claim to the throne.[6] Her advocate was Bishop Ulger of Angers. He argued that the English throne was lawfully hers by hereditary right and on account of the oath taken to Stephen. Worthy and competent that Ulger was, he was no match for his opponents, who won the day. Innocent was not prepared to nullify the original support he had given Stephen, who was now a properly crowned and anointed king. Moreover, Stephen's undertakings in his Oxford Charter had shown him to be suitable for kingship. Matilda was left with no option but to fight for the English throne.

It was, perhaps, an omen for the future that apparently, at Stephen's coronation, Archbishop William forgot to include the kiss of peace. The reign was dominated by war. There were three major conflicts: civil war with Matilda from 1139 to 1148, which continued as a struggle for the succession after Matilda had departed from England; Anglo-Scottish wars (1135–39); and French wars, involving Anjou, Maine and Touraine against Normandy (1135–44). There was also Wales to contend with, and problems with rebels who were not partisans but whose primary concern was to protect and extend their own interests with recourse to as much violence as they thought necessary. The second chapter of H.A. Cronne's *The Reign of Stephen* is a helpful narrative of events.

Nineteen long winters?

Few historians today would go along with the Peterborough chronicler when he wrote of 'nineteen long winters when Christ and his saints slept'. In reality, although this appears under the entry for 1137, it may well have been a piece of Angevin propaganda actually written early in the reign of Henry II. England never experienced the chaos that was a feature of eleventh-century France and which led to an attempt by the church to establish some control through the Peace of God and the Truce of God. Although Henry I had confirmed the provisions of the Truce for Normandy,[7] it was unknown in England. While for much of Stephen's reign there was a breakdown in strong central government, royal government did not collapse and the major institutions survived.[8] In three areas in England authority was maintained, albeit outside the south-east not Stephen's. Stephen retained the support of London even during his period of captivity in 1141, and the south-eastern counties and some parts like Kent and Sussex were rarely disturbed. Empress Matilda, with the support of her illegitimate half-brother Robert of Gloucester, Miles of Hereford and Brian fitz Count, maintained authority in the West Country, and King David of Scotland governed effectively those parts of northern England under his control. While the magnates welcomed the opportunity to further their own aggrandisement this was not necessarily to the disadvantage of those under them.

In the regions loyal to Stephen coinage was good; the fall of Roger of Salisbury notwithstanding, the exchequer system survived under the influence of the Beaumonts; the chancery issued writs; sheriffs responded to the king's commands;

justices were appointed to hear cases; the king's council continued to meet. Stephen's reign saw many monastic foundations, perhaps 175, not just Cistercian but Gilbertines and houses of Augustinian canons.[9] Nor was this an entirely bleak period for learning and scholarship. Archbishop Theobald's household became a centre for training young men in theology and law, canon and Roman.[10] He introduced Vacarius, the celebrated teacher of Roman civil law, to his household, and his young students, who included Thomas Becket and Roger of Pont l'Évêque, remained in contact with continental scholars. In 1154 John of Salisbury left papal service to join them while other English scholars like Robert Pullen, and Hilary, bishop of Chichester from 1147 to 1169, were prominent in the papal chancery. The only Englishman ever to become pope, Adrian IV, was elected in 1154.

While it would be wrong to take the Peterborough chronicler literally it would be equally wrong to deny that a great deal of lawlessness and violence prevailed in Stephen's reign. The words of *The Anglo-Saxon Chronicle* are echoed elsewhere. *Gesta Stephani* is full of accounts of violent disorder. Henry of Huntingdon[11] stated that the reign began well, but after two good years 'the third was mediocre and things were beginning to fall apart'. The years 1139–40 'were pernicious with everything torn to pieces'. William of Newburgh wrote of England being 'drained and crippled and wasting away through internal evils'. He claimed that both the empress and Stephen 'pandered to their supporters, denying them nothing so that they would not desert them'. He tells of numerous castles being built, and 'there were in a sense as many kings or rather tyrants as there were lords of castles. In a country once most fertile they virtually wiped out the bread which is the staff of life.'[12] Violence and disturbances were features of medieval life under even the strongest kings and all the kings since the Conquest had experienced baronial revolts. Much of the violence was due to the actions not of the greatest lords, but those of lesser men who built castles and terrorised the areas which they dominated. Private feuds were fought out, the lack of strong rule in parts of the country led to a collapse of law and order and people suffered the inevitable consequences of the civil war. Mercenary soldiers might rampage, towns were burned, crops and livestock were wrecked and parts of the country accustomed to peace like Berkshire, the Thames Valley and East Anglia suffered the consequences of prolonged fighting. Conditions in Wales undermined the authority of the lords of the Marches and made life bad for English settlers. On top of the chaos and distress caused by men, natural events aggravated the situation, with bad weather leading to widespread famine.

The bishops

The bishops of England and Wales were inevitably greatly affected by the civil war and lawlessness. Thirty-four men were English bishops in Stephen's reign, nineteen of whom were appointed in its course. Nineteen of the bishops were secular clerks who had worked their way up the ecclesiastical hierarchy; only six were specifically from the royal household, and twelve were monks. Of the appointments actually made in Stephen's reign ten were ecclesiastical clerks, eight were monks and only William fitz Herbert was a royal clerk. This compares significantly with Henry I's reign, when sixteen appointments were royal clerks, four were ecclesiastical clerks and eight were monks. The influence in these appointments of Archbishop Theobald of Canterbury, formerly a monk of Bec, was considerable, overshadowed only by that of Stephen's brother Henry. There was a significant number of his protégés among the appointments: Robert of Bath and Wells was a Cluniac, Hilary of Chichester had been a clerk in his household, Jocelyn of Salisbury had been one of his men, Hugh of Durham was a nephew. Henry was an unashamed nepotist and had no qualms ensuring that relations were also appointed as abbots. Even so, some care was taken to ensure that the chapter was given a genuinely free choice.

The Oxford Charter had by implication promised free elections – vacant sees and their possessions were to be entrusted to suitable guardians 'until a new pastor may be canonically appointed' – but in the years of civil war and Bishop Henry's legateship political considerations played a significant part, at the expense of the rights of the nominal electors, as did the dominant influence of Bishop Henry. There was some improvement when Henry lost his legateship in 1143, and Theobald as primate and papal legate in his turn had much greater influence. Avron Saltman states that six of the fourteen English and Welsh elections held between 1143 and 1154 were the result of the free choice of the chapter: Norwich, Lincoln, London, Coventry, Worcester and Durham.[13] True, the London chapter was required to pay £500 to Stephen before they were allowed a free choice. This was an enormous sum and made them open to the charge of simony, despite Stephen's undertaking in 1136 to have nothing to do with this, but they secured the man they wanted, Richard de Belmeis, archdeacon of Middlesex, despite the pope's original demand that they must elect a monk or canon. On several other occasions papal pressure was put on the electors, Theobald himself influenced elections and Cistercian interests played a part.

Not all elections were straightforward and were complicated by there being rival factions in the civil war. Moreover, Stephen as king was not always in a strong enough position to ensure with any consistency that his own nominees became bishops. After the death of the 'Magnificent' Alexander of Lincoln in February 1148 the attempt by Henry and Stephen to impose one more of their nephews was thwarted by Pope Eugenius, who rejected each of the three put forward. Instead, Robert, the archdeacon of Leicester, was freely elected by the dean and chapter of Lincoln. The procedure actually took place at Westminster in the presence of King Stephen and Queen Matilda and a number of bishops, including Theobald. Robert was consecrated by Theobald on 19 December 1148. 'With great jubilation he was eagerly awaited at Lincoln, and still more eagerly welcomed, being devotedly received by the clergy and people at the Lord's Epiphany', wrote Henry of Huntingdon, who enthused about him.[14]

An election fraught with some difficulty was that to Coventry following the death of Roger de Clinton at Antioch on 16 April 1148. Coventry was in the same diocese as Lichfield and Chester and the bishop's title fluctuated between the three. The monks of Coventry had had a bad time in the civil war. Robert Marmion senior, described by John of Salisbury as a despoiler of churches, came into conflict with Ranulf, Earl of Chester. In August 1144 he seized the cathedral priory of Coventry, expelled the monks and fortified the precinct against Ranulf. With the approach of the earl's men he rode forward but fell off his horse, broke his leg and suffered the ignominy of having his head cut off by a Chester foot soldier. His son continued the fight. When some peace was established and the monks had returned they claimed that it was their right to elect the new bishop of Coventry. This claim was contested by the canons of Lichfield and of Chester. Theobald summoned the monks to Leicester where they elected Walter, the prior of Christ Church, Canterbury, a man well known to Theobald. The canons of Lichfield and Chester appealed to Pope Eugenius III on the grounds that they had been wrongfully excluded from the election. Thereupon the prior of Coventry visited Eugenius in person and succeeded in persuading him to reject the appeal of the canons and confirm Walter's election. Having been enthroned at Coventry he went to Lichfield but could not obtain entry to the church. He thereupon excommunicated the canons. Walter was an appropriate choice, not merely a monk but a man with a reputation for learning and piety.

Most problematical of all was the election to York following the death of Thurstan in 1140. There was no obvious successor. The crisis attracted a number of interested parties, not just the king, his brother Henry and Archbishop Theobald but David of Scotland, William d'Aumale, a great Yorkshire landowner, consistently loyal to Stephen and created Earl of York after his contribution to the Battle of the Standard, the papacy, Augustinian canons, the Cistercians and their leader St Bernard. Possible successors to Thurstan were Waltheof, the Augustinian prior of Kirkham, the Benedictine abbot of Fécamp, Henry of Sully, William fitz Herbert and the Cistercian Henry Murdac. Waltheof was not interested and in any case unacceptable to Stephen as he was a stepson of King David. Henry of Sully, following the example of his uncle Henry, refused to surrender his abbacy, a stance that alienated Pope Innocent. William fitz Herbert, another nephew of Stephen and Henry, had the backing of William d'Aumale. He was far from ideal, being something of an amiable but idle libertine, but William d'Aumale put considerable pressure on the less than unanimous York chapter, and reluctantly they elected him in January 1141. He remained unconsecrated until September 1143 and then not by Theobald but by legate Henry.

William had not received the pallium so lacked metropolitan status, and his opponents refused to accept him. As well as the York chapter they included the Augustinian priors of Kirkham and Guisborough and the Cistercian abbots of Rievaulx and Fountains. They were supported by St Bernard, who said of William that he was 'rotten from the soles of his feet to the crown of his head'. Even so,

William remained in office until 1147. His fate was determined by the papal election on 15 February 1145 of Eugenius III, a Cistercian who had been at Clairvaux under Bernard and very much one of his disciples. In 1143 Henry Murdac had been elected abbot of Fountains. He was certainly cast in the mould of St Bernard, 'a man of strongly ascetic life, by temperament inclined to drastic and imperious action, at Fountains enforcing the full observance of every Clairvaux use and tradition'.[15] Under pressure from Bernard Eugenius deposed William and consecrated Murdac at Treves on 7 December 1147, giving him the pallium. Another of Bishop Henry's protégés, Hilary had also had aspirations to York and was granted the bishopric of Chichester as consolation. William retreated with dignity to Winchester where he put himself under the care of his uncle, joining the cathedral monastic community. Murdac's experiences as archbishop were far from happy. The king did not give him his backing and refused to invest him with his temporalities. William had been much liked by the laity of the diocese and they took their revenge by attacking Fountains Abbey. The clergy of York were also deeply hostile to Murdac and for much of the time that he was archbishop he was unable to reside in the cathedral city but was compelled to live at Ripon or Beverley. His unhappy episcopate came to an end when he died in October 1153, three months after Eugenius and two months after Bernard. William fitz Herbert was restored to York.

Before Murdac died he became involved in another controversy. On the death of the bishop of Durham, William of Sainte-Barbe, in November 1152 he was succeeded by Hugh de Puiset. Hugh was a precocious young man, for he was only 25 at the time of his election. He was then treasurer of York and before that had been at Winchester with his uncle Henry where he was clerk and archdeacon. In York he was a leader of the resistance to Henry Murdac. Not surprisingly Henry Murdac opposed him with characteristic vigour. It was more than he could bear to know that instead of a fellow Cistercian a relation of Henry of Blois and a personal enemy had been elected. He rejected the election and excommunicated the prior and archdeacons. He argued that Hugh was below the canonical age, which was true, that he was ignorant and worldly and that the election was invalid as it had not been approved by the metropolitan. But he did not take account of the citizens of York, who remained loyal to Stephen and who saw Murdac's attack on Hugh as an attack on the king. Once again they drove him out. The excommunicated prior and archdeacons appealed to Archbishop Theobald in his legatine capacity; he upheld their plea and ordered Murdac to absolve them. Anastasius in person consecrated Hugh on 20 December 1153 and he was enthroned in Durham a little more than four months later.

Stephen now had two nephews in northern sees, but not for long. Within a few weeks of William's return to York on 8 June he met a sudden and dramatic death. Rumour had it that Osbert, archdeacon of York, had poisoned the communion wine consumed by William at mass. That Osbert had done so was never proved, but although a nephew of Thurstan he had none of his uncle's spirituality and suspicions of his guilt persisted for some years.[16]

Henry of Winchester

For many years Henry bishop of Winchester, King Stephen's brother, was a dominant figure in English secular and ecclesiastical politics. He had an exalted view of the role of the church in Christian society while recognising the need for co-operation between the spiritual and secular powers. He had what David Knowles described as 'a high Gregorian attitude towards matters of church polity and practice'.[17] Following the line proclaimed by Pope Gregory VII he maintained that the clergy formed a distinct class from the laity, that the church had its own laws and its own courts, the clergy being answerable only there, and that the law and courts Christian were under the direction of the papacy, its decrees, legates and judges delegate.

Henry was no reformer. He was chaste but an unashamed nepotist and pluralist. He had no intention of yielding the abbacy of Glastonbury when he became bishop of Winchester. He was a brilliant administrator with special gifts for handling financial matters and dealing with landed property. William of Newburgh wrote of him: 'he was a man of great power in the kingdom, and was crafty and inordinately fond of money'.[18] His financial acumen was of great benefit to Glastonbury and Cluny and enabled him to amass a personal fortune. He was generous to the two abbeys but had no scruples about using his vast wealth in his own interests. He lived in enormous style and grandeur at Glastonbury and Winchester. He loved jewellery. He was a connoisseur and collector of examples of the art of antiquity, like his uncle Henry he had a menagerie of foreign animals, and he built and equipped a number of grand fortified palaces and castles.[19] He was also a benefactor, donating artistic treasures like the Winchester Bible and Psalter, and founding and supporting a leper hospital dedicated to St Mary Magdalen and the Hospital at St Cross, an almshouse for 13 ageing brethren and for feeding 100 poor people daily. He was truly a paradox. So much so that Henry of Huntingdon described him as 'a new kind of monster, composed part pure and part corrupt, I mean part monk and part knight'.[20] St Bernard's references to him were equally colourful – 'the old wizard of Winchester' and the 'whore of Winchester'.

With his long black beard he was doubtless an impressive figure whose presence was felt in many of the crises of Stephen's reign. Henry's military toughness was apparent early in the reign at the siege of Exeter. When William of Corbeil, archbishop of Canterbury, died on 21 November 1136, Henry of Winchester had little doubt that he would be the unchallenged successor. Only Robert de Bethune, bishop of Hereford, a man of far greater spirituality, could have approached him in stature. While Henry's spirituality may have been open to question, he had every other advantage and as a monk was acceptable to the Christ Church community. Indeed, Orderic Vitalis stated that he actually was elected. He then said that in order to obtain the papal permission required if he were to be translated from one see to another he went over to Normandy, where he wintered en route to Pope Innocent, who was then in Italy.

During the Canterbury vacancy of two years Henry acted as vicar responsible for its administration, thereby fulfilling one of Stephen's undertakings in the Oxford Charter. The papal legate Albert of Ostia, who arrived in England in summer 1138, held a legatine council on 11 December. He had made it clear in advance that the Canterbury appointment would be discussed with the object of finding a person whose election would be canonically valid, who would be acceptable to the suffragans of the province, and whom the king could not refuse. The strongest voice was to be with the monks of Christ Church, and it seems that they were to have the opportunity to hold a genuinely free election.

To the fury of Bishop Henry, the man chosen was the apparent nonentity, Theobald, abbot of Bec, whom Stephen found acceptable. There was no obvious reason for the choice except that he hailed from Bec, like his distinguished predecessors Lanfranc and Anselm. Possibly the Beaumont network had a part to play, for the Beaumonts had strong links with Bec and were no fans of Henry. Theobald proved to be a far more distinguished archbishop than might have been anticipated. Henry received a very potent consolation prize, his appointment by Innocent II as papal legate. This put his authority above Theobald. As legate Henry soon 'appropriated the totality of archiescopal authority. He confirmed the election of bishops and consecrated them, presided over councils, adjudicated on leading cases and cited the archbishop himself and subjected him to his jurisdiction.'[21]

On 30 September 1139 Empress Matilda landed at Arundel with her half-brother Robert, earl of Gloucester and 140 knights. She remained there while Robert moved to Bristol. Stephen arrived at Arundel from Marlborough and actually provided Matilda with an escort to join her brother. Angevin power became concentrated in the west. Among Matilda's principal supporters in addition to Robert of Gloucester were Miles of Gloucester and Brian fitz Count, lord of Wallingford, son of Alan Fergant, count of Brittany. These three were especially strong in the West Country and the Marches of South Wales. The significance of Matilda's arrival is that she was clearly determined to confront Stephen head-on with the consequence that unrest was turned into full-scale civil war, which continued at least until her departure from England in February 1148. Although Matilda failed to achieve her ambition of establishing herself as sole ruler of England, she persisted in championing the Angevin cause after her return to France, working with great determination to ensure that the succession would pass to her son Henry.

The civil war reached its climax in 1141. The events of that year were precipitated by the seizure of the royal castle of Lincoln by Ranulf, earl of Chester, in association with his half-brother William de Roumare, earl of Lincoln, shortly before Christmas 1140. Stephen initially made peace with the brothers then returned to London, where he was persuaded to change his mind and mount an assault on Ranulf. The major confrontation, the Battle of Lincoln, was fought on 2 February 1141 and ended disastrously for Stephen. Despite fighting with a courage that would have distinguished someone years younger, he was captured, taken to Empress Matilda at Gloucester and imprisoned in chains, appalling treatment for a consecrated king.

Henry's part in the events of 1141 after Stephen's defeat at Lincoln was decidedly controversial. Following advice that it was important for her to win Bishop Henry's support, 'because he was reckoned to surpass all the great men of England in judgement and wisdom and to be their superior in virtue and wealth',[22] a meeting was arranged for 2 March at Wherwell, near Winchester. Empress Matilda undertook to guarantee that she would grant Henry control of all appointments to bishoprics and abbacies if he received her formally in Holy Church as 'lady' (*domina*), a title that was intended to signal that she would then proceed to coronation as queen. The next day she was formally received in Winchester cathedral. She headed a grand procession with Henry on her right and Bernard, bishop of St David's on her left. Several other bishops were also present, the bishops of Lincoln and Ely, Robert of Bath and Robert of Hereford and possibly Seffrid of Chichester. William of Malmesbury says that several abbots were present as well. The archbishop of Canterbury was not there but was invited by Henry to join himself and Matilda a few days later at Wilton. To Matilda's request that he should swear fealty to her as his lady he replied that it would be inappropriate for someone in his position and harmful to his reputation to transfer his allegiance without consulting the king. He and several bishops and laymen were allowed to visit Stephen and discuss the position with him. He responded graciously that it would be in order for them to change their allegiance 'as the times required'. They therefore fell into line with Bishop Henry's policy.

Henry summoned a legatine council for the first Monday after Easter week, 7 April, at which, as papal representative, he required the presence of the archbishop of Canterbury, all the other English bishops and many abbots. Quite a number failed to appear and excused themselves in letters of apology. With those bishops who did respond to his summons Henry had a secret conference at which, it seems, they discussed the transfer of power to Empress Matilda, followed by another with the abbots and finally one with the archdeacons. William of Malmesbury was present throughout the council and gave a full account of its deliberations.[23]

The following day Henry, in his capacity as legate, spoke to the assembled company. He recited the circumstances of the oath exacted by Henry I from his great subjects to acknowledge the empress as his successor and explained how it came about that in disregard of that oath Stephen, his brother, was allowed to become king. However Stephen had utterly failed to honour his promises, neglecting his duty to God and thereby bringing the kingdom to a state of disorder. God had delivered his judgement on Stephen, so with God's help they should now turn to Matilda, the daughter of the great King Henry. However, Matilda's consecration and coronation could not proceed immediately but had to await the arrival of representatives of the commune of the city of London. Stephen had apparently granted London commune status which conferred special privileges on the citizens who had taken an oath to form a single corporation. William of Malmesbury described the Londoners as 'like nobles' on account of the greatness of their city. In the *Gesta Stephani* London is described as 'the capital of the whole kingdom'.

Empress Matilda was clearly in the ascendant. Much of England had gone over to her side; she was recognised by most of the magnates as she had been by the legate. He had handed over the king's castle at Winchester and to her obvious delight, for she most eagerly desired it, he gave her the royal crown along with such treasure as was still remaining. He commanded the people of Winchester 'to salute her as their lady and queen'.[24] Archbishop Theobald and some other bishops who had seen Stephen had his consent to transfer their allegiance. Most of Normandy had defected. The Londoners, however, remained defiant, and would not admit Matilda until more than two months had elapsed after the Winchester council.

Henry of Blois's conduct at this time may be open to the charge that he had been guilty of serious disloyalty to his brother. Although there may have been no great bond of fraternal affection between them, Henry had been instrumental in securing the throne for Stephen and would have sworn fealty to him. The author of *Gesta Stephani* addressed the problem.[25] As he said, 'the bishop was in a quandary'. There was no denying the grave weakness of Stephen's position, which was largely due to his own negligence, but even so, to turn to Stephen's enemies while he was still alive was, as Henry recognised, 'dreadful and unseemly'. In his defence, it was argued that he had come to terms with his enemies as a temporary expedient. He could then take advantage of the peace and watch how events developed. If the opportunity arose he would be able to act swiftly and effectively to support Stephen. It is also probable that while loyalty to his brother was important, even more important was freedom of the church. Without peace this would be in peril. At some stage in the summer Henry had written, as papal legate, to Innocent II. Apparently, in reply, the pope mildly rebuked him on the grounds that he had not worked hard enough for his brother's release, but he forgave him provided that he did everything in his power, ecclesiastical or secular, to obtain it.[26]

He was helped by the actions of Matilda herself, who very quickly threw away her advantages. Those who in 1135 had renounced the oath they had taken in 1127 had acted with prescience. Her demeanour was such that she succeeded in alienating many of those who were prepared initially to accept her or whose support she badly needed. Having managed to offend former adherents of Stephen who had come to her to offer homage, she alienated the King of Scotland and the Londoners. Their support was crucial and was not going to be given lightly. The Scots were outraged by her overweening manner, as were the Londoners, who were so alienated by her insensitive demands for taxes that they turned against her and drove her out in most humiliating circumstances.

Among those who were offended was Bishop Henry. Although Matilda had been urged to follow his advice she frequently failed to do so, she humiliated him in public, and he was embarrassed, to say the least, in the matter of the inheritance of Eustace, the son of Queen Matilda and Stephen. The queen had had the same experience. Eustace was the grandson of the count of Boulogne. It was

Queen Matilda's hope that her father's inheritance, Boulogne and Mortain, should be transferred to Eustace. This wish was shared by Henry, who considered these territories to belong lawfully to his nephew while Stephen was a prisoner. The empress would not hear of it. So enraged was Henry by the affront that he refused to attend the empress's court.

Had he hoped that Empress Matilda would honour the undertaking made earlier in the year at Winchester to safeguard the liberties of the church, he was to be disillusioned. Two sees became vacant during the period of Matilda's ascendancy, London and Durham. No immediate difficulty arose over London. Matilda favoured Robert de Segillo, formerly master of Henry I's writing office. 'Florence' of Worcester said that he was appointed after she had taken advice. He may well have been approved of by Bishop Henry for he had become a monk at Reading, a house with strong Cluniac associations. Problems arose in later years about Robert's appointment but are not relevant at this point. His election was approved by the abbot of Reading, he took a profession of obedience to Theobald and was consecrated by him. As Marjorie Chibnall wrote: 'there was nothing in his election to give offence to even the most ardent reformers in the church'.[27]

The Durham election was a different matter altogether. Following the death of Thurstan in 1140 York was still vacant. King David of Scotland took the view that the bishopric of Durham was in his power and he wanted it to go to his chancellor, William Cumin. The cathedral chapter would have nothing of this. They believed that such an intrusion would be contrary to the liberty of their church and their right to hold a free election. They sent envoys both to the empress and to Henry as papal legate to express their views. Henry gave the chapter his support and forbade William to accept the bishopric unless he was canonically elected. The empress took a contrary line. True to form, she rejected the request of the chapter and made arrangements to bestow the bishopric on William once she was queen. Not all historians accept the Durham chronicler's statement that she actually planned to invest him herself with the ring and staff. If it were true, this would have been an outrageous attempt to reverse the settlements agreed to by Henry I of England in 1107 and her late husband the Emperor Henry V of Germany in 1122. The attempted intrusion of William Cumin into Durham played into the hands of her opponents, particularly the bishop of Winchester.

Following her expulsion from London by the outraged citizens Matilda joined Robert of Gloucester in Oxford. She was admitted to London where she worked for Stephen's release, urging Henry to do the same. He promised to do his best and settled back in Winchester. The attempts of Empress Matilda and her brother Robert to assert their authority over the city caused great damage there and led ultimately to the humiliation of Matilda at the Rout of Winchester in September 1141, when she was driven from the city by Queen Matilda, who had gathered together forces loyal to Stephen. Robert of Gloucester was taken prisoner. With the king and the leader of the Angevin cause both in captivity, a period of negotiation followed during which an exchange was planned.

Archbishop Theobald and Bishop Henry played a prominent part as guarantors that Stephen, once released, would play straight. Stephen was released on 1 November, Robert two days later.

The following month Henry summoned a legatine council at Westminster on 7 December. Stephen himself was present and made his complaint before the assembled company about the treatment he had received. He then gave way to his brother. Henry attempted to justify his abandonment of Stephen earlier in the year and his positive espousal of Empress Matilda, then his subsequent return to Stephen's side. He argued that he really had no alternative but to support Matilda as his position was so weak, however, having given his support he had been enjoined by the pope to do everything possible to restore the king. Moreover, Matilda had broken all her promises concerning the freedom of the church and, he claimed, had intended to deprive him of his position and even kill him. The king had been anointed and had the approval of the people and the support of the Apostolic See. All who had supported the empress, now described as the countess of Anjou, should be excommunicated, although she should be spared that fate. Henry was then confronted in vigorous terms by an envoy from the countess, but he remained calmly unmoved. The eventful year concluded with a grand ceremony in Canterbury cathedral. Stephen was re-crowned not by his brother but, following established precedent, by the archbishop of Canterbury, and Queen Matilda also wore her crown.

While the restoration of Stephen put an end to any prospect that Empress Matilda might have had of becoming Queen of England, it did not guarantee peace and disorders continued in 1142–43. Henry seemed to have been fairly impassive in this period. As a result, claimed Henry, the clergy enjoyed a bare measure of tranquillity. The death of Innocent II on 25 September 1143 meant that Henry's legateship died with him, although before that Theobald was emerging as the more effective head of the English church. He was able to secure the loyalty of the bishops to Stephen while retaining Empress Matilda's respect. Before news of the death of Innocent and the election of Celestine III reached England Henry held his last legatine councils, on 10 and 30 November.

A legate no longer, Henry could not claim any kind of superiority over Theobald, a situation that doubtless rankled. Although he had hoped that the office might be restored to him by a later pope, the brief reigns of Innocent's successors, Celestine and Lucius II, were followed by that of Eugenius III, well known for his hostility towards the Cluniac Henry. If Henry's prospects of regaining superiority over Theobald were doomed he might, at least, become an equal, a fellow metropolitan bishop. There had been a third metropolitan see once before when in 788 Pope Hadrian I had sent a pallium to the bishop of Lichfield, but it was short-lived. However, it could be cited as a precedent for Henry's ambition to become archbishop of Winchester. An argument that could also be used in Henry's favour was that York had a mere two suffragans while Canterbury had seventeen, including the Welsh sees. This was out of line with what was normal in the west. In France it was usual to have five sees in a province. Such arguments seemed to find favour with Lucius II but his death meant he could do nothing for Henry, who had no alternative but to accept his subordinate position.

Archbishop Theobald

Once Henry of Blois had ceased to be a legate, Archbishop Theobald was in a much stronger position to play his part as head of the ecclesiastical hierarchy in England. He himself was appointed legate in 1150 and he was reappointed by succeeding popes. Although he owed his initial election to Canterbury to Stephen and Stephen's close associates, he came to see himself as much a servant of the papacy as of the king. Towards the end of 1143 Theobald set off for Rome to enable the new pope to become acquainted with him in the hope that he would be offered the legateship. He left England shortly before Christmas. He had hoped to be accompanied by Gilbert Foliot, who had shown his pleasure at the release of Canterbury from the grip of Bishop Henry, and whom he trusted enough subsequently to make him his agent in the west of England, but Foliot was too busy safeguarding Gloucester abbey from the earl of Hereford.[28] He was accompanied instead by the bishops of Ely and Coventry. Stephen raised no objection to their going. It was in his interests to remain on good terms with the pope, who was apparently sympathetic to the Angevins. Henry of Winchester had also set off for Rome in the hope that Celestine would look favourably on him and renew his legateship, but sensing that Celestine might in fact be ill disposed to him, he broke his journey at his beloved Cluny, where he spent the winter.

Not long after Theobald reached Rome Celestine died on 8 March 1144. It is possible that Celestine awarded Theobald the legateship before he died but, if so, his successor Lucius II promptly reversed the decision. Disappointed Theobald left Rome before mid-May. Lucius enjoyed as brief a reign as his predecessor, for he died on 15 February 1145. The new pope, Eugenius III, was in no hurry to do anything for Theobald. On the other hand his dislike of the Cluniac Bishop Henry had been fuelled by his mentor Bernard, so there would be no question of his granting him any favours. Moreover, Eugenius had problems of his own to contend with. He went to France in 1147–48 to play his part in organising the second Crusade and in Rome he was faced with Arnold of Brescia and his followers. In May 1147 Theobald met Eugenius in Paris, whence he had gone in a successful attempt to settle a dispute between the monks of Bec and the canons of St Frideswide, Oxford. Having dealt with this and possibly a matter concerning the bishop of St David's, he returned to England. A few months later he was called back to France by Eugenius to attend the Council of Rheims. This was due to open on 21 March 1148, and Eugenius had summoned all the English bishops and abbots to attend.

John of Salisbury's *Historia Pontificalis* tells of the relationship between England and the papacy at this time. Stephen decided that he should take a stance against the papacy in the manner of his uncle and grandfather. He had already provoked Eugenius by refusing to allow St Malachy, archbishop of Armagh, primate of Ireland and legate to pass through England on his way to Ireland from Rome. He refused to admit Archbishop Henry Murdac into England and he expelled the legates who had summoned the English prelates to the Council of Rheims. He then gave permission to only three bishops, Robert of Hereford, William of Norwich and Hilary of Chichester, to attend the council. This act of defiance was misjudged, for when Stephen subsequently needed the support of Eugenius it was denied him. Theobald had been determined to attend the council, and suspecting that Stephen would try by all possible means, both open and furtive, to prevent him doing so, he hired a fishing boat concealed in a hidden creek. This was scarcely seaworthy and was ill-equipped to sustain the archbishop and those he took with him, including a clerk in his household called Thomas Becket. He had, however, obtained Stephen's permission to send some of his clerks ahead of him, ostensibly on the grounds that they could present his excuses to the council, in reality to form a nucleus of a council if he was not allowed to return. John of Salisbury may have been one of these clerks. When, to everyone's surprise, Theobald landed, he received a most friendly reception. On receiving news of this Stephen angrily confiscated his estate.

Eugenius had every intention of punishing Stephen. In the final session of the council the candles were lit in readiness for the pope to excommunicate him. At that point Theobald begged for the sentence to be stayed. According to John of Salisbury, the pope was 'stunned and astounded at the archbishop's boundless generosity and after a little thought and a few sighs',[29] he admitted to being so impressed by this Christian demonstration of Theobald's love for his enemy that he suspended the sentence and gave him three months to make reparation. Failure to do so would lead to even more dire consequences. Although for the time being Stephen was spared punishment, those bishops who had failed to respond to the summons, none of whom was mentioned by name, were suspended. Theobald, however, was empowered to absolve them, and did so after a short while. Henry of Winchester was treated differently. He alone was named and only Eugenius could absolve him. Bearing no animosity towards Henry and not wishing to exploit the situation to his advantage, Theobald begged Eugenius to reinstate him. This he refused to do until Henry's brother, Count Theobald of Blois, intervened on his behalf. The sentence was relaxed for six months, and during that time Henry was to seek an audience of the pope.

Theobald's generosity towards Stephen was not reciprocated. Towards the end of April Eugenius left Rheims and, with his permission, Theobald returned to England and made for Canterbury, where he was enthusiastically received by the townspeople and the Christ Church monks. Stephen immediately banished him while retaining control of his temporalities. He settled in St Omer at the monastery of St Bertin where, John of Salisbury tells us, he was 'beloved by all for his honesty of character and from respect for his rank, but chiefly because he was mild of speech and devoted to the poor, and seemed to be a unique example of kindliness and generosity'.[30] He was accompanied on his travels by Gilbert Foliot, and it was while Gilbert was with him that he was consecrated bishop of Hereford.

Gilbert was one of Theobald's few friends among the bishops, most of whom remained loyal to Stephen, or, as John of Salisbury wrote: 'turned aside from the archbishop like a deceitful bow'. Eugenius had moved from France to Brescia, where he stayed from mid-July to 8 September 1148. There he met envoys from Theobald and responded positively to their plea that he should act on Theobald's behalf. He wrote to all the English bishops severally and jointly ordering them to warn Stephen that unless he welcomed Theobald back and restored his lands, they were to place his kingdom under an interdict. If that did not achieve the desired result Stephen would be excommunicated. At the same time he wrote to the bishops and lay magnates of France requesting them to give aid to the exile, while ordering all in the province of Canterbury to obey him as if he were present in his see.

There is no reason to think that the bishops were personally hostile towards Theobald; rather that they believed that the interests of the church were best served by their remaining loyal to Stephen. The pope's commands were ignored. Theobald promulgated an interdict on 12 September to very little effect. The see of Canterbury alone obeyed it and even in Canterbury the monastery of St Augustine's, with its history of awkwardness towards archbishops, continued to celebrate the divine offices. Stephen then decided that it would be judicious to moderate his attitude. He realised that if the Angevins were to work to achieve their ambition that young Henry of Normandy should succeed him he might be unwise to alienate the pope further. Queen Matilda and William of Ypres advised that he should make his peace with Theobald and welcome him back. Theobald had no wish to remain in exile and returned in October. He remained cautious, however, and felt it wiser not to land in Kent, where Stephen had staunch support. Instead he sailed to Gosford in Suffolk, a port now under the sea, and made for Hugh Bigod's castle of Framlingham. There he resumed his archiepiscopal responsibilities. Hugh Bigod, earl of Suffolk and Norfolk, was a partisan of the empress and Stephen had enough sense to recognise that it would not be to his advantage to find that the archbishop of Canterbury had become an adherent of the Angevin cause. He therefore made peace with Theobald, who returned to his diocese and to his property. In 1150 Eugenius recognised his loyalty and conferred a legateship on him. He could not be challenged by Bishop Henry. It is clear from the many charters that he issued he asserted his authority in all parts of the Canterbury province, not just those controlled by Stephen.[31]

Reeds shaken by the wind?

Few bishops receive much favourable comment in the chronicles. The Peterborough Chronicle dismisses them as ineffective: 'the bishops and the clergy always cursed them (those guilty of violence and disorder) but that was nothing to them'.[32] The *Gesta Stephani* is scathing. Having given a detailed and colourful description of the dire condition of the country in 1143, the author is contemptuous of the response of the bishops. He writes of them 'cowering in most dastardly fear, bent like a reed shaken by the wind'. He tells of some who, 'made sluggish and abject by fear of the plunderers, either gave way or lukewarmly and feebly passed a sentence of excommunication that was soon to be revoked'.[33] Others donned fine suits of armour and took their share of the spoils. Few bishops are mentioned by name, but the bishops of Winchester, Lincoln and Chester are specifically referred to as being particularly devoted to irreligious pursuits. Only one bishop, Robert of Hereford, receives unqualified praise for 'manfully setting himself like a shield of defence against the enemies of catholic peace'.[34]

Such criticism of the bishops is scarcely merited. Their churches and estates were threatened by the depredations of civil war, lawlessness and violence. In a letter to the pope Gilbert Foliot, when abbot of Gloucester, wrote: 'the churches of the whole of England wear a look of total devastation'.[35] Many of the people for whom the bishops had pastoral responsibility suffered desperate hardship at times, and they were faced with the issue of loyalty. As tenants-in-chief of the king they were required to produce knights for the king's service. According to the returns of Henry II's enquiry of 1166 Chichester owed only two, but Canterbury, Winchester, Lincoln and Worcester owed as many as sixty, Norwich and Ely forty.[36] While a bishop was forbidden by canon law to shed blood he could raise troops and rally them. Roger de Clinton, the crusading bishop of Coventry and therewith of Lichfield and Chester, fortified Lichfield during the civil war using the service of Coventry knights and was prepared to work to contain the aggression of Ranulf, earl of Chester.

Most famous from a military perspective is Archbishop Thurstan of York. Despite age and increasing infirmity he assumed responsibility for defending Stephen's interests on the northern borders threatened by David of Scots' intention to win Northumbria for his son Henry.[37] According to the chronicler Richard of Hexham his inspirational leadership turned this into a divinely inspired enterprise.[38] Poor health prevented him from being at the ensuing battle at Northallerton, but he was represented by Bishop Ralph of Orkney, who addressed the troops on the morning of the battle, 22 August 1138.[39] The Battle of the Standard, as it is known, resulted in a great victory for the English. Thurstan's health continued to decline and he died nearly six months later in the Cluniac monastery of Pontefract, clad in the habit of a Cluniac monk.

Whatever their personal views of Stephen, most of the bishops remained loyal to him. He was the crowned and anointed king. As such he had been recognised by the papacy and there was no way he could be lawfully deposed. They had no reason to believe that Empress Matilda would be more effective at maintaining law and order or defending the interests of the church. They appreciated that in difficult times they were looked to to provide some means of enforcing peace and stability. They tried to maintain order in the localities and support legitimate local government. Their ecclesiastical authority and spiritual influence, their established role in shire government and their association with the king helped in their attempts to oppose the aggressor and support the victim.

Some did indeed have difficulty in recognising Stephen, among them the Welsh bishops. Bernard of St David's had been loyal to Henry I but the political situation in Wales and the Marches led him to reconsider his relationship with Stephen; moreover, he had pretensions to establish himself as primate of Wales. Maurice of Bangor and Uchtred of Llandaff were consecrated by Theobald and made their professions of obedience to him. Maurice was reluctant to pay homage to Stephen but was persuaded to do so by the bishops of Hereford and Chichester. This alienated him from some of the Welsh princes and he was driven to seek refuge at Theobald's court.[40] The question of loyalty was particularly an issue for the bishops whose dioceses were in the part of the country controlled by Matilda and her brother Robert of Gloucester and their supporters, but they remained conscious of their responsibility to remain loyal to Stephen. Robert of Lewes, bishop of Bath, was steadfast in his loyalty. Robert of Bethune, bishop of Hereford from 1131 until his death during the Council of Rheims, owed his election to local leaders but was not prepared to accept the violence of Miles of Hereford and his ally Geoffrey Talbot.[41] When Maurice of Bangor refused to pay homage to Stephen at Worcester in 1139 Robert and Bishop Hilary of Chichester persuaded him to change his mind, with the words: 'seeing that we have paid homage, reason demands that you should as well'.[42] When Miles was killed in a hunting accident and was succeeded by Roger his young son, Bishop Robert remained loyal to Stephen and continued to be a strong spiritual force in the region.

Robert's successor was Gilbert Foliot, one of the outstanding bishops of Stephen's reign and the next. At the time of the death of Robert of Bethune Gilbert was abbot of Gloucester. He was a great letter writer, keen to communicate with members of the highest ranks of church and state. He was on genuinely good terms with Theobald, Bishop Robert and Ralph, the dean of Hereford. Gilbert was strongly supported by Theobald. John of Salisbury's words are important: 'Gilbert was elected bishop of Hereford with the advice and assent of the archbishop of Canterbury. This was highly pleasing on personal grounds to the Norman duke (who at this time was Geoffrey of Anjou, father of the future Henry II), in whose power the election to the bishopric then resided, but he would not give his consent or bestow the regalia until the bishop elect had bound himself by solemn oath to do homage to him within a month of his consecration and had undertaken not to do homage to King Stephen, whom the entire English Church acknowledged by a decree of the Roman Church.'[43] John of Salisbury then tells us that Theobald, supported by the pope, summoned Robert of London, Jocelyn of Salisbury and Hilary of Chichester to participate in Gilbert's consecration. They refused to attend on the grounds that such a consecration would be unprecedented and was contrary to their oath to Stephen. Moreover Stephen had not consented to the election and Gilbert had not sworn fealty to him. Theobald, undeterred, obtained permission from the pope to use the local bishops to assist at the consecration at St Omer on 25 September 1148. Gilbert then returned to England and swore fealty to Stephen. Geoffrey and Henry were not pleased, believing that Gilbert had deceived them. Further evidence of Gilbert's recognition of Stephen's authority is that in 1150 he responded to a royal mandate when hearing a case between Gilbert de Lacy and Roger of Hereford concerning breach of sanctuary.[44]

In the late 1140s Stephen continued to summon the bishops of Hereford and Exeter to councils in London, and he expected bishops in every diocese but Carlisle to act as leading members of the shire court alongside the earl and sheriff.[45] Where royal authority was weak the bishops could act as safeguards of law and order. Perhaps the most celebrated example of this is the part played by Walter Durdent, bishop of Chester and Robert de Chesney, bishop of Lincoln in guaranteeing the peace treaty drawn up by the earls of Chester and Leicester in about 1150.[46]

In spring 1143 Henry held a legatine council, according to Henry of Huntingdon because of the urgent needs of the clergy.[47] The clergy and God's church were the victims of plunderers. Clergy were being captured and ransomed like laymen. It was decreed at the council that anyone who attacked a clerk could be absolved only by the pope and that in person. Theobald held his first legatine council in London in March 1151.[48] According to Huntingdon Stephen himself and his son Eustace were both present. The canons of the council are in existence and show the need to seek out new remedies to the current problems.[49] The canons are decidedly anti-baronial in tone and convey the wish to restore royal authority and co-operation between the lay and spiritual authorities. Those who damaged church property were to be subject to interdict or excommunicated until they made reparations. Royal taxation was upheld but unjust levies by magnates were condemned. Churchmen were forbidden to answer to the local baronage in legal cases reserved to the crown. Stephen and Theobald were on good terms again. But it was not long before the issue of the succession tested their relationship to the extreme.

The succession issue and the peace settlement

Stephen's determination to ensure that he was succeeded by his son Eustace matched Empress Matilda's to secure the throne for her son Henry. The papacy and the archbishops of Canterbury and York played a significant part in the outcome. Despite Innocent II's support there was no promise that the papacy would guarantee backing for Stephen's heirs. Celestine II had actually declared in a letter to Theobald that 'there was to be no innovation in the kingdom of England with respect to the crown', an attitude adopted by Lucius and Eugenius.[50] This could be interpreted by the Angevins to mean that while the papacy would not countenance the deposition of Stephen it would not go further than that and declare in favour of his heirs.

The most effective way for Stephen to secure the succession would be to have his son Eustace crowned in his own lifetime. He did not need the pope's consent for this. There had been no precedent for an English king to require papal approval to be crowned but Stephen believed that to ensure that such a coronation would go unchallenged he should seek the approval of Eugenius III. Presumably, and this says little for his political judgement, he was confident that he would be given it. What he had failed to see was that if the pope refused he might establish himself as the arbiter of the future of the English monarchy. Resentful though Stephen was of the way that Henry Murdac had supplanted his nephew William as archbishop of York, he saw him as a means of securing the pope's favour, for as an old school friend and a fellow Cistercian Eugenius might listen to him. Towards the end of 1150 Stephen and Murdac were reconciled, and early the next year Murdac visited the pope and put Stephen's request to him. Old friends that Henry Murdac and Eugenius might have been, Eugenius had no wish to be accommodating towards a king who had been so uncooperative in 1148. Instead he summarily rejected Henry's request and according to Henry of Huntingdon, the pope wrote to Theobald forbidding him to crown Eustace.[51]

It is therefore not surprising that after Murdac came back empty-handed Stephen's attempt to get Theobald to agree to crown Eustace failed. In spring 1152 Stephen called a council at London attended by the bishops and barons with a view to securing Theobald's agreement to the coronation, and there Theobald proved to be uncooperative. So, too, were the other bishops. In some sort of desperation Stephen turned to them, but well aware as they were that the right of coronation lay with the archbishop of Canterbury, they refused to be disloyal to Theobald. The king was furious and in his rage imprisoned them and tried to force them to agree to his demands. They bravely refused to cave in and when Stephen had calmed down he released them and returned their possessions which he had confiscated. On 6 April Theobald escaped to Dover and once more retreated to Flanders. One account seems to anticipate the Becket murder. It says that while Stephen had no intention of harming Theobald personally he would not have objected to anyone else doing so. So a dozen knights pursued him down the Thames with the intention of mutilating or even killing him. Happily he escaped thanks to divine intervention. He did not remain in exile long. Stephen's attitude towards Theobald contrasts favourably with that of Henry II and Becket. Stephen could certainly be moved to anger, but he did not harbour grudges and was rarely vindictive. He was not moved by any sort of personal malice towards Theobald and, having calmed down, he was happy to be reconciled with him.

In that year Stephen suffered personal tragedy, for Queen Matilda died on 3 May. This was more than a personal tragedy for the queen had done so much to rally and sustain the royalist cause. Then, fifteen months later, his son Eustace also died. William, Eustace's brother, was far too young to be considered as Stephen's successor. The way was effectively open for the empress's son, Duke Henry of Anjou. However, a peace settlement had to be negotiated. According to Huntingdon, Theobald had frequent conversations with the king in person and with the duke through intermediaries. He was assisted in this by Bishop Henry. They made a good team. Theobald was wise and statesmanlike, and despite his Angevin sympathies he was capable of impartiality. Bishop Henry's inclinations were to his family, but as the events of 1141 showed, he had political skills and accepted the reality of circumstances. Stephen and Duke Henry had been campaigning in arms for much of 1153 and both bishops wished for peace.[52]

The settlement was embodied in the so-called Treaty of Winchester or Wallingford.[53] The role of the church in formulating the settlement was significant. The first two signatories were Theobald and Henry followed by twelve other bishops and one prior. Henry of Anjou was unconditionally recognised as Stephen's successor. Bishop Henry agreed to return his castles to the next king on Stephen's death. Archbishops, bishops and abbots were to swear fealty to young Henry. The whole agreement was sanctioned by the church. There are a number of references in the treaty to 'the advice of holy Church' and the 'counsel of holy Church', and the archbishops and bishops had each undertaken that if either Stephen or Henry departed from the terms of the treaty they would be visited 'with the justice of the Church until he has corrected his errors and returned to the proper observation of this pact'.

No one at the time, of course, knew how long Stephen would live. As it happened peace was guaranteed by his death on 25 October 1154. Six untroubled weeks elapsed before Henry was crowned. There was no taste for further disorder. Gervase of Canterbury wrote of the 'peace throughout England made by the will of God and the assistance of Theobald, archbishop of Canterbury'.[54] Theobald lived until 1162. His death precipitated one of the most dramatic and well-documented episodes in the whole of English history.

6

The Becket Conflict in Perspective

The conflict between Becket and Henry II is different from that between Anselm and his two kings. Much of it was about technicalities and it did little to alter the long-term relationship between the secular and spiritual authorities. Becket was archbishop for less than a quarter of Henry's reign and for much of that time in exile. He was not the first archbishop of Canterbury to be murdered. Aelfheah had been brutally killed by Danes in 1012, but these were heathen invaders. The murder of an archbishop in his own cathedral apparently on the orders of his king created a sensation that reverberated throughout Christendom. Very soon miracles were attributed to him and his reputation benefited from a great deal of subsequent sympathetic writing. Becket came to be revered as far away as Poland, Hungary, the Scandinavian countries and Iceland. His murder turned a problematical man into a martyr and a saint, elevating Canterbury to one of the leading centres of pilgrimage and inspiring one of the greatest works in English literature, Chaucer's *Canterbury Tales*. Tennyson and T.S. Eliot wrote plays about Becket, as did Jean Anouilh.

The relationship between Henry II and Becket is not susceptible of a simple interpretation, and the views of eminent historians working on the same material vary greatly. Anne Duggan, David Knowles and John Guy, for instance, while acknowledging his faults, are far more sympathetic than Frank Barlow or W.L. Warren. However momentous the fundamental and specific issues, the tragedy of the Becket conflict is that it became intensely personal, with king and archbishop each unable to moderate his stance because of personal pride and fear of loss of face. As impasse succeeded impasse acrimony and mean-spiritedness replaced rational debate, so that any prospect of reconciliation was doomed.

The setting

The Becket conflict must be seen in a European context and the interrelationship of the four great powers in Western Europe, Frederick Barbarossa, the Western Emperor and king of Germany (1152–90), Louis VII, Capetian king of France (1137–80), Henry II (1154–89) and Pope Alexander III (1159–80). Through his Norman and Angevin inheritance and then his marriage aged 19 to Louis's divorced wife Eleanor of Aquitaine, Henry was not only king of England but also lord of a vast agglomeration of territories in France. Although legally Louis had ultimate authority over Henry for his lands in France, his power to enforce it was limited. Consequently there was recurrent political tension between Louis and Henry, aggravated by personal feelings following the divorce. When Becket was in exile in France Louis was happy to give him his support.

The position of Alexander III was less straightforward. An enduring problem, one faced by Alexander's predecessor Adrian IV, was that of the pope's relationship with the Romano-German emperor Barbarossa. Alexander III and Barbarossa were at permanent enmity and Alexander immediately found himself challenged by a rival claimant to the papal throne. The anti-pope 'Victor IV' was recognised in Imperial territory, and for much of his long pontificate, faced with a rival supported by Barbarossa, Alexander was unable to establish himself in Rome. He could not support Becket wholeheartedly lest he provoke Henry II to withdraw his allegiance and turn to the emperor's side.

Although the authority of the papacy was challenged by prolonged schism and Hohenstaufen hostility, the increasing sophistication of the machinery of papal government enhanced its authority in practical and unprecedented ways. Fundamental to this were the developments in canon law following the appearance in 1140 of Gratian's *Decretum*. Canon law could not provide all the answers to the controversial matters confronting rulers like Henry II, for political problems which address the issue of where power ultimately lies do not necessarily admit of legal solution. Moreover the development of canon law and therewith the power and authority of the church courts did not always answer the fundamental problem of which law and which jurisdiction, secular or ecclesiastical, was appropriate for a specific matter. No attempt had been made to define precisely the nature of matters that 'pertained to the cure of souls', so the problem of which belonged to canon law and which did not was unresolved by Becket's time. However, the ecclesiastical courts were seeing the development of formal legal process which compared favourably with the king's more haphazard courts.

The fundamental problem was about jurisdiction and ultimate authority. It was encapsulated in the famous words of Becket to Henry: 'You are my lord, you are my king, you are my spiritual son.' It is misleading to see it as a conflict of 'church v. state'. That was not a twelfth-century concept. The church as a community of all Christians embraced everyone, laity and clergy. Leading churchmen were essential to the organisation and administration of the realm. They were great landholders with secular obligations and a commitment to maintain the integrity of their temporalities and exploit them. The logic of the reform movement associated with Gregory VII and developed by Urban II and Paschal II was to elevate the status not just of the papacy as monarchical head of Christendom, buttressed by a law and administrative system that touched both laity and clergy, but of all clergy as superior to laymen. The danger to secular rulers was that the clergy would become an increasingly privileged and exclusive corporation within the wider community. The challenge facing Henry II and his four predecessors was how to maintain ultimate authority.

We have seen that Eadmer had stated that the Conqueror had erected barriers against papal influence in England. To suggest that Henry II sought to restore the barriers that had collapsed owing to the weaknesses of Stephen's reign is to over-simplify, as it would be to imply that Stephen failed to assert any authority over the church. The Oxford Charter was far from a capitulation. The extent to which the bishops were loyal to Stephen has been considered. He was prepared to challenge the papacy and he was determined to take into his court one of the most notorious cases relating to a priest accused of crime, that of Osbert, archdeacon of Richmond, accused of poisoning Archbishop William of York by Symphorian, a member of William's household. Although the case remained unresolved at the time of his death, Stephen insisted that the crime should come before him because it was so heinous and he was actually in York when it was committed.

Henry and Theobald

Thomas Becket's professional career began in the household of Archbishop Theobald. He was born in 1120 or thereabouts, the son of a prosperous London merchant of Norman birth and ancestry. Following schooling in an Augustinian priory and a London grammar school he continued his education in Paris, but despite his considerable intellectual ability left without a master's degree. On his return he was employed for three years by a relation, a highly respected London financier, Osbert Huitdeniers.[1] Guided by Osbert, he learnt the administrative and financial skills that he employed so effectively as chancellor. Thomas's father Gilbert had powerful contacts, and through them he was able to meet Archbishop Theobald, whose household he later joined.[2] By 1146 he was well established as clerk to the archbishop and regularly appears as Thomas of London, witness to Theobald's charters. He was given the opportunity by Theobald to enjoy a sabbatical in Bologna and Auxerre studying civil and canon law.

Henry II's debt to the church in securing a smooth succession to the throne was as great as that of Stephen. Equally, there was optimism that the English church would benefit from the end of civil war and the arrival of a young king determined to maintain the peace. Henry quickly set about asserting his authority, banishing Stephen's Flemish mercenaries led by William of Ypres, destroying castles built unlawfully, reclaiming crown lands and appointing new judges. In January 1156 Henry crossed to the Continent for 15 months, returning there at the end of 1158 until January 1163. On his deathbed Theobald wrote to Henry in France: 'Surely my Christ will not deny me the sight of him whom He permitted me in answer to my desire to make an anointed king.'[3] As Anne Duggan has shown, in Theobald's last years there were warning signs of potential trouble on the horizon.[4] There was evidence of tension between king and archbishop in 1156–57 when John of Salisbury returned from the Papal Curia and John found he had lost Henry's favour. From about 1154 John's main responsibility had been to draft official correspondence with the Curia, particularly in connection with appeals. In the late summer of 1156 Henry was provoked to anger by a suspicion, nurtured by Arnulf of Lisieux, that John was too inclined to favour ecclesiastical independence.

The reality was not as clear-cut as that. The mid-twelfth century saw a significant development in the study of canon law in England. Archbishop Theobald attracted scholars to his household, among them the distinguished Roman lawyer Vacarius, and Z.N. Brooke said of Theobald that he was 'renowned for his learning, especially in the law of the Church'.[5] With the greater sophistication of canon law went an expansion of ecclesiastical courts and appeals to Rome. Many were inappropriate or trivial. Appealing was used to protract disputes, delay settlements and even avoid an unfavourable judgement. Theobald, no less than Henry, found much to dislike about this. He was convinced that it was best for many cases to be settled locally by those who were familiar with the circumstances of the dispute rather than by recourse to distant Rome. Archbishop Theobald and the king were both opposed to any papal intervention that might diminish their authority, but at the same time Henry was willing to leave final judgements to the church.

A potentially contentious matter was that of advowsons, the question of who had the right to present an incumbent to a church.[6] For a long time it had been accepted that disputes over this right were matters for the secular courts, but in the course of the twelfth century advowson was redefined and related issues were held to fall within the jurisdiction of the church courts. Because they were related to spiritual jurisdiction Archbishop Theobald was drawn by appeals into a number of such cases. Contentious, too, were cases with a penitential or pastoral side, such as those relating to marriages and wills. Civil lawyers saw handing over a woman in marriage as a civil contract comparable to transferring property, theologians saw it as a sacrament and canon lawyers, anxious to dispel the notion that a woman was property, stressed the importance of consent. This was hugely contentious for a society in which the marriage of heiresses and widows was so important, as was the fate of the issue of a marriage that was believed to be valid and subsequently declared not so. One of the best-known, protracted and expensive cases in the twelfth century was that of Richard of Anstey, which ran from 1158 to 1163. The case was heard both in the king's court and the papal court and demonstrates that Henry was not hostile to papal authority in principle, nor did he take a doctrinaire stance towards the church, provided always a subject's involvement with the pope in no way diminished his own rights or authority.[7]

Theobald recognised this and could handle the king, well aware that Henry expected to have his own way. There were several elections to bishoprics between 1155 and 1161: St Asaph twice, Exeter twice, Worcester and Coventry. There is little to suggest that Henry attempted to impose his will on the electors.[8] A fine example of the skill with which Theobald was able to handle Henry while ensuring that the king achieved what he wanted concerned the recognition of

Alexander III. From the days of the Conqueror it had been established that in the event of papal schism the king should determine who should be recognised as pope. Following the death of Adrian IV in 1159 the Imperialists backed Cardinal Octavian as Victor IV while anti-Imperialists like Louis VII supported Alexander. Theobald did not contest Henry's order to the English church to recognise neither, to ban appeals or to forbid travel outside the kingdom for any purpose connected with the schism. In May 1160 Louis and Henry agreed to support Alexander; then in June Henry summoned a church council in London to discuss the schism in his absence. Although the council was not unanimous, a majority favoured Alexander. Theobald wrote personally to Henry, anxious to stress that nothing had been decided to the prejudice of royal power and without saying whom the council had favoured. This was left to the messengers bearing Theobald's letter. They merely stated the council's decision, making clear that the final judgement must lie with the king. The Norman church had been less circumspect in publicly supporting Alexander, and only the intervention of Becket saved the archbishop and archdeacon of Rouen from the consequences of Henry's wrath. In conclusion Theobald, as papal legate, addressed a mandate to the English bishops ordering them to obey Alexander and condemn Octavian as a schismatic and heretic.[9] The king had retained his authority; his bishops had suffered no loss of face.

The new archbishop

Henry clearly appreciated Thomas's work as the senior member of Theobald's household after Roger of Pont l'Évêque's promotion to the province of York, for in 1155 he made him his chancellor. The fullest account of Thomas's time in that office was written by William fitz Stephen.[10] Thomas was secure in the king's support and fitz Stephen suggests that he was soon to find universal favour for restoring England's prosperity through his industry. He became immensely rich himself, leading the ostentatiously extravagant lifestyle appropriate to his office while enjoying a genuinely close personal friendship with the king. 'Never in Christian times were there two greater friends, more of one mind.' Proof of the regard in which Henry held Becket is that he entrusted the care of his young son Henry to him in his lengthy absences from the kingdom.[11] But close that their relationship was, warning signs for the future appeared. Above all it was not a friendship of equals, as was demonstrated by the incident of the beggar and the cloak.[12] Although 'second in the realm after the king', Henry never allowed Becket to forget his subordinate role, that he had raised him 'from a humble and poor rank to the highest peak of honour and distinction'.[13]

As chancellor Thomas had no option but to put loyalty to the king before friendship with the church. In 1159 Henry imposed a heavy war tax on those who owed military service but whose actual service he did not require. The burden fell on ecclesiastical tenants-in-chief as much as lay. Demands went beyond these scutages. So-called 'gifts' were required of a number of bishops, abbots and abbesses. The bishop of Durham, for instance, paid a scutage of 20 marks and was assessed for a 'gift' of 500. Becket's part in this is not clear, but the prelates believed that he had done nothing to help alleviate the burden and Gilbert Foliot, admittedly no friend of Becket, wrote to him when archbishop complaining that the taxes were as 'a sword plunged in the vitals of holy mother Church'.[14]

Becket was also seen as unfavourably disposed to the church in the dispute between the bishop of Chichester and Battle Abbey.[15] Disputes between abbots and diocesan bishops over the extent of their respective jurisdictions were common. There had been tension between the bishops of Chichester and Battle Abbey since its foundation by the Conqueror. Matters came to a head when Bishop Hilary (1147–69), with the full backing of Theobald, who greatly admired his intellectual ability and mastery of canon law, confronted Abbot Walter de Lucy, brother of one of Henry's justiciars. In 1157 Walter appealed to the king to help him refute Hilary's claim that the abbot must submit to the diocesan bishop. At a council held at Colchester in April the king came out strongly in favour of the abbey. Throughout he had the wholehearted support of Becket, who greatly discomfited Bishop Hilary by improperly suggesting that he had tried to use a papal mandate to nullify royal authority. Unsurprisingly, Hilary became Becket's sworn enemy. In considering the Battle Abbey case it is difficult to discern fact from fabrication. The abbey's early charters were forgeries and in 2001 Nicholas Vincent showed that much of the Battle Abbey chronicle is as spurious as the charters.[16]

Despite Thomas's unswerving loyalty to the king, John of Salisbury believed that Theobald retained his personal affection for him and actually favoured him as his successor. He hoped that Thomas would be able to protect the metropolitan see, resist the ambitions of York, maintain his authority over the suffragans and keep the Canterbury monks in their place. Even so, Becket was not an obvious candidate, for in other respects he had not shown the qualities an archbishop would expect of a successor and his worldliness was not mitigated by great learning or obvious piety. There were undoubtedly distinguished churchmen among the bishops, but probably only one, the Cluniac bishop of Hereford Gilbert Foliot, was a strong contender. He certainly considered himself to be.

There was no exact procedure for the election of an archbishop of Canterbury. The monks of Christ Church claimed an exclusive right and the bishops of the province reckoned, not unreasonably, that they should have a say, but there was no doubt that the final decision would be the king's. Considerable pressure was put on the Canterbury monks. The bishops of Chichester, Exeter and Rochester, along with the justiciar Richard de Lucy, went to Canterbury to ensure that their election accorded with the king's will. Thomas's appointment was confirmed on 23 May by a council of bishops and other senior clergy, magnates and royal officials chaired by Henry of Winchester. On 2 June, the Saturday after Whitsun, deacon Becket was ordained priest and the following day he was consecrated bishop in Canterbury cathedral by Bishop Henry. The one setback in the magnificent ceremony was the ominous prognostic '"May no fruit ever come from you again," and the fig tree withered away at once.' On 10 August, barefooted, Becket received the pallium at the high altar in Canterbury Cathedral.

Thomas's reluctance to become archbishop of Canterbury is well known. The somewhat worldly and extrovert but very scholarly Herbert of Bosham, Becket's former clerk and unfailingly loyal companion in exile, wrote of Becket's reaction when Henry informed him of his intention that he should succeed Theobald.[17] Unlike some chancellors, Thomas did not see the office as a step towards a lucrative bishopric. He was well aware of the burden of inheriting the place of Augustine and Theodore and his more recent predecessors. Lanfranc, Anselm and Ralph had been monks; William an Augustinian canon. Anselm, whom he greatly revered, was on an altogether different intellectual and spiritual plane. Thomas knew Henry's mind very well. He had the perception to appreciate that he and Henry could not enjoy their former relationship and that he lacked the innate statesmanship and political skills required to handle a demanding king.

In meeting the considerable challenges of reasserting royal authority in England and mastering his continental dominions Henry showed himself to be a man of considerable intelligence and formidable energy, ruthless in using his terrifying temper as a political instrument for achieving his way.[18] He was a master of chicanery and double-dealing, as Louis VII repeatedly discovered. He may not have been temperamentally bloodthirsty, although in 1165, when thwarted on a Welsh expedition, he had 22 Welsh hostages mutilated and hanged, and the following year one of Becket's couriers, a boy whom Herbert of Bosham had sent to the king with a letter, was subjected to appalling cruelty.[19] However, he was also capable of inspiring affection.[20] In appearance the contrast between Henry and Thomas was striking. Henry was short and stocky, inclined to stoutness, with a large round head and fiery countenance. His legs were bowed from constant riding. Becket was tall and dark with a handsome face, aquiline nose and long hands with exquisite fingers. He had a commanding presence which was impossible to disguise, however he tried.[21] He was courteous and generous, but not particularly warm or affectionate, and lacked a sense of humour. Nevertheless he inspired great loyalty from a number of people, including Herbert of Bosham, John of Salisbury and William fitz Stephen.

There has always been much speculation as to why Becket's transformation from chancellor relishing the fruits of office to masochistically ascetic champion of the church was so rapid and complete.[22] In fact he had been chaste all his life and was personally devout.[23] It may be that, having accepted that he had no alternative but to accept the office, he saw it as an opportunity to fulfil himself in a way that could be true to himself. Perhaps he was realising the need of an unconfident man to prove himself before his social and intellectual superiors and to assert himself in his own right, free from his occasionally humiliating dependence on the king. For in Theobald's household he was made uncomfortable by those who considered themselves his intellectual and social superiors, like Roger of Pont l'Éveque. John of Salisbury wrote of his difficulties at court, 'exposed to so many snares by the spite of courtiers'.[24] Such tensions may have aggravated his stammer and the digestive disorder, possibly colitis or irritable bowel syndrome, which disabled him at times of stress like the Northampton council. Moreover, he was well aware of current academic and scholarly thinking about the right order on earth and his role as archbishop within that right order.

Becket's episcopal colleagues

At the time of Thomas's consecration fourteen bishops were in office, two since the reign of Henry I, with two vacancies. Four sees fell vacant between 1162 and 1170 and remained so, providing Henry with welcome income. There were two consecrations, that of Robert of Melun to Hereford in 1163 when Gilbert Foliot was translated to London with Becket's support, and Roger to Worcester in 1164. Knowles[25] divided them into four groups. Nigel of Ely was the only royal official; the bishops of Durham, Coventry, Lincoln, Rochester, Salisbury and Worcester were clerical careerists; Hilary of Chichester, Bartholomew of Exeter and Robert of Hereford had risen to distinction outside England; Robert of Bath and Wells and William of Norwich were monks. Of the bishops only three consistently supported Becket: Bishop Henry, whose friendship never wavered; Roger of Worcester after his election in 1164; and the outstanding scholar Robert of Hereford (1163–67). The elderly William of Norwich, a man regarded with respect and affection, remained loyal to Becket but stayed detached from the later stages of the conflict.

Most of the bishops were indifferent or prepared to await events. Three were bitterly hostile to the end: Roger of York, Hilary of Chichester and Gilbert Foliot, bishop of Hereford then London. Roger had disliked Thomas in their days together with Theobald, frequently insulting and taunting him.[26] Knowles described him as 'an unattractive figure, wealthy, ambitious and unspiritual'.[27] John of Salisbury told of his guilt when archdeacon of an appalling act of paedophilia, which Becket actually helped him to conceal.[28] Foliot had appropriate credentials as monk, bishop, scholar and canon lawyer and undoubtedly saw himself as the man who should have been archbishop. He later bitterly remarked that Henry had worked a miracle, for he had transformed a layman and a knight into an archbishop. He maintained that Becket's route to the primacy smacked of simony; publicly he showed nothing but contempt for Becket: 'a fool he was and a fool he ever will be'. Gilbert was never entirely satisfied with his move to London and tried ineffectually to have the see elevated to metropolitan status. Later in the conflict he wrote a long letter severely critical of Becket, the self-serving and intellectually dishonest *Multiplicem*.[29] He was in reality something of a tortured soul, a disappointed man wracked by the inner conflict of one whose status required him to be loyal to the king and whose Benedictine vows enjoined loyalty to the church, its head the pope and its principal representative in England.

The questions at issue

Thomas soon disappointed Henry by resigning the chancellorship, so deny-ing the king his hopes of a partnership that Barbarossa enjoyed with Rainald of Dassel, worldly-wise chancellor and archbishop of Cologne. However, that can-not be seen as precipitating an immediate crisis, and for the first year or so their relationship remained harmonious. An issue throughout the conflict was that of the Canterbury estates. Thomas soon busied himself with the recovery of those Canterbury estates which he believed had been misappropriated. This is not evi-dence of avarice or worldliness. Lanfranc and Anselm had seen it as their duty before God to retain the integrity of the Canterbury estates and recover those that had been alienated. The monks of Christ Church expected it, and in 1156 Pope Adrian had threatened the bishop of Ely with suspension if he failed to recover lost property. In defending the rights of Canterbury Becket was acting properly but risked making enemies. Especially objectionable to him was that during his exile Henry confiscated Canterbury estates and property and put some of them in the hands of members of the actively hostile de Broc family.

The first warning of the potential fragility of the relationship between king and archbishop came at Woodstock in July 1163. It related to the matter of the Sheriff's Aid, a customary goodwill payment by the shires to the sheriff. It was not the king's money and Becket objected to Henry's proposal that it should be paid direct to the Exchequer. Henry reacted angrily, but sensing that he lacked general support, he dropped the matter.

Far more fundamental, striking at the root of the relationship between the secular and spiritual authorities, was the issue of whether clergy accused of a crime should be tried, and if found guilty sentenced and punished, in a lay court like a layman. This had been a subject considered by canon lawyers for centuries. The treatment of criminous clerks had featured in the laws of Ethelred and Cnut. What the church deemed a proper punishment was related to the belief that, at his ordination, a priest's body assumed a sacred character, and to inflict on it physical hurt or damage was to do so to the body of Christ. Clerks guilty of crimes did not get off scot free. They might be required to perform severe pen-ances or to go on long, demanding pilgrimages. They might be unfrocked, which would lead to loss of face and means of livelihood. They could be detained in a bishop's prison. However they could not be subjected to mutilation, castration or dismemberment of limbs, or sentenced to death. In Henry's mind they were getting off lightly. He had learned that since his coronation more than a hundred murders had been committed by clerks, along with many cases of theft and rob-bery with violence. If he was to fulfil a basic responsibility of a medieval king, 'the protection of his subjects in the quiet enjoyment of their lands and goods',[30] appropriate punitive action had to be taken against tonsured malefactors.

In his attempt to resolve the issue in the way he deemed proper Henry sum-moned the Council of Westminster in October 1163, seeking the support of the two archbishops and their fellow bishops.[31] Initially faced with implacable opposition, he demanded of the bishops whether they would undertake to accept the customs of the realm, or his interpretation of them. Unconditional assent would empower him to act canonically or uncanonically, as he judged appropriate. Speaking for them all, Thomas declared that they would indeed give their consent, so far as it was lawful for a clerk to do so, *salvo ordine suo*. They had effectively yielded nothing. In a misguided and futile attempt to soften Henry's anger Hilary of Chichester substituted the words *in bona fide*, which pleased no one. The council ended with the bishops exhausted and anxious, the frustrated king exhausted and furious.

Such was Henry's mortification that he changed the tone of the dispute to a personal level, and he determined to hurt and humiliate Thomas. He demanded the surrender of all the castles and estates which he had retained since resigning the chancellorship, and in a move calculated to wound he removed his son Henry from Becket's care. News of the rift was spreading abroad. The legally learned but duplicitous Arnulf, bishop of Lisieux, advised Henry to cause a split among the bishops by encouraging a group showing signs of lack of sympathy with Becket. Not long before this same Arnulf had preached the opening sermon at the Council of Tours, taking as his theme the defence of the unity and liberty of the church, its inevitable victory in the struggle and the spiritual blessings promised to those who suffered in the great cause.[32] Archbishop Thomas and many of the bishops and abbots would have heard this as Henry had allowed them all to attend the council. Alexander III, in anxious exile in Sens at the time of the Westminster Council, wished to see the quarrel resolved before it became worse. He sent the distinguished abbot of L'Aumone with Robert of Melun, once Becket's teacher and soon to be bishop of Hereford, to reassure Becket that if he could show some accommodation Henry would not take advantage of it, thereby confirming the assurance of Henry's own envoys, Arnulf of Lisieux and Richard of Ilchester, the archdeacon of Poitiers and later bishop of Winchester.

Determined to secure what he wanted, Henry summoned a council to meet at Clarendon, a royal hunting lodge near Salisbury, in January 1164.[33] It was well attended. All the bishops but three were present, as were Prince Henry, the two justiciars, ten earls and a large number of barons. Becket, still hopeful that the abbot of L'Aumone's reassurance would be fulfilled, was shocked to find that Henry was determined to force the issue to the conclusion that he wanted. The atmosphere was extremely tense but the bishops were prepared to unite behind Becket as long as he stood firm against the king and gave them strong leadership. Warned by allies of the king and the bishops of York, London, Chichester and Salisbury of dire consequences for himself personally and the clergy generally if the king were resisted, Becket promised to accept the customs 'in the word of truth', and ordered the bishops to do the same.[34] This was a stunning blow for the bishops who, leaderless, fell into shocked disarray. The bishops of Salisbury and Norwich were fearful of incurring the king's displeasure. The archbishop of York, the bishop of Chichester and the bishop of London, Gilbert Foliot, showed no inclination to support Becket, Foliot urging compromise. Henry, for his part, aggravated the situation by insisting that the customs of the realm should be put in writing. Some, including Henry's mother Matilda, believed that to do so was a mistake. It was unprecedented for bishops to be required to give their consent to a written statement and it would deny Henry the opportunity for subsequent flexibility. But it was Henry's way to codify important matters. Moreover, as Henry Mayr-Harting commented, he put them in writing to discomfort Becket and cause his leadership to be challenged.[35]

The royal clerks duly busied themselves and the written document was ready by 29 January. It was essentially a reactionary programme harking back to the past, albeit presented in a modern form.[36] It had 16 clauses dealing with ecclesiastical jurisdiction, relations with the pope, excommunication and church vacancies. Not all were controversial. When Alexander III received the Constitutions he condemned ten clauses but tolerated six. The most controversial from Becket's standpoint but not Alexander's was clause 3: 'Clerks cited and accused of any matter shall, when summoned by the king's justice come before the king's court to answer there concerning matters which shall seem to the king's court to be answerable there, and before the ecclesiastical court for what shall seem to be answerable there, but in such a way that the justice of the king shall send to the court of Holy Church to see how the case is there tried. And if the clerk be convicted or confesses, the Church ought no longer to protect him.'

For many years the accepted interpretation had been that of the great nineteenth-century scholar F.W. Maitland.[37] Recent historians have significantly modified it.[38] Specific crimes were not detailed; the wording was deliberately open-ended. There had been precedents, and it was established canonical theory that in certain cases, at the church's initiative, it was acceptable for degraded clerks to be delivered to secular judgement. It was Henry's demand for total control that was impossible for Becket to accept and Henry was impervious to Becket's objection, based on the statement of the prophet Nathan, 'God does not judge twice on the same offence.' The text of the Constitutions was presented as a chirograph, that is, it was written out three times, with each version separated by the word *cyrographum*. The document was divided into three parts with the breaks through the word *cyrographum*. The king and the two archbishops each retained a copy. Becket refused to add his seal to the parts, but the fact that he accepted one could be seen as a failure to resist the king. He left Clarendon profoundly depressed, with the bishops disillusioned and greatly troubled. In a state of remorse following a demand made by Pope Alexander on 23 February to 'make peace with God and the Church in respect of the unlawful promise',[39] he suspended himself from priestly duties. Subsequently absolved by Alexander III, he consecrated Roger of Worcester the following August. Twice Becket tried unsuccessfully to leave the country without the king's permission. It was preferable for Henry to keep Becket in England where, with the support of the archbishop of York and the bishops of London, Chichester and Salisbury, he could work at breaking him rather than have him establish himself with the king of France.

The setting for the humiliation and intended destruction of Becket was Northampton, where a council to be attended by the king, archbishops, bishops, earls and barons was convened for 6 October. William fitz Stephen wrote a full account of the council.[40] At times Becket showed a defiant spirit, as when he celebrated a votive mass of St Stephen, the first Christian martyr, with its introit 'Princes did sit and speak against me; but thy servant is occupied in thy statutes'. Then, as a reminder that royal vassal that he was, he was a consecrated archbishop with metropolitan authority, wearing his pallium he took the cross from the hands of his faithful crossbearer Alexander, perhaps intending to confront Henry in person. He had recovered from the flare-up of his digestive problems which had confined him to his bed the day before. However, as Henry planned, the council was a bruising and humiliating experience for Thomas. The king had acted disreputably throughout. Becket was confronted by a series of false charges unsupported by evidence. No defence was allowed. As Warren wrote: 'the council of Northampton reflects no credit on Henry II, Henry acted throughout with scant regard for decency, legality or justice'.[41] Amid a scene of turmoil, shame and disorder, Thomas managed to escape on the evening of Tuesday 13 October. His road to six years' exile was just beginning.

Exile

Following a circuitous route in a scarcely effective disguise,[42] Thomas and his companions reached territories directly under the control of King Louis and made for Soissons. Herbert of Bosham, travelling separately, had met Louis who, happy to exploit the diplomatic game played out between himself and King Henry, undertook to provide peace and security throughout his realm and protect him from his persecutors. He also promised financial support for as long as it was needed. Meanwhile, ironically perhaps in view of Clarendon, Henry turned to the pope. On 24 November Henry's ambassadors met Alexander in exile at Sens. The party consisted of some lay magnates and three notorious opponents of Thomas – Roger of York, Gilbert of London and Hilary of Chichester – along with the slippery Arnulf of Lisieux. Perhaps to add a semblance of fairness, Bartholomew of Exeter and Roger of Worcester joined them. Not only did they achieve nothing for Henry; Gilbert Foliot and Hilary managed to humiliate themselves. Foliot's diatribe against Becket was too much for Alexander, who subjected him to a papal put-down, reducing him to uncharacteristic silence. When the normally eloquent Hilary took the floor he made a nonsense of his Latin and was met with mocking laughter. The Earl of Arundel fared much better. He spoke in French rather than Latin and his tactful request to Alexander to send legates to England to resolve the problem was favourably received. Again Foliot was snubbed. When he asked that the legates be allowed to settle the dispute free from any appeal against their judgement, Alexander made it quite clear that only he could make decisions about appeals. The royal party left the Curia with nothing to mollify Henry.

Soon after, on 29 November, Becket and his party met Alexander, who recommended that they should take up residence in the Cistercian abbey at Pontigny, one of the first four daughter houses of Citeaux. There he remained for nearly two years until Henry vengefully threatened to expel the Cistercian order from England. Refusing the offers of comfortable grandeur made by some of the great French prelates, he established himself at the ancient Benedictine abbey of St Columba at Sens, where he stayed for two years. He was supported materially by King Louis and spiritually and intellectually by the archbishop of Sens, William of the White Hands, nephew of King Stephen and Henry of Winchester and a patron of scholars. Herbert meanwhile relished the more worldly delights that the beautiful and civilised city had to offer.

In exile Thomas devoted himself to study. John of Salisbury wrote to him advising him to concentrate on spiritual studies rather than civil or canon law: 'I would rather have you ponder on the Psalms and turn over the moral writings of St Gregory than philosophise scholastically.'[43] Even so, in addition to his spiritual studies with his tutor Herbert of Bosham, who declared himself well satisfied with his pupil's progress, better to equip himself in forthcoming struggles with the king he studied civil and canon law under a learned scholar from Piacenza known as Master Lombard.

Thomas also pursued a life of rigorous asceticism while at Pontigny and Sens, that at Pontigny he saw as penance for his weakness at Clarendon. At St Columba he subjected himself to a life of intense spiritual devotion, wearing a hair shirt infested with lice, eating and drinking very sparingly and subjecting himself to physical disciplines that, to modern sensitivities, read like extreme forms of sado-masochism. His practice of submerging himself in an icy stream there caused a severe throat infection which resulted in an ulcerated abscess which recovered only after two bones had been extracted from his jaw.[44] This immoderate way of life, long hours without sleep, severe mortification of the flesh and unbalanced diet must have had a profound effect on his mental and physical wellbeing and his friends were constantly anxious about him.

The period of exile was also a period of blast and counter-blast by Thomas and Henry and attempts at reconciliation which proved abortive. The course of events was influenced by the political situation in Europe and the fluctuating relationships between Henry, Louis, Barbarossa and Alexander. Henry had much more to deal with than Becket, both in England and Europe, while Thomas's whole life revolved around his relationship with the king. Before settling at Pontigny Alexander had confirmed Thomas in his office after he had removed his ring and resigned his archbishopric. The confirmation delivered Becket from any taint of impropriety associated with his original election. Secure as archbishop, he had effectively outmanoeuvred Henry.

Henry's response to this and the failure of the mission to the pope was to lash out not just against Thomas but his relations, his friends and their servants, several hundred people. Members of the de Broc family were involved in the king's vindictive actions. In the sources favourable to Becket the de Brocs represented the least attractive side of baronial power. Ranulf and Robert appear as ruthless but efficient thugs, and apparently one of the family had been hanged. Henry ordered the confiscation of all Thomas's possessions and all estates pertaining to the archbishopric. The Canterbury estates were granted to Ranulf de Broc, who was still in occupation when Becket returned in December 1170. Day-to-day administration was entrusted to Robert, who built a house at Canterbury of timber taken from the archbishop's woods and, allegedly, the Canterbury estates were ravaged. All the churches and revenues of Thomas's clerks were seized and put in the hands of Gilbert Foliot, who used some for religious purposes. Payment was demanded from all who had stood surety for Thomas at Northampton. Thomas was forbidden any aid; he was even to be denied prayers on his behalf. But retribution was not reserved for Thomas alone. All his relations, members of his household, clerks and laymen, and their families were proscribed and exiled. Henry's conduct did him no credit. He showed himself capable of acts of vindictive spite, bringing real hardship to several hundred people who had no involvement at all in the dispute. Even so, as Anne Duggan wrote, 'it was clear by the end of 1165 that the king's strategy of sequestration and expulsion had failed to break his adversary'.[45]

Striking evidence of the archbishop's firmness of purpose was manifested at Vézelay on Whit Sunday 1166, 20 years after St Bernard had preached the second crusade there. To the astonishment of his companions, he preached a momentous sermon from the pulpit of the church of the ancient Cluniac abbey. He launched a devastating attack on Henry, condemned the Constitutions of Clarendon and anathematised in general terms all who observed and enforced them. Several men were excommunicated, but not the king.[46] Letters were despatched between Becket and the English bishops and the bishops and the pope. The essence of the latter was a strong defence of the king and blame of Thomas for turning the dispute over criminous clerks into a massive crisis by his own outrageous behaviour. Acerbic correspondence followed between Becket and Foliot in which personal feelings and animosities were only too apparent. The exchanges concluded with Foliot's *Multiplicem nobis*, deeply felt, but 'a tissue of half-truths and inconsistencies'.[47]

During 1167 and 1168 attempts were made at reconciliation through envoys and representatives, but mutual suspicion thwarted them. Alexander III's fortunes had changed for the better since the summer of 1167 when members of the imperial army and Rainald of Dassel succumbed to plague. Frederick abandoned Rome and the following year retreated ignominiously from Italy. Aware that this might encourage Alexander to act more forcefully, Henry appreciated the wisdom of acting more circumspectly. We do not know how much he feared the spiritual consequences of interdict and excommunication, but the political consequences were certainly unwelcome.

Towards the end of 1168 papal commissioners chosen for their religious reputation worked to achieve the first meeting between Henry and Thomas since the Council of Northampton. The meeting was to be about more than church issues. It was to be a peace conference to settle relationships between Henry and Louis and to consider those between France and the Empire and the Empire and the papacy. The papal emissaries were not involved in the negotiations between the two kings. Bosham's account inevitably focuses on the archbishop and the king.[48] Henry and Thomas met on 6 January 1169 at Montmirail, a hilltop town just within French territory. This was the first of three meetings between king and archbishop in that year. After initial optimism each came to nothing. Facing each other in a field below Montmirail, the archbishop fell on his knees before the king. Henry immediately raised him up, and although he did not offer a kiss of peace, discussion proceeded amicably and seemed to conclude with Thomas prepared to accept the customs of the realm. Bosham quoted him as saying: 'regarding the entire cause between you and me, I now submit myself to your mercy and judgement in the presence of our lord king of France, and the bishops, nobles and others'. Then came the bombshell. To the dismay of all, perhaps prompted by a whispered remark from Bosham, Thomas added the words 'saving God's honour'. Furious that Henry was, he nevertheless asked that Thomas should give his assent to observing the ancient customs of the realm in the manner of his Canterbury predecessors. Becket refused. There was to be no repeat of Clarendon.

On 7 February Louis and Henry met again at St Léger. Henry and Thomas also met once more, but to no avail, and a possible meeting a fortnight later did not materialise. On Palm Sunday, two months later, Thomas formally excommunicated Bishop Foliot and Bishop Jocelyn of Salisbury and seven of his enemies occupying Canterbury property. Further excommunications followed on Ascension Day. In October Henry reacted by ordering that anyone who brought an interdict decree into England would be punished as a traitor. The ports were closed and communication with pope or archbishop forbidden. To avoid submission to these decrees some English bishops retired to monasteries and the bishop of Chester sought refuge in the Welsh mountains. England was bereft of spiritual and pastoral leadership.

A further meeting was arranged by the papal nuncio, Master Vivian, at Montmartre on 18 November 1169. According to Herbert King Louis, along with some nobles and bishops, joined them and 'intervened painstakingly and attentively, pursuing peace with great diligence'. After much wrangling and discussion there seemed real hope that a settlement might be achieved. But once again, just when peace seemed at last within reach, another blow was delivered to frustrate it. Perhaps aware of the fact that Henry had once sworn in anger that he would never allow the archbishop a kiss of peace, Becket demanded one as a sign of reconciliation. Henry replied that he would gladly give it but for a previous oath that he had taken against it, a specious argument from one not usually conscientious about keeping oaths. 'For no other reason would he deny him the kiss, certainly not because he harboured any anger or resentment in his heart.' Herbert wryly adds: 'When the king of France and many of the mediators heard this, they were immediately suspicious that under the honeyed speeches which had gone before, there lay poison'.[49]

The coronation of young Henry

Henry's true attitude to Becket can be seen from the next development, which ultimately proved to be fatal for the archbishop. On 3 March 1170 Henry returned to England after four years' absence, determined to have his roistering teenage son young Henry crowned as soon as possible to prevent his sons fighting over the succession. He had no intention of delaying the ceremony, although he knew full well that if someone other than the archbishop of Canterbury performed it Becket would see it as a major and deliberate personal affront. The insult would be made worse in the likely event of young Henry being crowned by Becket's old enemy Archbishop Roger of York. Not only would it be a personal affront, it would raise the old spectre of the primacy. Most people were weary of the issue, and in the minds of the papacy and papal lawyers and theorists primacies were anachronisms running counter to the centralising tendencies of the church. For the monks of Christ Church and Becket himself, any attack on its primacy 'struck at the roots of Canterbury's divine authority'.

Although precedents were important, canonically a coronation performed by any duly consecrated bishop was valid. Politically it was altogether different. Alexander hoped to turn Henry's determination to have his son crowned by Archbishop Roger to political advantage. He felt secure enough to stand by Becket, hoping that Henry would be spurred on to make concessions to the church. He therefore wrote at the end of February to both archbishops and their suffragans forbidding the coronation unless Henry revoked the Constitutions of Clarendon, removed some of the anti-papal barriers and allowed the ceremony to be conducted by the archbishop of Canterbury. The letters were sent to Becket to forward to England. He added a covering letter of his own and arranged for Roger of Worcester, then in Normandy, to deliver them.

Before their dispatch Henry arrived back in England. Aware of Alexander's letters, he reacted against them by reinforcing the anti-papal barriers and ordering Roger of Worcester to stay in Normandy. A splendid coronation duly took place, with Roger of York officiating in the presence of ten bishops, English, Welsh and Norman. The coronation was an affront not only to Becket, but to King Louis, as for some unknown reason his daughter Margaret, young Henry's wife, was not present even though appropriate ceremonial wear had been made for her. Alexander reacted by authorising Becket to excommunicate those who had taken part in the coronation and to impose an interdict whenever he thought fit. Anticipating this, and conscious that Louis was reasonably aggrieved, Henry sent a letter to the archbishop of Rouen stating his readiness to make peace with Becket. On 21 July the two kings met near Fréteval. After an exchange in which Henry spoke churlishly of Thomas he mollified Louis by promising a second coronation at which Margaret would certainly be present. The following day king and archbishop met while Louis deliberately absented himself to avoid any impression that he was putting pressure on Henry.

Fréteval and Canterbury

The meeting went well. Perhaps Henry was genuine or simply dissembling. Perhaps for a brief while the two men felt a return of their old mutual affection and regret for the way events had developed. In the presence of many magnates, lay and ecclesiastical, Thomas stressed his indebtedness to the king for the many great honours bestowed upon him. Henry agreed to allow Thomas to return to England in peace and restore the property and see of Canterbury. Nothing was said of the Constitutions of Clarendon, for while Henry had no intention of abandoning them he hoped that Thomas would assume that they had been dropped. Thomas remained aggrieved by the coronation but was cheered by the prospect of the second coronation at which he would certainly officiate. According to Herbert, the kiss of peace was neither sought nor granted, but fitz Stephen reported that despite being absolved by the pope from his oath Henry declined to give the kiss, preferring to delay until it would seem 'to spring from grace and benevolence while here it would seem to be prompted by necessity'. This apparently satisfied Thomas. A warm scene followed, concluding with the king holding the archbishop's stirrup for him as he went to mount his horse. Everybody was happy.[50]

Despite Becket's apparent joy at the reconciliation, issues still rankled. He brooded on Henry's failure to give him the kiss of peace and he could not put young Henry's coronation behind him. His frustration that Henry, detained by a life-threatening illness and a renewal of hostilities with Louis, was unable to return to England with him was aggravated by his learning that an old enemy, John of Oxford, dean of Salisbury, was to accompany him rather than Rotrou, archbishop of Rouen. Following the crossing on 1 December they landed at Sandwich. Seeing the archbishop's cross a crowd of poor folk gave him an emotional reception, but only the presence of John prevented the sheriff of Kent, Gervase of Cornhill, Ranulf de Broc and Reginald of Warenne from physically assaulting him. He suffered further threats from the de Brocs, and on one occasion the particularly repellent Robert ordered one of his younger relations to insult him by cutting off the tail of one of his packhorses. The archbishop was further insulted by finding he was forbidden to make contact with young Henry.

On 2 December Thomas was rapturously received in Canterbury by people overjoyed at the return after six years' absence of their pastoral and spiritual leader. The suggestion that he had returned bent on martyrdom should be dispelled by the knowledge that he had with him a considerable library of scholarly books and collections of sermons and treatises which would help his preaching.[51] Moreover, with the exception of Archbishop Roger, most of the bishops, even Foliot and Jocelyn of Salisbury, looked to be reconciled with him. But before his landing in England Becket had already suspended the bishops who were present at young Henry's coronation and renewed Foliot's excommunication. He confirmed these sentences in his sermon in the cathedral on Christmas Day.

Already two groups had travelled to Henry at Bures near Bayeux, where he was preparing for Christmas. Royal officials reported, without a shred of evidence to support them, that the archbishop had been leading a force of knights around the country preparing to attack cities and drive young Henry from the kingdom. The archbishop of York, who was also present with the bishops of London and Salisbury, raged against Becket and was reported to have said, 'You will never have peace as long as Thomas is archbishop.' Henry reacted with a characteristic outburst of rage, uttering the fatal words which four household knights, Reginald fitz Urse, Hugh de Morville, William de Tracy and Richard le Bret, took at their face value. Hopeful of winning favour with the king, they crossed to England, and on 29 December they reached Canterbury. When they realised Becket had no intention of submitting to them they barbarously hacked him to death, seriously wounding Edward Grim in the process.[52]

The King's reaction[53]

Henry received the dreadful news at Argentan on 1 January. Bishop Arnulf of Lisieux, adroit master of spin, wrote to Alexander III to inform him of the king's reaction, reporting that his grief and distress, stupefaction, wailing and groaning shocked all around. He shut himself up for three days, refusing food or callers. Some feared he had died of grief. When he had recovered some composure he was at pains to stress that whatever his enemies might say, the crime had been committed without his knowledge. He had never wished for such an outcome but he acknowledged his ultimate responsibility and was prepared to submit himself entirely to the judgement of the church.[54]

When news reached Louis he wrote to the pope: 'Such unprecedented cruelty demands unprecedented retribution.' His brother-in-law Theobald of Blois, no friend of the Angevins, wrote: 'The blood of that righteous man cries out for revenge.' Theobald's brother, Becket's friend Archbishop William Whitehands of Sens, spoke with considerable intensity of feeling: 'Of all the crimes we have ever read or heard of, this easily takes first place – exceeding all the wickedness of Nero, the perfidy of Julian, and even the sacrilegious treachery of Judas.' He put words into action by imposing an interdict on Henry's continental territories that were within his jurisdiction.

Alexander III's reaction was more restrained. After his initial shock he acted in a statesmanlike way that characterised all his subsequent dealings with Henry. While he confirmed the interdict imposed by Archbishop William and excommunicated the murderers and all who had in any way given them support, there was to be no interdict laid upon England and Henry was not excommunicated. Instead he was forbidden to enter a church until legates could confirm that he was truly humbled. Legates departed from Rome for this purpose later in the year, but Henry was preoccupied by affairs in Ireland and not until May 1172 did he submit to papal legates at Avranches.[55] On Sunday 21 May a ceremony of reconciliation was held in the cathedral. There, before everyone present, Henry laid his hand upon the Gospels and swore that he had neither ordered nor willed the murder of his archbishop of Canterbury. He claimed that it had caused him greater distress than the death of his father or mother, but acknowledged his responsibility and undertook to atone by whatever actions were deemed appropriate. He then performed an act of penance, was led to the door of the cathedral and publicly absolved. He was readmitted into the cathedral as a sign of his being fully restored to the arms of the church.

Henry had been accompanied by his irresponsible 17-year-old son Henry. The following year he joined a rebellion against his father led by his mother Eleanor and two of his brothers, Richard, aged 15 and the 14-year-old Geoffrey. This delayed King Henry's return to England until summer 1174 and at last, on 12 July, he performed his famous act of penance. According to William of Newburgh, 'He prayed before the tomb of the blessed Archbishop Thomas, shedding copious tears. Having entered the chapter of the monks he prostrated himself on the ground and most humbly entreated their pardon: at his own urgent request this man who stood so high in rank was beaten with rods by all the brethren in turn.'[56] More details are provided by Gervase of Canterbury and Edward Grim.[57] While it would perhaps be cynical to doubt the sincerity of Henry's public gestures, in no way did they harm him politically at a time when he was forced to deal with various crises.

After Becket

Following the Becket debacle Henry had no wish to find himself with any more problem bishops, but he did not impose a repressive control on the episcopate. His nomination of royal clerks who had not been Becket men was approved by Alexander III. The fact that they were royal nominations did not make them poor bishops. Moreover, Henry was not ruthless in controlling appointments. The elections of John of Greenford to Chichester and Robert Foliot to Hereford were freely made by their cathedral chapters. Henry did not want time-servers and he had the courage to appoint men who, he knew, might be difficult. Baldwin, abbot of Ford and subsequently bishop of Worcester and archbishop of Canterbury (1184–90), was an eminent canon lawyer who, it might be supposed, could put the objectivity of the law before the interests of the king. John of Oxford, bishop of Norwich, excommunicated a royal official without the king's consent, for which he was reprimanded by Henry. One of Henry's most inspired and remarkable appointments was that of the Carthusian monk, Hugh of Avalon, to the see of Lincoln.

Henry's concern was that the monks of Christ Church should not appoint another Becket as his successor. Their prior Odo, whom they favoured, was not the choice of the suffragan bishops, who wanted Richard of Dover, former chaplain to Archbishop Theobald and currently prior of St Martin's. Henry presented no objection. Alexander III confirmed Richard's election on 2 April 1174, consecrated him on 7 April and conferred the pallium on him.[58] Like Theobald before him, Richard was promoted from relative obscurity. He does not merit A.L. Poole's dismissal of him as 'feeble and ineffective', although this was the view of some contemporaries, who hoped for an unflinching champion of church liberties. Richard of Ilchester, the successor to Henry of Blois in the see of Winchester, judged that he threw away the gains made by Becket, a view shared by Gerald of Wales, and an anonymous commentator dismissed him as 'unworthy of the name of archbishop, both in word and deed'. In truth, like Theobald, he achieved far more than he initially promised. Although not a trained lawyer himself, he encouraged the development of canon law in England. He attracted to his household a number of scholarly men of considerable intelligence, including Peter of Blois and Gerard Pucelle.[59]

Richard saw no real conflict between his duties as papal legate, conferred on him by Alexander, and head of the English church and his responsibilities in serving the king. In 1175 he collaborated in deposing the abbot of Peterborough and supported Henry's appointment of 12 abbots and a number of bishops. He actually incurred the displeasure of Alexander III, who censured him for confirming episcopal elections made in the king's chamber. As one of the greatest tenants-in-chief he was often in Henry's company attending councils and courts. He also represented the king on diplomatic missions on the Continent. He took the view that co-operation with the king was possible without being subservient to him, and as archbishops and bishops were of this world they had an important part to play in secular affairs.

Of Richard of Canterbury William of Newburgh wrote: 'he was a man of only modest learning but worthy of praise for the innocence of his life, prudently keeping within the measure of his own capacity and not straying into the field of great affairs'.[60] This is to underestimate his importance. The intellectual snobbery of some of his contemporaries led them to be rather dismissive of him, and to underplay his understanding of difficult legal matters and his ability to achieve a working relationship with the king, while in no way capitulating to him. Indeed he had the qualities needed to restore some equilibrium in the English church after the previous tumultuous years. It is to Henry's credit that he allowed the election of such a man and to Richard's credit that 'his cultivation of Henry II's goodwill enabled him to pursue canonical policies that consolidated the jurisdictional position of the English church in harmony and co-operation with secular authority'.[61]

Among his suffragans were the distinguished canonists Bartholomew of Exeter and Roger of Worcester. They were regularly employed as papal judge delegates in the 1160s and 1170s. Three suffragans, Ely, Norwich and Winchester, became chief justices in 1179. This did not earn the wholehearted approval of some members of the Papal Curia but the archbishop, through his secretary, declared them to be honourable men who would serve the church's interest by holding such office. Ralph of Diceto, the dean of St Paul's,[62] declared that the king had had difficulty in finding competent and honest judges from other sources and trusted the bishops, with the fear of God before them, to act impartially and with integrity untainted by bribery and to be fair to the poor. If they were to be accused of acting contrary to canon law they could cite the king's great need as justification and the virtue of their conduct in fulfilling it.[63] As the great Maitland wrote in 1895: 'Henry's greatest, his most lasting triumph in the legal field was this, that he made the prelates of the realm his justices. English law was administered by the ablest, the best educated men in the realm. It is by "popish clergymen" that our English common law is converted from a rude mass of customs into an articulate system.'[64]

Henry was able to work harmoniously with men who displayed a reasonable independence provided that they recognised that he was without question the master. One such man was Richard, the subject of the famous writ addressed to the monks of Winchester, apparently leaked to Alexander III as a deliberate act of mischief-making by Prince Henry (see Chapter 1). Henry's trust in Richard was thoroughly justified. Long before his election to the see of Winchester he had shown himself to be a very able and loyal royal servant. His origins could not have stood in greater contrast to those of his predecessor at Winchester, Henry of Blois. He was a relation of Gilbert Foliot, and although he lacked real social standing he had the talent to advance himself as a royal clerk. Early in Henry's reign he had the king's ear, and from 1163 he was known officially as archdeacon of Poitiers. He was one of Henry's principal advisers in the crisis with the bishops over the Constitutions of Clarendon but although, inevitably, Becket denounced him, John of Salisbury respected him and sought his help in an attempt to moderate the king's anger. He was regarded by the monks of Christ Church as 'a friend and protector of the convent in its troubles'.

Richard of Ilchester was a classic example of one of Maitland's 'popish clergymen'. Until he became a bishop he had been an itinerant justice working on every eyre, and while a bishop he continued to take his place in the Exchequer as he had done since at least 1165.[65] For two years he was seconded to Normandy, where he was responsible for reorganising judicial and financial procedures along English lines. In such regard was he held by the king that he had witnessed Henry's will, and in 1182 Henry stayed at his manor house at Waltham in Hampshire. We hear far more of Bishop Richard as a royal servant than a bishop, and no doubt much of his diocesan work was delegated to archdeacons, rural deans and to *officiales* – 'bishop's deputies', a functionary apparently introduced to England by Richard.

Assessment

It must be asked whether Becket had actually achieved anything by his death. Certainly, in the matter of criminous clerks he gained something. Henry no longer demanded automatic degradation for an offending cleric or the imposition of a secular punishment for one who had been degraded. 'Benefit of clergy' became an established privilege and remained so, theoretically at least, for more than 650 years. At Avranches Henry agreed to abolish the evil customs he had introduced and the Constitutions of Clarendon were not referred to again. Henry also promised not to forbid appeals to Rome, unless they were detrimental to him, or visits to the pope. Perhaps what was subsequently achieved could have been brought about without the turmoil of the 1160s, had Becket been the sort of archbishop that Henry was hoping for and had Henry himself acted more temperately. On the other hand, perhaps a major crisis was needed to bring about a recognition that the interests of the secular and ecclesiastical powers were best served by a pragmatic response to potentially divisive problems. The period between the death of Becket and that of Henry showed that the working relationship between the secular and spiritual authorities in England which Henry wanted, the papacy wanted and the English bishops wanted, could be achieved without any diminution of royal authority within the framework of an effectively developing system of canon law and papal government.

Henry's vision was that of a regional church – *ecclesia anglicana* – under his personal control with a hierarchy of his own appointing. This vision Becket looked to thwart with incomplete success. Becket's critics, like Foliot, maintained that he should have been prepared to compromise, but that was fundamentally to misunderstand him. He could be provocative, histrionic even, and obstinate, but his understanding of his role as archbishop made compromise impossible. Foliot and Hilary of Chichester were lawyers. Foliot was well versed in Roman law and as Mayr-Harting pointed out, 'lawyers had a much stronger instinct for compromise than had theologians'.[66] Although he lacked a master's degree, Becket read works of theology in exile. Herbert of Bosham had been taught by the great Peter the Lombard, and his loyal supporter Bishop Roger of Worcester had studied theology at Paris with the future bishop of Hereford and perhaps Peter the Lombard. In the first, 1973, edition of *Henry II* Warren described Becket as 'a theological dinosaur'. He subsequently recanted this. He cited Beryl Smalley, who demonstrated that the arguments he advanced were the common coin of lecturers in the Schools at the time. However lacking formal training in theology, 'he pressed the arguments with all the unsubtle dogmatism of the dedicated amateur'.[67]

Thomas Becket's achievement was posthumous. Elevated to martyrdom and sainthood, he became associated with miracles and Canterbury drew countless pilgrims from throughout Christendom. Not that everyone was swept along by the tide of public emotion which flowed after his death. He had always had his critics. Few of the bishops gave him unequivocal support, and the opposition of Gilbert Foliot, Roger of York and Hilary of Chichester is well recorded. While many were doubtless reluctant to go against the current of public opinion, a few were prepared to express openly their scepticism about his achievements. We are told of a debate between Peter the Chanter, a canon and distinguished professor of theology at the cathedral school of Paris and Roger, one of the masters.[68] Peter had no doubts about Becket's sanctity or the justice of the claim that he was a martyr who had died for the liberty of the church. Master Roger maintained that he had been perversely obstinate, and he went along with those who judged him to be a damnable traitor to his kingdom, worthy of death even if not in the actual form it had taken. The balanced and independent-minded canon of Newborough, William, accepted Thomas's sanctity but was critical of some of his actions. It was the myth of Thomas Becket that survived 350 years or so until that scourge of the historic church, Henry VIII, declared of Becket: 'there appareth nothing in his lyfe and exteriour conversation whereby he should be callyd a saint'.[69]

7

England without a King

Richard I's approach to the church

In one of C.R. Cheney's aphorisms he stated: 'The church's government, as then constituted, required the service of sinners as well as saints.'[1] The king's government did, too, and Richard I was dependent on the work of the bishop of Ely and the archbishops of Rouen and Canterbury. This is not the place for a philosophical debate on the nature of sin, but loyalty, hard work and efficiency were virtues to offset such faults of character as shown by these three men. Hubert Walter was clearly the greatest of them, William Longchamp the least attractive, but if their actions at times invited criticism or even contempt, their concern was the king's business and the maintenance of order in the kingdom from which he was absent. Twenty-six different men held sees in the reign of Richard I, of whom sixteen were elected in his reign. It would be too easy and wrong to claim that, as Richard I was absent from England for all but six months of his reign, he had no interest in English affairs or appointments. As John Gillingham makes clear, Richard was a far more complex and sophisticated person than the traditional image of the macho warrior suggests.[2] That centralised government did not break down in his absence, as it had in the reign of Stephen, but positively flourished was due partly to the legacy that Richard had inherited from his father, and very much to the quality of the men who were entrusted with the responsibility of making it work. Richard was responsible for their appointment, which suggests that he had an understanding of the complexities of government and administration and had the interest and ability to appoint men of the calibre to make it work. Even when in captivity he was in communication with his officials. No ransom could have been raised otherwise.[3] As M.T. Clanchy wrote, Richard I was 'a man of business and through his choice of officials he proved an able as well as heroic king'.[4]

Despite his readiness to take the cross and the alacrity with which he sought to fulfil his crusading vow, Richard was not a particularly devout person. He took a pragmatic approach to ecclesiastical affairs and there were those, largely his political enemies, who saw him as a traitor towards Christianity. Although he recognised that he was a member of Christendom and that bishops were fundamental to its existence, he did not welcome ecclesiastics meddling in secular matters.

Nevertheless he knew that among the senior clergy were the best-educated men in his realms, many of whom held master's degrees from the emerging universities, with the expertise and experience to be distinguished royal officials. There was only one saintly bishop in his reign and he had inherited him from his father. For Richard, like Henry, one saint was enough. He was determined to control elections to sees and he preferred men who had already shown their worth as royal servants. A bishopric was a suitable reward for such a man. He inherited some, like Gilbert de Glanville, bishop of Rochester. He created others, like Richard fitz Nigel, a member of the Salisbury dynasty and author of *Dialogus de Scaccario*, who became bishop of London, and Godfrey de Lucy, son of a chief justiciar, to be bishop of Winchester. Master Philip of Poitou, who became bishop of Durham in 1197, had been a clerk of the king's chamber; Master Eustace, consecrated bishop of Ely in 1198, had been vice-chancellor and keeper of the king's seal since 1194. The most notorious of his mitred civil servants was William Longchamp, bishop of Ely, and the most eminent was Hubert Walter, who became archbishop of Canterbury.

It is clear from the available evidence that Richard intended to be firmly in control of the English church and was inclined to take a more authoritarian stance than his father had adopted in his latter years. He defended the barriers against undue papal influence. A feature of the period is that in those sees where the cathedral was run by the monastic chapter rather than the lay canons there was friction between the bishop and the monks. One of the issues which Richard inherited and was drawn into was the dispute between Archbishop Baldwin and the Canterbury monks. Like Bishop Glanville of Rochester and Bishop Hugh of Coventry, Baldwin aimed to replace the monks with a college of secular canons. Naturally the monks contested this, and in November 1189 Richard instructed the Christ Church monks to submit to arbitration by the English bishops and abbots rather than trust in the papal legate. Nine years later, in an extension of the conflict, the new pope Innocent III ordered that Archbishop Hubert's chapel at Lambeth should be destroyed. Richard wrote to two cardinals urging them to persuade the pope that, as a consequence of his not being fully informed of the facts, he had made the wrong decision, which should be revoked. His letter concludes: 'We would like you to know that we cannot allow a mandate of this sort, which has been issued to the prejudice of our dignity and of the liberty of our realm, to be put into effect in our realm.' The tone was courteous, but Richard's intent was clear.[5]

Richard was determined to control the entry of papal legates into his kingdom. He insisted that the legate John of Anagni should not attend his coronation lest the papacy take the view that it was proper for English coronations to come within its sphere of influence. This was in marked contrast to Stephen's attitude regarding the coronation of Eustace. Cardinal John did eventually land but was warned to hold back by Richard's aged mother, Queen Eleanor. The bishop of Rochester, Gilbert Glanvill, was unequivocal: 'before he has the licence of the lord king to enter the realm, he cannot be legate'.[6] Richard was equally adamant that English envoys should not go to Rome without his approval. For instance, he refused to allow representatives of Geoffrey, archbishop elect of York, to go to the curia to collect his pallium. They had to return empty-handed.

Unlike his father, Richard resisted any temptation to prolong episcopal vacancies so that he could enjoy the benefits. On 13 September 1189 he was crowned in Westminster Abbey. Two days later he held a great council at Pipewell Abbey in Northamptonshire. One-third of the 15 suffragan sees were in need of a bishop. Carlisle continued to remain vacant throughout the reign, but at Pipewell Richard took steps to fill four of the vacancies: London, Winchester, Salisbury and Ely. Although due forms may have been observed, the electors were very careful to select men known for their loyal service to their king. London went to Richard fitz Nigel, Winchester to Godfrey de Lucy, Salisbury to Hubert Walter, dean of York, and Ely to William Longchamp. All four were described by the chronicler Richard of Devizes as men of considerable virtue and fame.

Hugh of Nonant of Coventry and Savaric of Bath

Undoubtedly William Longchamp saw royal service as a means to personal aggrandisement and at times he found himself in predicaments that were highly discreditable, but it should be said, in fairness, that some of the criticism made of him was due to the snobbery of those contemptuous of his ignoble birth. As the twelfth century approached its end many of the aristocracy were coming to see themselves as English rather than Anglo-French, and some held Longchamp in disdain as a low-born foreigner.

One of his principal critics was Hugh of Nonant, bishop of Coventry, hardly an exemplar of the virtues himself.[7] Hugh seems to have shared some of the qualities of his uncle Arnulf of Lisieux, that notorious political fixer and master of spin. John Gillingham referred to him as bishop of Coventry 'in his spare time'.[8] Hugh was educated at Canterbury in the archbishop's household where he showed himself to be a skilled linguist and ready student of forensic debate. For much of the conflict with Henry II he remained loyal to Becket, and although he did not immediately go into exile with him he joined him in due course. In 1170 he appreciated the wisdom of becoming close to the king and he remained a friend and adviser. In 1184 Henry sent him on an important diplomatic mission to intercede on behalf of his son-in-law the duke of Saxony, Henry the Lion, who was having problems with Emperor Frederick and the German princes. King Henry was much impressed by Hugh's diplomatic skills and appointed him to the vacant see of Coventry in January 1185. So valuable was Hugh to the king that he was sent on a series of diplomatic missions which delayed his consecration until 31 January 1188. Even then he spent more time with Henry on the Continent than in England. Richard ordered him to return in August 1189 and he was present at the coronation and the Council of Pipewell.

Another bishop consecrated in Richard's reign who put personal ambition and a career in the diplomatic service above spiritual and pastoral care was Savaric of Bath. His relations included Jocelyn de Bohun, one-time bishop of Salisbury; Reginald de Bohun, himself a bishop of Bath; and even the emperor, Henry VI, of whom he was a distant kinsman. Although Savaric appears to have fallen out with Henry II he quickly ingratiated himself with Richard, took the cross and accompanied him on his journey to the Holy Land. While in Sicily he extracted from Richard, possibly with the help of a bribe, letters addressed to the justiciars in England stating that if Savaric were canonically elected to a vacant see the king's assent could be taken as given. One of the recipients was cousin Reginald. Canterbury had been vacant since the death of Baldwin in November 1190. Savaric's plan was that Reginald should be elected in Baldwin's place and he would succeed to Bath. The emperor and Philip Augustus actually wrote to the monks of Canterbury strongly recommending Reginald and speaking well of Savaric. Reginald was indeed elected to Canterbury, visited Bath to commend Savaric to the cathedral priory and became fatally ill on the return journey. He had been archbishop for a month. Cousin Savaric duly succeeded him as bishop of Bath – despite objections from the canons of Wells, who claimed that they had not been involved in the election – was ordained priest and consecrated in Rome on 19 September 1192.[9]

William Longchamp[10]

There is no doubt that in his verbal assault on Longchamp Hugh was indulging in propaganda, for at the time of writing he had gone over to the side of John against Longchamp. In an attempt to redress the balance Peter of Blois, archdeacon of Bath and London, referred to Longchamp as 'amiable, kind, generous, wise, meek, bounteous and liberal to the highest degree'.[11] That was perhaps too fulsome. He was not the grandson of a servile peasant, as Nonant alleged, but came from a modest knightly background. He had the ability to become one of the 'new men raised from the dust' and began his professional career as one of Geoffrey Plantagenet's clerks. Richard, then count of Poitou, made him his chancellor in Aquitaine. On becoming king he promoted William to the office of chancellor of England in return for a fine of £3000 which William may have offset by increasing the fees for sealing chancery documents. He was one of the four created bishop, in his case Ely, at the Pipewell council.

Senior to the chancellor was the justiciar, the king's deputy in his absence. Ranulf Glanvill had fulfilled this role, but perhaps because of his loyalty to Henry II, Richard removed him. He was a member of the advance party that went to Acre, and shortly after his arrival succumbed to the rampant disease that was the scourge of many. The bishop of Durham, Hugh de Puiset, was appointed in his place, but Richard did not trust him to rule alone and appointed as co-regent

William de Mandeville, earl of Essex. When the earl died a few weeks later Richard appointed Longchamp. He had been further exalted when Clement III made him papal legate in June that year. He was not a prepossessing person. Physically he was unattractive, described by Gerald of Wales as more an ape than a man. He was short and ugly and walked with a limp. His looks did not conceal an attractive personality. He was said to be overbearing, obsessed with power and unwavering in his pursuit of advancement for himself and his family. He was tactless and regarded the English with contempt, making no attempt to learn the language. He claimed that lechery and drunkenness had caused them to lose their literary and military pre-eminence, and he made little attempt to understand or speak English. He was also criticised for attempting to introduce French customs into England. Rumour had it that he had an unwholesome predilection for boys and young men. In spring 1193, having been out of England for a while, the captive Richard sent him back to England to assist with organising the ransom and to bring back hostages to Germany. The barons would not entrust him with their sons. While much of the criticism of Longchamp is derived from Hugh of Nonant, the more judicious William of Newburgh also said of him: 'The laity found him more than a king, the clergy more than a pope, and both an intolerable tyrant.' Longchamp was skilled at causing offence.

The earl of Essex died prematurely and the bishop of Durham's authority as justiciar was confined to the territory north of the Humber. Even so, Longchamp had no wish for any partner in office, and determined to break him. He had already removed him from his position as sheriff of Northumberland when, about Easter 1190, for no clear reason and without provocation, Longchamp placed de Puiset under arrest. The ageing bishop was taken to London and forced to surrender castles and lands and to give hostages for good behaviour. Returning north, he had reached Howden, where he was seized by Longchamp's brother Osbert, whom Longchamp had imposed on the region as sheriff following the terrible massacre of the Jews in York. Among the ringleaders were close associates of the bishop of Durham, whom Longchamp punished.

Although Longchamp's position was unchallenged more and more people were coming to revile him. The exchequer clerks made jokes about him and drew caricatures of his brother in the capital letter O of his name. Richard's absence from the kingdom and the increasing unpopularity of his justiciar provided an opportunity for John to exploit. John had no reason to feel any regard for Longchamp, who had recently agreed with Richard that in the event of his dying without an heir he should be succeeded not by John but by his nephew Arthur. In the winter of 1190–91 John embarked upon a military campaign seeking, with the support of the bishop of Coventry, to gain control of the Midlands. In the course of 1191 John's position grew stronger. A blow to Longchamp was the death of Clement III in the spring, for his legation died with him. Richard, in Messina, felt the need to respond to hostile reports of Longchamp's conduct.[12] He therefore commissioned Walter of Coutances, archbishop of Rouen, to go to England, investigate and sort out the situation. Walter took his time and arrived in England at the end of June. John and Longchamp had meanwhile come to some agreement whereby Longchamp would abandon his support of Arthur in favour of John. An arrangement brokered by Walter on 28 July confirmed Longchamp in control of England and John as heir apparent.

The bishop of Ely's ambitions were soon shattered by an act of folly of his own doing. Geoffrey Plantaganet, the archbishop elect of York, was on the Continent and banned by Richard from returning to England. In May 1191 he was consecrated and three months later received the pallium. He was a fully-fledged metropolitan archbishop but an absentee. He therefore determined to break his embargo and return to England.[13] His concern was by no means just for his diocese, so long without a pastor, but to deal with his enemies. Celestine III had made it clear that the bishop of Durham was to make a profession of obedience to him and he was to be subject to no authority below that of legate *a latere*. This freed him from the jurisdiction of the bishop of Ely, *legatus natus*, who could be made to answer for his unlawful detention of the temporalities attached to York. Geoffrey was also strengthened in his resolve to sort out his contumacious canons. This was a fine opportunity for John to indulge in some more mischief-making and he encouraged his half-brother to return to England.

William Longchamp determined to prevent this. He gave orders to the sheriff of Sussex to obstruct Geoffrey if he tried to land and he also sought the help of the countess of Flanders, whom he asked to detain him if possible. Nevertheless the archbishop managed to reach Dover. There Geoffrey was met by Longchamp's sister, the wife of the constable of Dover. He refused to take an oath of fealty to the king and, not surprisingly, also refused to take one to Longchamp. He then sought refuge in St Martin's priory, where he remained for four days. Longchamp, having learnt of this, was determined to take him by any means necessary. He therefore sent a group of the toughest mercenaries, '*bragmanni* and hired Flemish mercenaries' to the priory to arrest him. On 18 September they broke in and pulled Geoffrey from the altar, dressed as he was in his sacerdotal regalia. He was then dragged along muddy streets and lanes to Dover castle, where he was imprisoned. This was a monstrous act of sacrilege, made even worse that it was inflicted on one consecrated bishop in the name of another. Memories of the martyrdom of Becket were evoked; those who had witnessed the appalling scene or subsequently heard about it were outraged. Longchamp's reputation sank to its nadir.

According to Howden, Geoffrey was released from Dover on John's orders. John then summoned Longchamp to account for the grievances done to Geoffrey and also the bishop of Durham. Not surprisingly Longchamp refused to respond to John's party, which included Hugh du Nonant and the three justices, William Marshal, Geoffrey fitz Peter and William Brewere. They assembled first at Marlborough, whence they moved to Reading via Oxford. From Reading writs of summons to a council to meet a few miles away at Loddon on the first Saturday after Michaelmas, 5 October, were dispatched. Not surprisingly, knowing that everything was stacked against him, Longchamp failed to appear or even send

a message excusing himself. Instead he fled to London, not without an alterca-
tion with some of John's supporters en route, and took refuge in the Tower. The
council met in his absence and having agreed to a number of charges that could
be laid against him, concluded that he must be deprived of the office of justiciar.
The following day the archbishops of York and Rouen and the other bishops who
were assembled excommunicated Longchamp and his associates.

The Londoners, believing it would be in their interests to admit the John party,
opened their gates to them. At a meeting at St Paul's on 8 October Longchamp's
opponents repeated the charges against him. The citizens were granted the status
of 'commune', the right to organise their municipal self-government. As Matilda
had earlier discovered to her cost, it was essential for a would-be ruler to keep the
Londoners on side. John was appointed regent and Walter of Coutances chief
justiciar. An oath of fealty was taken to King Richard and John was recognised
as his heir in the event of his dying childless. Then followed one of the most
humiliating episodes in William Longchamp's career. He was forced to surrender
the castles in his custody and give up his brothers, Henry and Osbert, as hostages
before he was released. From London he went to Dover via Canterbury, accompanied by Gilbert Glanvill, the bishop of Rochester, and the sheriff of Kent.

What happened next is best told in the words of Roger of Wendover.[14] There
may be an element of fabrication here, for Wendover was prepared to sacrifice
exact truth in the interests of a good story. Longchamp 'exchanged his priest's
robes for the harlot's gown'. Thus attired, he went down to the beach and waited
for a favourable wind. A sailor, eager for some amorous sport, tried to impose
himself on the bishop but was astonished to find the woman's dress conceal-
ing men's breeches. 'Look at a man in woman's dress', the sailor called to some
women who had gathered, interested in buying the cloth which Longchamp was
carrying as part of his disguise. 'Not understanding the English language', he
was unable to answer their enquiries about the price of the cloth. Suspecting
that he was an impostor, they threw themselves on him and began to tear off his
disguise, revealing that he was indeed a man. They dragged him over the sand
and stones, causing him a great deal of discomfort. In vain some of his supporters tried to rescue him and he was forced to suffer more blows and insults before
being shut up in a cellar. Eventually Longchamp escaped or was released and
at the end of October crossed the sea to Normandy. Wendover is in little doubt
that he had received his just deserts, and if his account is true it makes the point
that one of the reasons the disguise did not work was that Longchamp was unable
to communicate in English.

Without doubt William Longchamp had grievous faults and his powerful
enemies made the most of them. The massive onslaught on his character and
achievements made by the bishop of Coventry has already been mentioned.
It occupies six pages of the Llanerch Press edition of *Roger of Howden*.[15] But these
are the words of a man well known as a self-interested politician, whose personal
record does not inspire confidence in his integrity or trustworthiness. Indeed it
was said of Hugh that on his deathbed he was unable to find a confessor prepared

to absolve him of his sins. John, whom he supported out of political opportunism, was always motivated by the desire to make mischief and the career of Geoffrey, archbishop of York, was riddled with blemishes. That the action of Longchamp at Dover served temporarily to turn Geoffrey into something of a hero demonstrates how ill-judged it was. Nevertheless William Longchamp had his supporters and admirers. The attack on him by Nonant was met with a strong defence by Peter of Blois.[16] Longchamp was respected by the monks of Canterbury and Winchester, and Celestine III was a staunch defender, in due course confirming him as legate.[17]

Longchamp is something of a paradox. Enormously ambitious both for himself and members of his family, he had neither the social background nor the ability to ingratiate himself with an aristocracy in England that was seeing itself as more Anglo than Norman. Yet from his relatively humble origins he had the ability to reach the very highest positions in government and to retain the confidence of the king. Gerald of Wales described him as 'Caesar and more than Caesar'. He was capable of inept conduct that descended to the ludicrous but was respected by popes, the king of France and the Emperor. He was well educated and scholarly, a canon lawyer of repute who wrote the treatise *Practica legum et decretorum.*

To the end of his life Longchamp remained loyal to Richard and had worked hard during the period of Richard's imprisonment to secure his release. Although in 1191 Richard seems temporarily to have lost some confidence in him he was fully restored to the king's favour when Richard returned to England from his captivity. John, anticipating wrongly that his brother would never return, had proved as feckless and irresponsible as ever but to no lasting effect. Hugh of Nonant was punished by Richard for his alliance with John and retired to Normandy where he died in 1198. Richard restored Longchamp to his chancellorship but the bishop decided that he would be happier returning with Richard to Normandy in 1194. He never came back to England, and died at Poitiers three years later. The diocese of Ely had become accustomed to an absentee pastoral leader, for Longchamp's involvement in English and international politics left him little time for diocesan affairs.

Walter of Coutances[18]

In the period of William Longchamp's eclipse England was in the hands of the archbishop of Rouen, Walter of Coutances. Walter, like William, was of relatively modest origins, a Cornishman of Norman ancestry. He came to be typical of those who saw the Angevin 'empire' as a unit and he worked for the institutions that transcended territorial boundaries, the king/duke/count and the church. His brother, Roger fitz Reinfrid, was in the royal service and through him Walter was introduced into the royal household. He was a scholar, a Paris master. He served

the church as a canon and later treasurer of Rouen cathedral and became archdeacon of Oxford in 1173 or 1174. He was also a royal clerk who rose to be vice-
chancellor when Ralph de Warneville, bishop of Lisieux, was chancellor. Until
the outbreak of the rebellion of 1173–74 he worked in the household of the
young Henry, but after the rebellion returned to the household of Henry II. In
1183 Henry supported his election on 2 May to the see of Lincoln on the resignation of the bishop-elect Geoffrey Plantagenet. Walter's progress from deacon to
bishop well illustrates the nature of the Angevin 'empire'. Ordained priest by the
bishop of Évreux on 11 June, consecrated by Archbishop Richard on 3 July – not
at Canterbury but at Angers – and enthroned at Lincoln on 11 December, he was
bishop of Lincoln for a mere 18 months. The following year, again supported by
Henry, he was elected archbishop of Rouen. He did not rush to accept Rouen. To be
a metropolitan would bring him greater status; to remain in Lincoln would make
him richer.[19] Eventually he opted for the senior office and the pope, Lucius III,
confirmed his election on 17 November 1184.

Walter continued to combine secular duties with spiritual and was active in
the diplomatic negotiations of Henry II and Philip Augustus. When Richard succeeded his father Walter invested him with the duchy of Normandy at Rouen and
came to England for the coronation. He then returned to Normandy and prepared
to go on Crusade. He had not gone beyond Messina when the Longchamp crisis
erupted in England and Richard sent him, along with the queen mother Eleanor
of Aquitaine, to sort things out. If Longchamp was co-operative he was to act as
his colleague, otherwise he was to take over altogether. Following Longchamp's
disgrace Walter held the office of justiciar from September 1191 to the end of
1193. He was determined to conduct himself very differently from Longchamp.
Roger of Howden reported that he declared that 'he would do nothing in the rule
of the kingdom except by the will and consent of his associates and by the counsel of the barons of the exchequer'.[20] Richard also gave him the responsibility of
supervising the election of a successor to Archbishop Baldwin. The early death of
Reginald led to a second election, that of Hubert Walter. Following Richard's capture and imprisonment Walter of Coutances's presence was required in Germany
to assist in the negotiations for the king's release. He accordingly surrendered the
justiciarship, and although he returned to England briefly in 1194 his future lay
in Normandy, where he became much involved in the conflict between Richard
and Philip Augustus.

Hubert Walter[21]

Following Coutances's departure, authority in England passed to Hubert Walter,
who proved to be one of the greatest and most innovatory of all medieval administrators. Like Walter of Coutances he was born an Englishman, in Norfolk, the
son of a knight. His debt to his aunt's husband was very considerable, for he

was no less than Ranulf Glanvill, sheriff of Yorkshire and, after 1178, Henry II's justiciar. Although never a master of the schools, Hubert received an invaluable alternative education in his uncle's household. There he enjoyed an administrative and legal training that led him to prominence in the king's court in the 1180s. It is unlikely that he spent some time at Bologna, as has been suggested, for his lack of a formal education in the schools was said to have earned the mockery of those whose Latin was better than his. There was even a story that Richard I corrected his grammar on one occasion. Nevertheless he was far from unlettered and had immense practical knowledge of the law learnt by experience. It is possible that the legal treatise *Tractatus de legibus et consuetudinibus regni Angliae*, formerly attributed to his uncle and generally known as *Glanvill*, was actually his work. Certainly some of his legal opinions are cited in it. Working with his uncle Hubert, he learnt to handle a wide range of business; administrative, judicial and financial. He served as a baron of the exchequer and sat as a justice of the exchequer court. In his final years Henry II engaged his services in chancery and diplomatic work.

In 1186 Henry appointed Hubert Walter dean of York, and shortly after the canons of York presented his name to the king as a candidate for the metropolitan see. However, the leap from chancery clerk to archbishop of York was deemed too great. He gained a see in 1189 when on 15 September 1189 Richard I appointed him to Salisbury. He was consecrated by Archbishop Baldwin at Westminster on 22 October. In the meantime he had acknowledged the considerable debt he owed his uncle by founding the Premonstratensian abbey of West Dereham for the benefit of Glanvill's soul. Hubert was another absentee bishop. Salisbury saw little of him, because from his consecration to spring 1193 he spent only a brief time in England. He went first with Richard to Normandy and then became actively involved in the third Crusade.[22] Before that he had spent some time touring parts of Wales with Archdeacon Gerald, preaching the Crusade.[23] Following the deaths of his uncle, his friend Baldwin, for whom he became executor, and the earl of Derby, Hubert emerged as the leader of the English contingent in Acre (now in Israel). He acquitted himself with exemplary energy and effectiveness in grim circumstances. As executor of Baldwin's will Hubert was enabled to use his possessions to pay wages and buy food for the desperate common soldiers. He was concerned by the lack of sentries and spent Baldwin's money on wages for 20 knights and 50 sergeants who were thus enabled to carry out the work. According to Ralph of Diceto, dean of St Paul's, he 'made the care of the poor his business, casting the eye of compassion on the helpless'.[24] He pricked the consciences of the wealthier pilgrims by preaching moving sermons which encouraged them to give generously to the needy. During Lent 1191 Lenten discipline had to be enforced, but Hubert appreciated that it was not in the troops' best interests to give up meat during that season. Those who ate meat were subject to penance, but Hubert was no harsh disciplinarian and corrected the penitent with 'three gentle strokes with a rod as a pious father should'. He was an inspirational leader, and the significant rise in morale in the English camp, attributed to Richard's arrival the following Whitsun, owed much to Bishop Hubert.

The presence of Richard far from diminished the importance of Hubert Walter. For 16 months the two men were inseparable. Not only did Hubert distinguish himself as a pastoral and spiritual leader, but he showed himself to be a fine soldier. In July 1191 he took part in a bold assault on the walls of Acre. In June 1192 he led his troops to come to much-needed assistance of the French at Beit-Nuba. Two months later, when Richard was ill at Jaffa, he maintained morale, summoned a council of war and presented the case for a truce with Saladin. Once the truce was secured he led one of the four convoys of pilgrims who went up to Jerusalem with a guarantee by Saladin of safe conduct. Cheney printed a translation of a moving interview that Hubert had with Saladin in September 1192.[25] In October king and bishop left Syria in different ships and went separate ways. Richard's journey culminated in his captivity and imprisonment. The next we hear of Hubert he is with the imprisoned king in Germany, at Speyer on the Rhine, about to set off for England. According to William of Newburgh he had hurried there from Sicily as soon as he heard of Richard's fate. En route he probably passed through Rome and met Celestine III. After a few days with Richard, which doubtless did much to raise the king's spirits, Hubert and the exchequer clerk, William of Sainte-Mère-Église, who was with him, left for England where he landed on 20 April 1193.

On 30 March 1194 Richard had sent letters to his mother Eleanor, the justiciars and the monks of Canterbury. Following the deaths of Baldwin and Reginald in rapid succession the see was vacant. His letter to the monks was expressed in general terms. They were urged to elect an archbishop acceptable to God and man and to follow the advice of Queen Eleanor and William. He made it clear to both of them that the man for the job was Hubert Walter. However there were other contenders. Both William Longchamp and Savaric of Bath aspired to the metropolitan see. There is some evidence that at one stage the captive Richard wavered and actually backed Savaric, but on 8 June he sent another letter to Queen Eleanor confirming his support for Hubert, and stating that if by chance the monks and prior of Canterbury had received anything from him on behalf of Longchamp, Savaric or anyone else they were to quash it. 'It is our fixed and unchangeable wish', he wrote, 'that the bishop of Salisbury be promoted to the church of Canterbury. We want this and nothing else.'[26] Richard need not have worried, for the monks had already elected Hubert on 28 May, somewhat to the chagrin of the bishop of London, who was aggrieved that he and his fellow suffragans had had no say in the election. It remained necessary to secure the approval of Celestine III. He granted it readily and sent the pallium to England. On Wednesday 3 November Gervase, who as sacristan of Christ Church had the responsibility for arranging the formalities of the new archbishop's induction, met Hubert at Lewisham, spoke to him of his responsibilities and presented him with his cross. The enthronement was scheduled for the following Sunday. Once an almost inevitable dispute between the Canterbury monks and the bishops of

Rochester and London about their respective roles in the ceremony had been settled it went ahead with no further problem. The diocese had a new bishop, the province a new metropolitan and England a new primate. After March 1195 they also had in Hubert a papal legate whose authority ran throughout England.

Great though his responsibilities as archbishop were his duties came to extend far beyond episcopal office. He was chief justiciar of England from January 1194 until 31 July 1198 and chancellor from 28 May 1199 until his death on 13 July 1205. With two absentee kings in succession, Hubert Walter was its effective ruler. Richard had left England for the last time in May 1194 and John was out of England for most of the first four and a half years of his reign. One of his first responsibilities before actually being accorded the title of justiciar was to make the necessary arrangements for collecting, storing, dispatching and delivering Richard's ransom.[27] By the end of 1193 a substantial part had been collected and sent to Germany. Although England alone did not have to bear the burden it is a tribute both to the country's prosperity and the effectiveness of its administrative system that so much money was raised. The available evidence for how this was done is limited. The exchequer documents known as the Pipe Rolls are unable to tell us much, as the receipts were accounted for in a special department set up specifically to handle the ransom money. It seems that the cash collected was handed over to special custodians appointed by Hubert and the treasurer, Richard fitz Nigel, and locked up in St Paul's cathedral. A charge, known as an aid, of 20 shillings was imposed on every knight's fee, and a general tax of a quarter of the estimated worth of each individual's revenues and possessions was imposed on the whole population, with the exception of the parish clergy, who were required to pay only one-tenth. The Cistercian and Gilbertine sheep farmers had to surrender their entire crop of wool and the plate of churches and cathedrals was taken. The value of these could be immense. Bishop Hugh of Durham contributed £2000 cash in preference to yielding his cathedral plate and ornaments. Even so all these measures proved inadequate. Further taxes were raised and fines were imposed to enable those who had supported John's rebellion to be restored to the king's pleasure. Ultimately the full amount was never collected. In 1195 the Emperor remitted 17,000 marks to encourage Richard not to make peace with France.[28] The duke of Austria saw little of the 25,000 marks due to him.

As justiciar Hubert Walter's main responsibilities were to restore and maintain law and order after the problems caused by John and to provide the means of financing Richard's wars on the Continent. For most of the twelfth century the standard rate of pay for a knight was eightpence a day. Inflation trebled this early in the next century and by the end of Henry II's reign it had risen to one shilling. Out of his own resources a knight had to equip himself with the war horse and his arms and armour. Good horses cost at least ten marks and quality armour and equipment were expensive. In a sense, however skilled, knights were largely amateurs. The men-at-arms were professionals recruited, often from Wales, at the rate of fourpence a day if they were mounted, with an additional twopence for a second horse. Infantrymen earned twopence a day. In addition there were foreign mercenaries. Some were highly skilled, like the crossbowmen from Genoa; some were honourable soldiers, like the favourite of King Stephen, William of Ypres; but many mercenaries, like those used by Longchamp against the archbishop of York, were ruthless and brutal thugs, like the notorious Mercadier. On top of this was the cost of building and maintaining castles and the defence works protecting towns and cities. Siege engines had to be constructed and repaired. The greatest of all Richard's castles, Château Gaillard, cost Richard dear not just in terms of the actual building but in making his peace with Walter of Coutances on whose land it was erected.[29] Hubert Walter claimed in 1196 that 'after examining his books and auditing his accounts in the last two years he had acquired for the king's use eleven hundred thousand marks of silver from out of the kingdom of England'.[30] An excess of one million marks is a huge sum, but there is no precise evidence as to how it was raised.

In September 1194 the justiciar inaugurated a great inquest to investigate judicial, financial and administrative procedures. There was a precedent for this in Henry II's inquest of sheriffs of 1170. Hubert sent royal judges through the shires with a list of the matters which they were to look into, 'the articles of the eyre'. There were 25 articles of instruction which covered crown pleas and other lawsuits, enquiries into the submission of John's supporters and the confiscation of their property, advowsons, wardships of boys and marriages of girls and widows, collection of the aid for Richard's ransom and complaints of extortionate conduct by various royal officials such as justices, sheriffs, constables and foresters. The stocking of royal manors was to be scrutinised and adequate inventories and accounts were to be prepared. The assets of the Jews were to be recorded and kept under control. The power of the sheriffs was to be curbed. Sheriffs were forbidden to act as justices in their own counties or any other county where they had held office since Richard's accession. The chronicler Roger of Howden, himself a sometime royal justice, gave a detailed account of the procedures.[31]

The answers to the questions presented by the commissioners were to be given by what is known as a Grand Jury and the procedure for forming and sitting on the jury added considerably to the responsibilities of the knights of the shire. Four knights were to be chosen from each county. Upon their oaths they were to choose two lawful knights 'from every hundred and wapentake' who were to choose a further ten knights from each. In the event of there not being enough knights available the numbers were to be made up by 'free and lawful men' of the locality. Three knights and one clerk were appointed to keep the pleas of the crown. In the work of these knights we have the origins of the office of coroner. Hubert himself took an active part in the enquiry working with the judges in East Anglia, Cambridgeshire and Huntingdonshire.

The enquiry was intended to achieve three main goals: the control of local administration by the central authority, the realisation of all available assets and the restoration of law and order. In an attempt to reduce crime and lawlessness Hubert in 1195 gave new life to the ancient 'frankpledge' system. Under this system, pre-Conquest in origin, groups of males over the age of 12 were formed into 'tithings' with responsibility for each other's good behaviour. In the event of one or more member of the tithing disturbing the peace the other members had to 'raise the hue and cry' with a view to catching the malefactor and bringing him to justice. Hubert required all those over the age of 15 to take an oath whereby they undertook to play their part in maintaining law and order. The oath was to be taken in the presence of knights, who were to receive wrongdoers.[32]

Several chroniclers give us an account of a potentially very serious breach of the peace that occurred in London in 1196.[33] A lawyer called William fitz Osbert who rejoiced in the nickname 'Longbeard' presented himself as a champion of the harshly oppressed poor. He claimed that the demands for taxes were falling heaviest on those least able to pay while the rich, the London oligarchs, were paying very little. He demanded that people should pay according to their means and sought the protection of the absent king. Hubert Walter sensed serious trouble and ordered that if any of the common people were found outside London's walls they should be arrested as enemies of the king and kingdom. When a citizen went, duty bound, to arrest fitz Osbert as a troublemaker, fitz Osbert killed him. He and some of his associates then fled and sought sanctuary in the church of St Mary-le-Bow. When they refused to come out and hand themselves over, Hubert, controversially, gave the order to set fire to the church so that they would be smoked out. 'Forced by the smoke and vapour', they eventually emerged. Fitz Osbert was arrested and someone stabbed him, but not fatally. The accused was led to the Tower and he and his associates were sentenced to death. By prompt action Hubert had forestalled a potentially dangerous situation, but the way he caught his man opened him to the charge of sacrilege. Certainly, according to Howden, the Christ Church monks were not slow to accuse him of it and, on the eve of the impending storm over the perceived threat to them by the archbishop's proposal for a collegiate church at Lambeth, 'they were unable to hold communication with him on any matter in a peaceable manner'.[34]

For some months in 1197 Hubert was in Normandy helping to settle the dispute with the archbishop of Rouen about Château Gaillard.[35] He subsequently had to attempt to act as peacemaker between the kings of England and France.[36] Back in England he became involved in a controversy about the demand for a tax to pay for 300 knights to serve in France for a year. Among the critics of the proposals was Hugh of Lincoln. At this time Hubert was extremely busy with exchequer and judicial matters. The financial demands on the country were so great that he was regularly attempting to find new means to raise money. Shortly before he resigned as justiciar in 1198 Richard, as desperate for cash as ever, imposed a tax of 5 shillings on every carucate or hide of land throughout the country. This involved complex procedures which were much resented. First the country had to be surveyed county by county. The money had to be collected, in two stages. Records had to be maintained of the various processes and finally the cash had to be delivered to the exchequer.[37] The pressure of all this may have hastened Hubert's retirement.

As justiciar he was responsible for the entire judicial system. One of his most celebrated innovations was the introduction of the 'foot of the fine'. On the same principle as the tally stick Henry II had offered to litigants the 'final concord'. At the conclusion of a case the judgement was recorded on parchment. This 'final concord', as it was known, was divided in two and each party thereby received a statement of the judgement. The date 15 July 1195 was a significant one in the history of legal record-keeping. For the first time the indenture was cut into three parts, two vertically and the third, the 'foot of the fine', horizontally. The concord of that day was endorsed with the words: 'This is the first chirograph that was made in the lord king's court in the form of three chirographs according to the command of his lordship of Canterbury and other barons of the lord king, to the end that by this form a record could be made to be passed to the Treasurer to put in the Treasury.'[38] One of the beneficiaries of this innovation was Hubert's brother Theobald. Henceforward the officials as well as the parties in the case had a written record of the judgement. True, there had been precedents for this, even in Anglo-Saxon times, and it is well known that in 1164 Henry II had personally insisted that a third copy of the Constitutions of Clarendon should be kept in the royal archives. However, as Clanchy wrote, the importance of the feet of fines should not be underestimated. In his words: 'For the first time, a form of record had been deliberately inaugurated as a continuing series for archival purposes. The feet of fines gave private individuals the opportunity to have transactions kept on permanent record in the royal treasury. What had in the past been exceptional practice now became the rule.'

The stress of office was very considerable, particularly as, in addition to the king's business, Hubert could not neglect his responsibilities as archbishop of Canterbury and, from 1195–98, papal legate.[39] While there is no evidence that he was a great spiritual or pastoral leader, he was not just a titular archbishop. It is true that he made enemies of the monks of Christ Church, but much of the blame must be attributed to them. The Canterbury monks apart, he was seen as a friend and benefactor. He assumed the Augustinian habit on becoming archbishop and evidence of the esteem in which he was held by the Cistercians is that they admitted him to their confraternity in 1195. He was known to be generous and made gifts of costly vestments to monastic houses. He was conscientious in reorganising Canterbury's estates and increased their revenues. As metropolitan he visited monasteries and vacant sees. As papal legate he headed commissions of enquiry for the canonisation of Gilbert of Sempringham and Wulfstan of Worcester, and although he lacked formal training in canon law his considerable legal experience must have made him an invaluable judge delegate. Legislator as well as judge, he issued canons for the archdiocese of York in 1195[40] and for Canterbury in 1200.[41]

It is hardly surprising that, in time, Hubert sought to retire as justiciar, particularly as his health was not robust. He may have first thought about it in May 1194. The appointment as legate undoubtedly added to his burdens. He was now servant of two masters and he had to keep a balance by ensuring that while he had to look to the interests of the church he had also to ensure that the interests of the crown were not sacrificed to them. This inevitably led to conflict. Richard was very fond of tournaments and Hubert had to regulate and supervise them, contrary to a decree of the Third Lateran Council forbidding them. In 1196 it appears that he began to increase his pressure on the king to relieve him of high secular office.[42] Roger of Howden reported that he frequently sent messengers to Richard urging him to relieve their master of his responsibilities as justiciar. The king was reluctant as he could think of no one who could adequately replace him. When eventually he agreed to Hubert's request the archbishop decided to change his mind and carry on. He assured Richard that if his services were really needed he would continue and would not use his age as a reason for giving up. This earned him the censure of Roger of Howden, who complained of his neglecting his priestly duties rather than abandon the king.

He continued for two more years, in the face of mounting pressures of work and increased criticism. One of his last duties as justiciar was to supervise Richard's 'Assize of Measures', an attempt to standardise the weights and measures of food and drink when they were sold and the dimensions of woollen cloth.[43] This extensive involvement in secular matters gave the monks of Canterbury the welcome opportunity to complain about him to Innocent III. They grumbled about the fact that, as justiciar, he had to deal with offences which merited corporal or capital punishment, and they cited the fitz Osbert case. Innocent at first supported the monks against their archbishop in the Lambeth dispute[44] and was no doubt moved to do so having been influenced by their reports of him as being unsatisfactory. He refused to renew Hubert's legation and actually asked Richard to relieve him of the post of justiciar. According to Roger of Howden,[45] Innocent wrote to Richard, 'with a fatherly exhortation', recommending him, 'as he valued the safety of his soul', to relieve the archbishop from his secular duties. He also stressed that in future neither Hubert, nor any other priest or bishop, was to assume secular responsibilities. On 11 July 1198 Richard did indeed issue letters patent from Château Gaillard giving notice of Hubert's resignation. He stated first that he had not responded to Hubert's request to be allowed to resign because he was doing such invaluable work. He went on to say that in view of his poor health he would release him from 'the intolerable burden of his labours'.[46] It is most unlikely that this was in response to pressure from Innocent III. Even so, Hubert's successor, Geoffrey fitz Peter, was a layman. This was far from the end of Hubert's involvement in secular affairs, for on the day of John's coronation he accepted the office of chancellor.

A saint: Hugh of Lincoln[47]

The monks of Canterbury were not Hubert Walter's only critics. Among his most severe was Hugh bishop of Lincoln. Historians are fortunate in that, like Anselm, he had someone close to him, in Hugh's case his chaplain Adam, a monk of the abbey of Eynsham, who had the ability to write extensively about the master whom he admired. There are some other lives of Hugh, including a brief one by Gerald of Wales, but Adam's *Magna Vita* is by far the most important. By 1186 the see of Lincoln was in desperate need of a bishop as it had been vacant for 20 years, a scandalously long time. It was an enormous and relatively heavily populated see extending from the Humber to the Thames and comprising nine counties. When Bishop Robert of Chesney died in 1166 no attempt was made to find a successor until Henry's illegitimate son, Geoffrey of Plantagenet, was nominated in 1173. He was quite unsuited for episcopal office and had not been ordained priest. It was said that he refused ordination in the hope that he would one day become king, ordination being a disqualification. William of Newburgh was particularly scathing about him: 'being ignorant how to feed the Lord's flock though skilled in shearing them, he deferred the hour of canonical consecration in order to indulge his pleasures more freely'.[48] He was not consecrated and resigned in 1181. Walter of Coutances, a canon of Rouen and royal clerk, was freely elected in 1183 but the following year returned to Rouen as its archbishop (see above) and for two further years Lincoln remained without a bishop.

For a week at the end of May and beginning of June 1186 Henry held a council at Eynsham, the home of the community of Benedictine monks of which Hugh's biographer Adam was a member and subsequently prior and abbot. At this council William de Northall was elected bishop of Worcester and William de Vere bishop of Hereford. There were several candidates for the see of Lincoln: Geoffrey de Lucy, who declined Exeter on the grounds that the income was inadequate to meet episcopal needs and eventually became bishop of Winchester; Richard fitz Nigel, the author of *The Dialogue of the Exchequer*, who became bishop of London; and Herbert le Poor, who in due course became bishop of Salisbury.

Hugh was concerned to search his conscience and observe the due proprieties before agreeing to assume responsibility for the biggest diocese in England and one of the richest. As bishop he ensured that in his household there were young men of intellectual distinction like Master Robert of Bedford and Master Roger of Rolleston, a future dean. His clerks were rewarded with cathedral canonries, but under Hugh these were to be no sinecures. His canons were required to live in Lincoln and to be conscientious in fulfilling their pastoral responsibilities.

He had no fears about standing up to Henry, particularly if he was concerned for the king's spiritual health, and with a combination of firmness and humour he was able to win round the king, a king admittedly chastened by his experience of the consequences of Becket's murder. Adam told of several occasions when he resisted demands made by Richard or his justiciar Hubert. He recounted a story to demonstrate that Hugh's respect for the Heavenly King was greater than that for the king on earth. Once Hugh was invited by Richard to dine with him at Rouen. Before he could go he had to attend to a number of burials in the city. As a result he was late and the king, the magnates and their attendants were obliged to wait for their meal. Attempts by some of the king's men to urge Hugh to hurry up were unavailing. 'There is no need to wait for me, he said, let them eat with God's blessing. It is better that an earthly king should dine without me than that the command of the King of Heaven should be left undone by his unworthy servant.'[49]

He had little sympathy for bishops who heavily involved themselves in secular affairs, and he told Hubert Walter that while he would obey him as his archbishop he would not do so as his justiciar. Adam recorded a number of examples of the friction between the two men.[50] His first recorded dispute with Richard involved Hubert and concerned the payment of tribute in the form of a mantle. One of his predecessors, Robert Bloet, had apparently made an annual gift to the king of a cloak worth 100 silver marks. Hugh discontinued the practice and Richard demanded that he should pay a large sum in lieu of the arrears which had accumulated. Hugh found himself confronted by Hubert Walter, 'his bitter enemy',[51] who apparently drove a very hard bargain of a one-off payment of 3000 marks. Hitherto Hugh had been accustomed to give any surplus income to charitable causes and he was loath to relinquish this practice. Nor did he wish to take money from those for whom he was pastorally responsible. His plan was to retire as a hermit to Witham and use his income from the diocese to pay the amercement. His clergy would not permit this as they could not bear the prospect of Hugh leaving them. He therefore yielded to the proposal that they should contribute from their own resources while he would also contribute as much as he could.

One of the best-known occasions when Hugh resisted the king's demands presented to him by Hubert Walter was at the Oxford Council held in December 1197.[52] The prolonged war with France was making ever-greater demands on England's resources and the traditional methods of raising, equipping and financing armies were proving quite inadequate to meet them. Hubert sought advice from the magnates, including the bishops, as to what best might be done to meet Richard's needs. It was proposed that they should all provide from their own resources the means of funding 300 knights to fight on the Continent. Hubert Walter and Richard fitz Nigel gave wholehearted backing to the scheme. Their enthusiasm was not shared by Hugh. He explained that he was a stranger in England who, before being raised to the episcopate, had been a monk living in seclusion and ignorant of English customs and privileges. He had therefore taken every step to inform himself about them as fully as he could. He acknowledged that the see of Lincoln was bound to serve the king in war, 'but only in this country, and it is a fact that no service is due beyond the frontiers of England'. He made it clear that he would rather return to his native Burgundy and resume the Carthusian way of life than allow his church to break with precedent and shoulder a new type of burden. When Hubert Walter heard this he was furious and his lips trembled with rage as he sought the opinion of Herbert le Poer, bishop of Salisbury. Herbert gave his full support to Hugh. Archbishop Hubert could contain himself no longer. He stormed at Bishop Hugh, closed the council and reported to Richard that the bishop of Lincoln was responsible for the failure of the proposal.

Richard reacted by ordering the confiscation of the temporalities of Salisbury and Lincoln. In reality Richard was in the right and Hugh was not correct in his absolute assertion that his church did not owe military service abroad. Confiscation was the normal penalty for failing to fulfil feudal obligations. After a humiliating experience and the payment of a large fine the bishop of Salisbury was allowed to recover his temporalities. However, 'no one dared to lay hands on the lands and goods of the bishop of Lincoln, because they feared to offend him, and dreaded his excommunication as much as the death sentence'. Despite frequent demands by the king, the Exchequer officials failed to confiscate anything belonging to Hugh and in some despair they urged him to visit Richard in Normandy.

On 28 August 1198 Hugh arrived at the chapel of the new castle at Andely, Château Gaillard.[53] Richard was sitting on a throne near the entrance, and Philip of Poitiers, Hugh de Puiset's successor at Durham, and Eustace, bishop of Ely, stood at his feet. Three other bishops were also there, as well as the archbishops of Rouen and Canterbury. Richard received the bishop of Lincoln's greeting in silence, frowning at Hugh before he turned his face away. The King's response to Hugh's request for a kiss was to turn his face further away. At that, the courageous bishop seized Richard's tunic with the words, 'You owe me a kiss, because I have come a long way to see you', at the same time shaking him violently. When Hugh was told by Richard that he was owed no kiss by him he shook him even more vigorously, boldly demanding the kiss which he claimed he rightly deserved. So struck was Richard by Hugh's courage and determination that, after a little while, he relented and, with a smile, kissed him. Subsequently Richard bestowed various favours on Hugh, including a pike for his dinner, and tried unsuccessfully to pass the blame for the dispute on to Hubert Walter who, said the king, had misrepresented him. In a later discussion of the incident with members of his household Richard remarked: 'If the other bishops were such as he, no king or ruler would dare raise up his head against them',[54] not a prospect that Richard relished.

Hugh's involvement in public affairs did not always bring him into conflict with the king but, reluctantly, he found himself drawn in to other contentious matters. Roger of Howden does not specifically mention him as being present at Richard's coronation in 1189, although he surely was and at the Council of Pipewell. Roger certainly includes him as among those who were present at Richard's second coronation held on 17 April 1194.[55] He was also present at Richard's burial.[56] He frequently acted as a papal judge-delegate and in that capacity was drawn into the dispute between the bishop and monks of Coventry. He was spared by illness from attending the settlement of the Canterbury affair. A few years before, in 1194, he was among those who excommunicated the rebellious John. His subsequent misgivings about John as king were recounted at some length by Adam of Eynsham.[57]

Even so, John visited Hugh on his deathbed in November 1200. Hugh had not changed his opinion of the king. In Adam's words, 'he had no illusions about John, and therefore spoke very little to him, knowing that his exhortations would be wasted'.[58] He was equally unforgiving of Hubert Walter, despite the archbishop's qualified attempt at reconciliation. Hugh's response to Hubert was to recall the number of occasions when, to appease him, he weakly suppressed matters on which he should not have been silent. 'My sin', Hugh apparently said, 'was that I preferred to offend my heavenly father and not you.'[59] Hugh died at his London house on 16 November 1200. His body was taken back to Lincoln and he was buried in the cathedral on 23 November. Miracles were soon associated with him and in 1220 he was canonised. When in 1886 Elizabeth Wordsworth, the great niece of the poet and daughter of a nineteenth-century bishop of Lincoln Christopher, founded St Hugh's College, Oxford, she named it after his saintly predecessor.

8

Stephen Langton, the Bishops and *Magna Carta*

European politics

Despite his earlier plans to retire, Hubert Walter continued to play a prominent part in John's reign, both as archbishop of Canterbury and chancellor, until his death on 13 July 1205. For much of this time John was in Normandy. Hubert's death led to a prolonged crisis which was not finally resolved until May 1213. This was one of a number of crises besetting John culminating in baronial rebellion, civil war and the imposition of *Magna Carta*, followed by a French invasion led by Louis, son of King Philip Augustus, in May 1216. The relationship of Philip Augustus (1180–1223) with John is fundamental to the understanding of his reign. Philip was shrewd and coldly calculating, prepared to bide his time until the opportunity arose to assert and establish his control. He could take advantage of Norman and English traitors when it suited him and it was related that when the great William Marshal, earl of Pembroke, asked Philip why he bothered to have anything to do with contemptible traitors, Philip replied that such men were torches, to be used and then thrown in the cesspool.[1]

John's claim to succeed Richard was not unopposed. Norman custom favoured John, as Richard's brother; Angevin tradition favoured Richard's nephew, the 12-year-old Arthur. Norman custom prevailed. John was invested with Normandy in June 1199, having been crowned king of England on 27 May. Philip saw himself as Arthur's protector and defender of the lands between Normandy and the Loire. Conflict between the two kings soon broke out, leading to a peace settlement at Le Goulet on 22 May 1200.

The peace may have been conceived as a lasting settlement, but in reality it proved to be a trap into which John fell. It emphasised John's subordination to Philip for all the lands he held in France. In acknowledgement of his status as a vassal John performed homage to Philip and paid him the considerable sum of 20,000 marks as a relief. It is significant that Philip had the confidence to make such an unprecedented demand, and John agreed to acquiesce. Although a king of England was in no way subordinate to a king of France, John's regal status was no barrier to his being answerable in the court of the king of France for any breaches of law and practice that might be held against him. When John offended the most important baron of Lower Poitou, Hugh le Brun, count of Lusignan, by snatching his fiancée Isabella from him and marrying her himself, Hugh appealed to King Philip, who summoned John before his court in Paris shortly after Easter 1202. When John failed to appear Philip declared him a contumacious vassal.

This was, in effect, a declaration of war. Although in the course of the war John showed himself capable of launching a spirited offensive, as when he captured Mirebeau castle in August 1202, he lacked the stamina and leadership needed to turn one victory into permanent success. Moreover, his excessively harsh treatment of the captives at Mirebeau was widely condemned, even by his allies. Among the victims was Arthur, who subsequently disappeared. His fate was mysterious but it was generally believed that John had arranged his murder, a monstrous crime held against him to the end. Arthur's fate gave the Bretons cause for war, and Philip energised himself in their support. In 1203–04 he concentrated his efforts on Normandy and achieved considerable success while John remained inert. In June 1203 the fortress of Vaudreuil on the left bank of the Seine, guarding the approaches to Rouen, surrendered when Robert fitz Walter and Saer de Quency, 'the noblemen to whom the charge of the castle had been entrusted, delivered it up to the French king'.[2] On 8 March 1204 Chateau Gaillard fell to Philip, and three months later Rouen was occupied unopposed. The Anglo-Norman realm had come to an end and all that remained were the Channel Islands. In 1206 and 1214 John led two expeditions to Poitou. The first failed. The second began promisingly for John, the Lusignans coming to terms with him for a while, although they subsequently defected. It ended disastrously, with John's fate decided by events not in Poitou but Flanders.

Pope Innocent III, 1198–1216

Although his political judgements were not always sound, as in his support of Otto, and despite controversies and disasters like the Fourth Crusade, Innocent III is regarded as one of the greatest medieval popes. He had such a strongly held view of his position as head of a Christian society that it has been contended that in reality he wished to be 'lord of the world', stopping at nothing, spiritual or secular, to achieve that goal. In his defence, it can be argued that he viewed power as the means of achieving the highest spiritual aims. He saw himself not as the vicar of St Peter, but as the vicar of Christ Himself, with *plenitudo potestatis*. He had no doubt that it was his duty to intervene in secular matters where sin was involved, *ratione peccati*. He described himself as 'lower than God but higher than man, who judges all and is judged by no one'. He declared that Peter was given 'not only the universal church but the whole world to govern'. He wrote that 'the priesthood was as superior to the kingship as the soul to the body and that just as the moon derives its light from the sun the royal power derives the splendour of its dignity from the pontifical authority'.

Innocent had a vision of a reformed Christendom united politically and doctrinally, extending into the Holy Land and the Byzantine Empire, a vision expounded at the Fourth Lateran Council of 1215, attended by 369 bishops from 81 provinces and 800 abbots. It was one of the greatest reform councils of the Middle Ages and its canons made an impact on the Catholic Church for centuries to come. Innocent had no qualms about telling kings how to behave. He imposed an interdict on France as punishment for Philip Augustus's hasty rejection of his wife Ingeborg of Sweden on the morning after their wedding night. He imposed a similar penalty on England when John refused to accept his choice of archbishop of Canterbury, Stephen Langton.

John: an awful king (*1066 and All That*)?

King John received as bad a press from the chroniclers and nineteenth-century moralising historians as did William Rufus. The difference is that John probably deserved it, up to a point. No one can deny that John was a flawed prince and an equally flawed ruler. He was capricious, inclined to fecklessness and cruelty. He was, however, capable of being energetic and militarily successful. The Barnwell annalist wrote: 'in Ireland, Scotland and Wales there was no one who did not bow to the nod of the king of England'.[4] He took an intelligent interest in running the country, enjoying the part he played in it. He was well-read, with an incisive mind. He often involved himself in Exchequer business and actually attended its meetings at times. He was particularly interested in judicial matters, sitting with his barons and judges to determine legal cases. His judgements were considered to be well worth the cost, not because he could be bought, but because they were respected as just, and even sometimes compassionate. As D.M. Stenton wrote: 'He should be given credit for his readiness to fulfil his royal duty of ameliorating the rigour of the law for the helpless, women, children, the poor, and the idiot.'[5] Moreover, he personally travelled to parts of the kingdom that had not seen a king for many years. But in the process he offended individuals and their grievances were not forgotten.

Among those offended were tenants-in-chief who had not benefited from John's interest in judicial procedures.[6] Henry II is renowned for his reforms in the administration and application of justice. As John Hudson pointed out,[7] these reforms had established controls over lords' actions and their courts, but few enforceable controls existed over the king and his courts. While lesser lords could use the new procedures to establish their rights there was no procedure whereby a tenant-in-chief could take action against his lord, the king. If the king failed to do justice there was no legal way by which he could be brought to account and disaffected lords might sometimes consider that justice had not been done even at a very considerable price.

To this day we can gaze on John's effigy in Worcester Cathedral; John apparently greatly admired St Wulfstan of Worcester, although the cynical would doubt his sincerity. While it is clear that John was no great friend of the church unless it suited him, he was not an enemy on principle provided he had his own way in his dealings with it. John certainly had his critics. Adam of Eynsham was far from complimentary, depicting him as a sacrilegious mocker who was disrespectful during church services, jesting with his friends like an adolescent schoolboy, rarely receiving the sacraments and keener to satisfy his bodily hunger than his spiritual. Matthew Paris presents him as a far from devout sceptic who sent an embassy to the sultan of Morocco and Spain with the purpose of communicating his interest in being converted to Islam.[8] However, there is evidence that John was a benefactor of small and obscure religious houses, often convents, and made grants totalling about £1450 a year to monasteries. In addition to money he made gifts of vestments and altar cloths. He arranged to feed hundreds of paupers annually, albeit for not wholly altruistic reasons but as a penitential offering which enabled him and his friends to eat meat and go hunting during Lent and on other fast days, or 'because he went fishing at Marlborough on the feast of St Leonard'. He gave money to the abbey at Reading to fund a shrine for its precious and important relic, the hand of St James. One of his most enduring acts was the foundation of the Cistercian abbey of Beaulieu. Unfortunately the first abbot, Hugh, did not bring lustre to the new foundation, for it seems that John was more concerned to have someone who would be useful to him than an abbot distinguished for his spirituality and learning. In 1215 he was charged with indulging in excessive drinking bouts with three earls and forty knights, of having his bed guarded by a dog on a silver chain and eating off silver plate. He was actually deposed within months of John's death but ended up as bishop of Carlisle.[9]

John was as determined as any of his predecessors to control appointments to episcopal sees, and of the bishops elected in John's reign a significant majority were curialists. There were eight elections before the imposition of the interdict in 1207. Five sees went to curialists: Bath, Chichester, Norwich, Winchester and Worcester. John had no difficulty in ensuring that his man was elected to four of these. Jocelin de Welles, bishop of Bath, was very active in a range of government activities; Simon de Camera, bishop of Chichester, was, as his name suggests, a clerk of the king's chamber; John de Gray, bishop of Norwich, was a senior chancery clerk and bearer of the royal seal; Mauger of Worcester had been Richard's doctor. Of the other appointments, that of Giles of Briouse was entirely political. John was in debt to his father William and he used the grant of the see of Hereford to Giles as a means of repaying the debt. Sidney Painter wrote: 'there is no reason for thinking that he was not simply a wild marcher lord covered with clerical vestments'.[10] It has been shown that this is not wholly fair, and that until John turned against the family he was a conscientious papal judge delegate enforcing the provisions of canon law.[11]

The appointment to Winchester was less straightforward.[12] A number of members of the monastic chapter dissented from John's choice of Peter des Roches, a leading member of the household financial department, and despite pressure from John a group went to Rome to state their case. Innocent ordered another election to be held under his supervision and this time the monks were reconciled to the practical sense of electing des Roches. He was the archetypal curialist bishop, unswervingly loyal to John both as bishop and, for a while, chief justiciar. He was as at home on the battlefield as in the Exchequer, less so at the altar or in the pulpit. Clanchy quotes a contemporary satirist: 'The warrior of Winchester, up at the Exchequer, sharp at accounting, slack at Scripture, revolving the royal roll.'[13] This view is not entirely just. The Winchester Episcopal Acta for his period as bishop provide testimony of his indefatigability in the service of his diocese, as well as the king.[14] Although it is not necessarily proof of religious devotion, he founded religious houses in Hampshire and supported the Dominicans when they first came to England in 1221.[15] He even joined the Fifth Crusade.

The Canterbury election

Innocent III's involvement in the Winchester election set an important precedent for his involvement in that in Canterbury following the death of Hubert Walter. This time John did not get the man he wanted. The pope insisted that it was his responsibility to determine the result of a contested election, if necessary using in the process the sanctions of interdict and excommunication. This was unprecedented for England. As a trained lawyer Innocent cared about correct procedures. Elections had to be canonical and valid. As the head of Christendom he was mightily concerned to ensure that he had the right calibre of men in key positions. He was attentive more to suitable qualities than personalities, and recognised that those of Mauger of Worcester compensated for his illegitimacy.[16] Even so, he did not initiate investigations into disputed elections. He became involved as an arbiter once he had received an appeal. The Canterbury election was not unique; it was one of many cases relating to elections throughout Christendom.[17] The health of Christendom required as bishops men of unimpeachable character who were learned and experienced. Innocent's object was to ensure that the law as formulated by conciliar edict, papal decree and decretal was superior to local custom as expressed, for instance, in the Constitutions of Clarendon. The Canterbury election tested the new system against the old tradition.

The question of who should succeed Hubert Walter was of concern to several parties. John wanted a loyal and effective royal servant to succeed Hubert. The ideal man in his view was the bishop of Norwich, John de Gray. In the words of Painter: 'There was no man in England whom King John trusted so completely and consistently as he did John de Gray.'[18] Strictly speaking, kings had no formal part in the election procedure beyond giving the electors the authority to go ahead, the *congé d'élire*. In practice they had the means of ensuring that the man elected was the man they wanted. The monks of Christ Church believed strongly that the right to elect lay exclusively with them and they had no intention of having an archbishop imposed on them. While the suffragan bishops of the province of Canterbury made no claim to have the exclusive right of election, they certainly believed that they were entitled to play a part in the choice of the man to whom they would be required to profess obedience.

A group of monks made a clumsy and uncanonical attempt to thwart John and the bishops by secretly choosing their sub-prior Reginald,[19] who headed a delegation to Rome to present their case. At the same time a representative of the bishops went to Rome to put the case for John de Gray. The pope was to adjudicate. When John heard of the monks' duplicity he rushed to Canterbury and terrified them into transferring their allegiance to John de Gray. At the end of 1206 Innocent decided on his own candidate, Stephen Langton, whom he consecrated at Viterbo on 17 July 1207, at the same time giving him the pallium. To John's fury the pope had imposed upon England an archbishop of Canterbury of his choice. His reaction was judged by Innocent to be 'insolent, impudent, threatening and expostulating'.[20]

There is little doubt that in terms of suitability Stephen Langton was a far stronger candidate than Reginald the sub-prior, and had the potential to be an archbishop of far greater stature than the worldly curialist bishop of Norwich. His training at Paris gave him the vision to provide for the English church the pastoral and spiritual leadership that Innocent longed for. But as Stephen proved to Innocent's later discomfort, he was a man of considerable moral and intellectual independence and integrity. Until he was drawn into ecclesiastical politics he had pursued an academic career of distinction and certainly knew Innocent when a student at Paris. Between around 1165 and 1180 he had studied arts and theology and then became a teacher who attracted some very able pupils. There is a great deal of extant evidence of Langton's career as a Paris master, his disputations on theological issues, his sermons and his biblical commentaries. His arrangement of the books of the Bible and their division into chapters was basically as they are known to this day. Langton's teaching career came to an end when Innocent made him cardinal-priest of St Chrysogonus early in 1206.

John was adamant in his refusal to recognise the new archbishop and it was not until 9 July 1213 that Stephen was admitted to England. By then the church in England had been leaderless for eight years. In that period Innocent imposed an interdict on England on 23 March 1208 and when John remained intransigent on 30 August 1211 Innocent declared him excommunicated, releasing his subjects from oaths of fealty to him. Sees remained vacant, the bishops in office went into exile and by the end of 1211 only one remained in England, Peter des Roches of Winchester. John's quarrel was with the pope personally and not the English clergy, whom he actually put under his protection. Even so, he sought to make as much money as he could from the situation, arguing that the clergy held their property to enable them to fulfil their spiritual functions. As these were now suspended their tenure of property was no longer justified, and it was appropriate for him to seize it all. It is highly likely that the devout were seriously distressed by the interdict. It was imposed for far longer than Innocent ever intended, remaining in force until July 1214.

John's eventual submission was due to a number of forces. Although, as the great William Stubbs wrote, John 'grew richer and stronger as he grew more contumacious', all was not well in England. The Welsh were not prepared to submit for long and broke into revolt in 1212, their leader negotiating a treaty with Philip Augustus. Rumours of treasonable activity reached John's ears at Nottingham in September and Roger of Wendover told of a Yorkshire hermit who prophesied that John's reign would shortly come to an end.[21] At the same time John learnt that two barons had fled, Robert fitz Walter to France and Eustace de Vesci to Scotland, and they were declared outlaws, justifiably so. Fitz Walter's conduct was undoubtedly treasonable. He tried to justify it to the sceptical king of France by claiming that John had attempted to violate his daughter. Innocent, whose knowledge and experience of the reality of English affairs were very limited, was persuaded of the sincerity of fitz Walter's pious claim that he could no longer serve an excommunicate king, and he included fitz Walter and Eustace de Vesci with the clerical exiles whom John was required to restore to favour. They were subsequently among the leaders of the northern barons who played a prominent part in the events leading to *Magna Carta*. The atmosphere was becoming increasingly tense and John was growing increasingly distrustful of all those in positions of power. In the circumstances all manner of gossip and rumour could flourish and abound, which may be why Roger of Wendover went so far as to allege that the pope had 'definitively decreed that John should be deposed and that another, more worthy than he, be chosen by the pope to succeed him'.[22] While it is true that Philip Augustus was formulating plans to invade England, Wendover's 'alleged deposition of King John' was effectively shown by C.R. Cheney to be a fiction.[23] There is no definitive proof that Innocent deposed John. Moreover, in his letters Innocent continued to address John as 'illustrious king of the English', and it was as a king that John was eventually received back into the fold. Nevertheless, feeling that his position was growing increasingly precarious, John saw the wisdom of negotiating a settlement with Innocent.

In autumn 1212 John sent an embassy to Rome to seek peace with Innocent. On 27 February 1213 the pope laid down his terms for a settlement.[24] On 15 May John capitulated and, through the papal nuncio Pandulf, offered his kingdom to Innocent as a papal fief. Not only was John fully prepared to comply with the pope's terms, he was ready to bind himself to the papacy with a plan that must have surprised many. His enemies on the Continent and in England were becoming increasingly threatening. He would resign the kingdoms of England and Ireland to Pope Innocent and receive them back as a papal fief. He would confirm the nature of his relationship in the traditional way by performing homage and fealty and making an annual payment of 700 marks for England and 300 for Ireland.

This was neither as audacious nor outrageous as later writers, who anachronistically saw it as a betrayal of English nationalistic pride, might have us believe. There were precedents for it. Sicily, Sweden, Denmark, Aragon and Poland had not been damaged by such a relationship. It is not known whether the initiative for the action came from Innocent or from John. It is assumed that it came from John, and, if so, he must have been giving thought to it for some before 13 May. But it is possible that the idea came from Innocent through the legate Pandulf. John's submission was put in writing in a charter dated 15 May 1213.[25] On 9 July Stephen Langton arrived in England to take up his position as archbishop of Canterbury.

On 20 July Langton and the returned exiles met John at Winchester cathedral. For the time being all was cordial. John received absolution from him and the excommunication was lifted. After exchanging the kiss of peace Langton led him into the cathedral to hear mass, although as the Interdict was still in force the Eucharist could not be celebrated publicly. According to Roger of Wendover, John swore to love Holy Church and its ordained members and undertook to defend them against all their enemies. He promised to renew all the good laws of his ancestors, especially those of King Edward, and annul bad ones and judge his subjects justly according to the decrees of his courts. Everything concluded with a great feast in an atmosphere of joy and festivity.[26]

The spirit of bonhomie was somewhat illusory. John did not like or trust Langton and the lack of trust was mutual. There was certainly a mean and vicious side to John's character. Powicke, quoting Gervase of Canterbury, stated that Stephen's father Henry, fearing reprisals from John, had in 1207 gone into hiding before travelling to Scotland where he found refuge in the priory of St Andrews. He stayed there until his death, being honourably treated on account of the love and esteem in which his son was held.[27] Langton was far from convinced that John would fulfil his undertakings and he took a stern line with those of John's officials who had been unmoved by the ecclesiastical censures. One suspects that Langton would much have preferred the academic life at Paris to being thrust into the world of church government and politics. Shortly after his consecration he had written to the English people, from which can be deduced his reasons for accepting the post. He felt a deep pastoral concern for the English, and having been ordered by the pope to accept the office he had no alternative but to obey him. Like Anselm a century before he had a powerful sense of obedience to duly constituted authority, Anselm's springing from his sense of obligation as a Benedictine, Langton's as a consequence of his studies and teaching. He also identified closely with Thomas Becket, acknowledging the considerable challenges that he would face. As Alexander III proved a disappointment to Becket, so did Innocent III to Langton. Langton may well have seen himself as an agent of Innocent's plan to enhance his own authority by securing the election of an archbishop of Canterbury of his choice. John, through his envoys at the Curia, found ways to foster Innocent's doubts about Langton's suitability for the metropolitan office and Langton was increasingly dismayed to find that Innocent was prepared to subordinate principle to expediency while remaining ignorant of the reality of the situation in England.

The appointment of Nicholas, cardinal bishop of Tusculum, as legate in England was an affront to Langton's authority. Although it had not been a rule, his predecessors had become accustomed to accepting the office of legate themselves, but Innocent's letters of 6 July 1213, both to John and to himself and his fellow bishops, made it quite clear that they were to see themselves as subordinate to Nicholas.[28] Any concerns that Langton may have had were confirmed by the pope's instruction to Nicholas to ensure that the vacant sees were filled with men acceptable to John. Undeterred by events, John at first aimed to continue the objectionable process of summoning electors to his chapel. When he went abroad in February 1214 he put the supervision of elections in the hands of five men: two lay curialists and three abbots, including his friend the abbot of Beaulieu. Langton was much concerned.[29] On John's return, realising the strength of mounting opposition, he may have begun to appreciate the wisdom of adopting a conciliatory approach towards Langton and the church. On 21 November John issued a charter promising freedom of ecclesiastical elections. This was sealed by the chancellor and fully attested.[30] It appeared to be a victory for Langton and his colleagues and the fulfilment of Innocent's earlier aspirations. It was another matter whether John would actually stand by it.

Langton was displeased to find that John was let off very lightly in meeting the condition for the lifting of the interdict which had required him to make restitution of and reparation for the confiscations of land and property. At the end of August two or three royal agents were sent into each diocese, and in conjunction with the ecclesiastical authorities and clerks sent by Langton, they were to summon to their presence the custodians of ecclesiastical property in an attempt to work out how much had actually been taken. By the time of Nicholas's arrival little had been achieved. To short-circuit the procedure Nicholas held a conference in London at which John agreed to pay 100,000 marks. If it was subsequently discovered that the king owed more, that could be resolved later. The bishops were unhappy with this proposal, preferring to wait and be certain of being paid what was owed in full and in one instalment. A letter from Innocent dated 23 January 1214[31] made it clear that they would have to be satisfied with the 100,000 marks, and once that had been paid the interdict could be relaxed.

For John, now planning an invasion of France, the prospect of finding that sum and using it for purposes other than military was alarming and he sought more favourable terms through an embassy sent to Rome. As a result the 100,000 marks were reduced to 40,000, including any payments already made. Once paid the interdict would be lifted. John would then pay 12,000 marks a year until the full amount had been redeemed. Even the 40,000 were soon reduced to 27,000, the remainder being postponed on the guarantee of the bishops of Winchester and Norwich. The king's official particularly associated with manipulating the arrangements in John's favour was Richard Marsh, a man hated by the clergy, seculars and regulars alike. After early experience as a chamber clerk in 1209 he was appointed senior chancery clerk. He had remained loyal to John throughout the interdict and been rewarded by him with a number of lucrative benefices and ecclesiastical offices, as well as his appointment as sheriff of Somerset and Dorset in 1212. On 29 October 1214 he was promoted to chancellor, nearly three months after the lifting of the interdict on 2 July.

John had suffered nothing from it and enjoyed considerable financial advantage, but he needed all he could raise to finance his Poitevin expedition. He was away from England from 9 February until 13 October 1214. The unfortunate outcome was a conclusive end to all his continental aspirations. John's hapless ally was his nephew Otto IV. Otto had become emperor as a consequence of the premature death of the Hohenstaufen Emperor Henry VI in 1197, which led to a disputed succession. The future Frederick II was a small boy, so a majority supported Henry's Hohenstaufen brother, the 'honourable and clerkly' Philip of Swabia. A minority backed the more disreputable Guelf, the second son of Henry the Lion, duke of Bavaria and Saxony and son-in-law of England's Henry II, whom they elected as Otto IV. When in June 1208 Philip was murdered in a private quarrel Otto's prospects became greater, and on 4 October 1209 Pope Innocent III crowned him emperor in Rome. Among Otto's supporters was his uncle King John. They were probably well matched, for Otto has been described as 'glib in tongue, lavish in promises, big in size and somewhat stupid'. Certainly he lacked any political sagacity. The catastrophic Battle of Bouvines demonstrated the ineffectiveness of the alliance. In July 1214 Philip Augustus met Otto IV, supported by John's half-brother, the earl of Salisbury, at Bouvines. John was 400 miles away. Victory, as conclusive as William's at Hastings 148 years before, went to Philip.

Magna Carta

The final period of John's life and reign was dominated by his relationship with his great subjects, civil war and *Magna Carta*. Stephen Langton was to play a prominent part in these developments. It is as well at once to dispose of grandiose and anachronistic Whiggish notions of the sanctity of *Magna Carta*. The adjective *magna* does not imply a philosophical greatness. In 1217 it was reissued with the forest clauses removed to make a separate charter of the forest, the little charter. *Magna Carta* was an attempt to put an end to the civil war which had broken out in May 1215. It failed to do so. John appealed to his feudal superior Innocent III, and on 24 August Innocent obliged by releasing him from it.[32] Civil war resumed.

The Charter was a response to the way John was governing the country and, more than that, a reaction to 60 years of Angevin government. It did not condemn in principle the constructive achievements of the Angevins, like Henry II's innovations for the practice of the law. It required John to play by the rules rather than act arbitrarily and inconsistently. It was about privileges which the Angevins had made available, particularly the legal privileges enjoyed by those who could afford them. It was about the constitution of society and the proper relationship of the government to the governed. It was about the title to property and the terms on which property was held by a vassal from a lord. It was also a reaction to the personal offences committed by John and unpopular agents acting on his behalf, his cruel and improper treatment of great men and members of their families. Chapter 39, the chapter which states that no free man shall be taken, or imprisoned, or dispossessed, or outlawed, or in any way ruined except by the lawful judgement of his peers or by the law of the land, is often regarded as perhaps the most important and enduring principle enshrined in the charter. It was not novel. As Walter Ullmann taught,[33] there was a precedent in the constitution of Conrad II issued in May 1037 which stated that no military tenant *miles* was to lose his fief 'except by the laws of our ancestors or the judgement of his equals'. Whether one can go further with Ullmann, and see *Magna Carta* as an attempt to resolve a conflict between theocratic principles of kingship espoused by John and feudal principles espoused by his vassals, is a matter of debate. What one can say, emphatically, is that it was a written affirmation of the principle that the king was under the law and, in theory, he was as answerable to it as all his free subjects. Arbitrary action by the king was outlawed; judgement must be in the courts according to the law of the land.

John faced a threatening situation on his return from Poitou. Much of the mounting hostility was due to the resentment caused by the activities of Peter des Roches. It is also likely that, like Longchamp, he was regarded by many with suspicion as a foreigner intruded into English affairs. Hostility towards John personally and to his approach to ruling England was becoming evident well before he went to Poitou. Although there was no formal attempt to depose John, there may have been less official attempts to remove him. According to Roger of Wendover,[34] in 1212 he was in Nottingham engaged in preparations to rebuff Welsh aggressions. Having arranged for 28 young Welsh hostages to be hanged, he prepared for dinner. While at table messengers from the king of Scotland and the king of Scotland's daughter rushed in with letters. These letters bore news of a conspiracy led by Robert fitz Walter and Eustace de Vesci to have John killed by his own men in battle or to hand him over to the enemy.

The nature of military service, where and for how long a tenant should serve, was a recurring source of friction between a king and his great vassals. Shortly before Hubert Walter's death John had been obliged to abort his plans to lead an expedition to the Continent. In 1213 he was determined to try again, but men in the north of England were contesting the king's claim that they should serve overseas in Poitou. They argued that they could not serve an excommunicated king, and also claimed that they had run out of money while preparing for a feared invasion and that they were exhausted by their expeditions in Wales and Ireland. The root of their objection was their claim that their obligation to serve overseas was limited to Normandy and Brittany. John found himself in the humiliating position of setting sail unsupported. In fury he returned to shore, determined in his wrath to exact an appropriate punishment on those who had failed to support him.

At this point Stephen Langton intervened. It was his first move in the national politics of the final period of John's reign and he showed himself to be just, statesmanlike and impartial. He also learned of the bitterness that can befall a man of integrity who aims to act rightly rather than serve the interests of particular groups. He ended up abandoned by the pope, reviled by the king and thanked by no one. When John gathered a band of loyal mercenaries and headed north to punish the recusants Stephen Langton urged restraint. Those who had refused to fight had raised objections on a point of law. It would be wrong of John to inflict upon them an arbitrary revenge. The validity of their case had to be tested in his court and judgement had to follow accordingly. News of John's movements reached Langton in the summer. He immediately went after the king and met him at Northampton. Shortly before Langton would have received a letter from Innocent III[35] dated 15 July. Innocent had commanded him 'as a prudent and loyal man zealously to do all that you believe helpful to the salvation and peace of the king and kingdom, not forgetting the honour and advantage of the Apostolic See and the English church'. Langton reminded John of the oath he had taken at Winchester and of his undertaking to act according to just laws. John was unmoved, so Langton followed him to Nottingham, threatening with excommunication anyone who acted violently. Reluctantly John agreed to do as Langton advised.

This should be seen in the context of two earlier meetings that Stephen Langton had held in 1213. On 4 August he held a council at St Albans. There, in the company of Peter des Roches and Geoffrey fitz Peter, it was ordained that the laws of Henry I should be observed and royal servants should desist from unlawful exactions and other unlawful practices.[36] Three weeks later, on 25 August, Langton headed an assembly at St Paul's to deal with the ending of the interdict. Roger of Wendover gave a very full account of this meeting.[37] The distinguished medievalist F.M. Powicke, lecturing in 1927, attached some credence to it.[38] He also told an interesting story from another source. Early in the council Langton preached a sermon which was heckled. He was still optimistic after the reconciliation at Winchester and took as his text 'My heart hath trusted in God, and I am helped, thereupon my flesh has rejoiced'. He was interrupted by a voice from the crowd: 'Thou liest: thy heart never trusted in God and thy flesh never rejoiced.' There is no means of knowing whether this remark should be taken seriously. It is found in only one source, the Waverly Annals. Recent research by David Carpenter has shown that certainly in the later part of his pontificate Langton did not always act as a man of complete integrity,[39] and perhaps the anonymous heckler was making that point. It may, of course, be that he had a particular grievance against the archbishop or that he harboured anti-clerical sentiments. Perhaps he found Langton difficult to understand. F.M. Powicke stated that 'in all his work there seems to have been some curious double strain in Langton. At one time he was simple and direct, at others far-fetched and allusive, running after conceits and hair splitting refinements'.[40] There have been admirable archbishops in recent times not immune from such criticism.

The inventive Wendover told of Langton's dramatic revelation of a charter that had been long forgotten.[41] In reality the coronation charter of Henry I was well known. However, Langton may have pointed out its significance to the barons 'in its formal abrogation of the bad, and establishment of good customs, and its value as indicating a sound line of policy'.[42] As Painter wrote,[43] Langton was trained to think of law, rights and privileges in general terms, and he may well

have used the occasion to explain that his ambition was to have England governed by an orderly regime based on generally accepted legal principles. He was
no more interested in redressing personal grievances or securing specific favours
for individual barons than he was in supporting the government of a king who
chose arbitrarily to disregard feudal custom and the laws of the land.

Langton's philosophy may have found expression in a document known by
the strange title *The Unknown Charter of Liberties*, so called because it remained
hidden in the French archives until 1863. It was not generally known in this
country for another 30 years. It is not properly a charter so much as a draft or
some heads of proposals.[44] Its first point is an undertaking by John not to take
men without judgement, nor accept anything for doing justice nor perform injus-
tice. There are clauses dealing with reliefs, wardships, heiresses, baronial legacies,
widowers and debts to Jews. The forests and forest offences are included. There
is also a statement that the king will no longer demand military service outside
England except in Normandy and Brittany. It probably dates from the period of
negotiations and discussions that were taking place in the autumn and winter
of 1213–14.

The legate Nicholas of Tusculum had arrived in England on 20 September
1213, and reported to Innocent that he had been very well received by the
king and the archbishop. Innocent could not possibly keep abreast of events
in England and, influenced by royal envoys, he remained convinced that the
reports of discontent that he had learned about were all related to his quarrel
with John. On 31 October he despatched three letters to Nicholas based on the
belief that the mounting disaffection in England was, in part at least, due to the
interdict and that once it was lifted peace would return. He ordered to be 'torn
to shreds or burnt to ashes' any of his previous letters that might now be used
against John. Nicholas was also required to take control of vacant sees and abbeys
and to ensure the election of men not only distinguished by their lives and learning 'but also loyal to the king'.[45] To Langton's concern and frustration it became
apparent that Nicholas, whose presence was in any case unwelcome to him, was
intent on giving wholehearted support to John and filling vacancies with men
whom he favoured. To make matters worse, early in 1214 Nicholas sent Pandulf
to Rome, where he praised John to the heights and vilified Langton. Stephen's
brother Simon, keen to stand up for Stephen in the Curia, was unable to have a
sympathetic hearing.[46] John was reaping the rewards of his submission.

From February to October 1214 John was out of the country. He returned,
humiliated by the defeat at Bouvines, to face mounting opposition. A particular source of grievance was the demand made in the previous May from Poitou
that those who had not joined him should pay a scutage instead. This demand
was not at all well received, and Essex, Hertfordshire, Lancashire and Yorkshire
contributed nothing. Well aware of this, the king seems to have granted concessions here and there and a key part of his policy was his attempt to detach
the bishops from the discontented barons.[47] It seems, however, that the sort of
concession that he was prepared to make either to individuals or to the bishops

generally was designed not to hit himself too hard financially. He did pay the 6000 marks' compensation due on All Saints' Day, but promises of further payments in six-monthly instalments seem to have come to little. He sought to mollify a number of individual bishops by making them specific grants. He issued a charter confirming that the see of Rochester should come under the patronage of the archbishopric of Canterbury, but this hardly established anything new. The bishopric of Ely was granted the patronage of Thorney Abbey and release from a long-standing debt of £100. The bishopric of Lincoln was awarded a number of manors and tenurial rights, and the bishopric of London was granted the manor of Stoke by Guildford. John also undertook to restore the bishop of London's castle at Stortford. The bishop of Worcester was granted an annual fair at Stratford and the rights of the bishop of Bath in Glastonbury were confirmed. These grants were intended to compensate the bishops for the losses they had incurred during the interdict without actually hurting John. On 21 November John issued the charter limiting his influence in episcopal and abbatial elections to the grant of the right to elect and the right to give his assent to the elected candidate. In reality it did little to prevent John and his successors securing the man they wanted, sometimes with papal acquiescence.

The first part of 1215 was a period of meetings and negotiations. Towards the end of the previous year Innocent summoned Nicholas back to Rome, somewhat to the legate's surprise. According to the source attributed to Walter of Coventry,[48] before he departed he mediated between John and those northern barons who had refused to pay the scutage. The barons asked John to confirm Henry I's coronation charter, and in response John proposed a meeting in London at Epiphany 1215, when he would give them an answer. A copy of the elections charter dated 15 January 1215 was sent to Innocent for confirmation. Lest there should be any doubt about it he included the charter in full in his grandiloquent and fulsome response dated 30 March.[49] It was addressed to all the prelates of churches in England. By the time that it actually arrived the prospects of a peaceful settlement between John and his opponents must have seemed remote. Epiphany duly came. The northerners, other magnates and the bishops met in London 'to petition the king about their grievances'. The barons had come armed 'in gay military array'.[50] Among them was a significant northern group including Robert fitz Walter and Eustace de Vesci. John was far from pleased at their demand that he should confirm their ancient liberties with references to King Edward and Henry I's coronation charter. He was also reminded of the promises he had made at Winchester in July 1213. Rather than give an immediate answer he proposed to hold a great council at Northampton on 26 April, the Sunday after Easter, and guaranteed safe conduct to and from the assembly for his opponents.

John used the ensuing three and a half months in several ways. He made concessions to individuals in an attempt to draw them away from the main body of his opponents. At the same time he prepared for war by calling up troops from abroad, stocking his castles with food and ammunitions and building new siege engines, while continuing negotiation. He had meetings with Stephen Langton, some of his suffragans and William Marshal, who acted as mediators in discussions with the northerners. On 19 February the northerners were granted letters of safe conduct to meet the Earl Marshal with the archbishop and his fellow bishops at Oxford on 22nd, and another meeting was held on 14 April, again at Oxford. John also sent envoys to Innocent III, as did his opponents, to apprise him of developments. Then on 4 March he took a step that was as cynical in its hypocrisy as it was politically clever: he took the cross as a Crusader. He and his possessions were now under the special protection of the church. Any who dared oppose him risked ecclesiastical censure.

The effectiveness of this step soon became apparent. The king and his opponents each wished to keep Innocent informed of English affairs, and naturally presented highly subjective accounts to a pope who had little grasp of the reality of the situation. Not surprisingly, Innocent was impressed by the royal line that the barons had risen against John because of his submission to him. This argument appealed to Innocent, who had difficulty understanding how the men who had supported the king when he was oppressing the church could turn against him now that he had renounced his ungodliness.

The two English parties were subsequently joined in Rome by representatives of Stephen Langton. They had arrived ostensibly to seek confirmation of the free elections charter, but they also knew that Langton believed that there was some merit in the baronial case. They were mindful of the oath which John had reportedly taken at Winchester on the occasion of his reconciliation with the church and Stephen Langton. In receiving this oath the archbishop was obliged to intervene if he believed that John was acting in such a way as to break it. Unhappily for Langton, the reception of his envoys at the Curia was lukewarm. He seems to have been the victim of a campaign of vilification in Rome led by Nicholas of Tusculum while Innocent was in no position to check the veracity of allegations made against him. To add to the general hostility shown towards him, another figure, Alexander, abbot elect of St Augustine's Canterbury, arrived in Rome. He was not actually involved in the political disputes, but abbots of St Augustine's had long been unfavourably disposed to the archbishop of Canterbury. He came seeking papal blessing and confirmation of his claim not to be bound by obedience to the archbishop. Stephen's only positive friend was another English cardinal and Parisian master, Robert Courzon, who played so significant a part in drafting the first statutes of the university of Paris, but he, too, was apparently out of favour. The fundamental problem that Langton faced was that once John had become a papal vassal Innocent expected him to support papal policy unequivocally and this entailed giving unreserved support to John.

Innocent's attitude is apparent from separate letters dated 19 March 1215, one to the magnates and barons of England and one to Stephen Langton. In his letter to the barons he stated categorically that he condemned the formation of leagues and conspiracies against the king and he deplored the use of arms. He feared that their attitude would thwart John's plan to go on Crusade. He therefore declared as null and void all leagues and conspiracies; anyone who presumed to hatch such plots in future was threatened with excommunication. They must demonstrate their loyalty to the king by rendering him the customary services which they and their predecessors had paid to him and his predecessors and any future demands that they might make of him were to be respectful.[51] Langton could only have been profoundly disappointed by the letter sent to him. Innocent expressed his surprise and annoyance that Stephen had ignored the differences between John and some of the barons 'when peace to the honour of God and the Church has been happily restored between you and our well-beloved son in Christ, John illustrious king of England'. The unfortunate archbishop was accused of wilfully shutting his eyes and making no effort to achieve a settlement, and worse, Innocent gave credence to those rumours which had reached his ears that Stephen was giving help and favour to John's opponents. He therefore commanded Langton to do all he could to restore agreement between the two parties, and he was to excommunicate those guilty of hatching plots in the future.[52] These letters were delivered to their recipients by the king's envoys, and so satisfactory were they from his point of view that he had them copied on to the back of the patent roll. The letter that Innocent sent John at the same time does not survive, presumably because he saw no need to preserve it. It was probably these three letters that papal commissioners had in mind when, a few months later, they spoke of *triplex forma pacis* (threefold peace terms) 'which were thoroughly honourable and reasonable and worthy of acceptance by God-fearing men'.

Innocent could not understand that the archbishop's apparent sympathy with the king's baronial opponents did not mean either that he had allied wholeheartedly with them or that he had turned against John. Certainly Langton was rightly prepared to criticise the king and it was becoming increasingly apparent that John was not a man of good will. Above all Langton sought a solution to the current problems that was just and lawful and in accord with the customs of the realm. He considered himself obliged to be fully involved, as a disinterested party, in the political developments in England. Unfortunately Eustace, the bishop of Ely, with whom Langton could work well, died on 3 February, but he was happy in his positive relationship with the earl of Pembroke, William Marshal.

As Easter approached and went it became clear that John had no intention of fulfilling his undertakings to meet his opponents. A peaceful solution was not in sight; the barons were fortifying their castles and preparing for war. By early May the prospects of a settlement were as remote as ever, with neither side prepared to yield anything significant. John saw no reason why he should. He was king and lord of the hostile barons from whom fealty was due, he himself was a papal vassal and England was part of the patrimony of St Peter and the Roman church. As a crusader he was free from attack. His offer to abolish such evil customs as had arisen in his reign and that of his brother and to submit the customs which had arisen in his father's time to the advice of his faithful men was rejected. John then called upon Langton to excommunicate his opponents for disturbing the peace. Langton refused. On 5 May John was approached at

Reading by an Austin canon with the news that the hostile barons had formally renounced their allegiance to him, an act of *diffidatio* defiance. Moreover the rebels had appointed Robert fitz Walter as their commander-in-chief with the title 'Marshal of the army of God'. A false crusader was now faced with a baronial militant, some might say 'disreputable thug', bearing a self-styled title reeking with sanctimonious piety.

To break faith was legitimate if those who did so could demonstrate that the actions of their lord had been such that they no longer owed allegiance to him. In reality it was a declaration of war and the rebels began to lay siege to Northampton castle. Nevertheless John did not act immediately with violence. He may not have had as many on his side as did his opponents, but among their number were men of distinction and integrity like William Marshal and the earl of Chester. Not all his supporters were royal favourites; even some who had grievances put loyalty to their king and lord above personal feelings. There was also a significant number, perhaps more than a hundred barons, committed to neither side. Among them were Stephen Langton and his fellow bishops. Several sees were vacant at the time and only one bishop, Giles of Briouse, put family before loyalty to the king. His brother, sister-in-law and nephew had all been treated appallingly by John; Matilda and her son William were starved to death in a royal castle on John's orders.[53] Not surprisingly he allied himself with the rebels. Rather than plunge straight into conflict, John sought to ensure that the moderates remained on his side. In the second week of May he made conciliatory gestures. He offered to seek papal arbitration and undertook to repudiate arbitrary action. Anticipating chapter 39 of *Magna Carta*, he promised to his baronial opponents that he would not 'take them or their men, nor disseise them, nor go upon them by force of arms, *except by the law of our realm or by the judgement of their peers in our court*'. To show that he meant it he offered to have reviewed in court by their peers the fine imposed on the earl of Essex, Geoffrey de Mandeville, for his marriage to John's first wife Isabella of Gloucester, and the relief exacted from Bishop Giles for his inheritances. He also granted a charter to the citizens of London giving them the right to hold an annual mayoral election. Nevertheless he took the precaution of simultaneously strengthening the city's fortifications and manning his castles nationwide.

Such precautions were needed. On 17 May the rebels took London. Ten days later John asked Langton to negotiate a truce. According to Roger of Wendover, routine government was becoming paralysed by events, and 'the pleas of the exchequer and of the sheriff's courts ceased throughout England'.[54] Before John met the rebels at Runnymede on 15 June he had met some of their leaders at Staines and committed himself to a draft schedule known as *The Articles of the Barons*. This is something of a hodgepodge of detailed clauses, draft headings and notes. John pledged his faith by allowing the Great Seal to be attached to it. Five days later John's baronial opponents moved to Runnymede where they met the king and joined in a formal ceremony of acceptance. Although *Magna Carta* concludes with the words 'Given in the meadow that is called Runnymede between

Windsor and Staines, on the fifteenth day of June', historians have not been unanimous in agreeing that that was the actual day on which it was sealed.[55] No one arrived at Runnymede with copies of the charter already drawn up and ready for sealing. Following discussion and verbal agreements, the chancery clerks had to get down to the business of working out the precise legal form of words and putting them in writing. A number of copies had to be made, of which four survive. On 19 June, before the final copies were sealed and distributed, the rebels renewed their oaths of allegiance to John. John issued letters patent formally notifying his officers that peace had been made 'between us, our barons, and the freemen of the realm' and directing them to enforce the provisions of the charter, which was to be read publicly in every shire court.

Magna Carta was attested by Archbishop Stephen, Archbishop Henry of Dublin, bishops William of London, Peter of Winchester, Jocelin of Bath and Glastonbury, Hugh of Lincoln, Walter of Worcester, William of Coventry and Benedict of Rochester. The suffragan bishops had all at various times been royal servants in the chamber, chancery, Exchequer or as justices. Bishop Giles of Hereford was with the rebels; Simon of Exeter and Herbert of Salisbury were not present, nor were any Welsh bishops. The remaining sees were vacant. Pandulf and the Master of the Temple also attested. The preamble to the charter states that it was drawn up 'for the honour of God and the exaltation of Holy Church', but that was a formality. The first chapter grants that 'the English church shall be free, and shall have its rights undiminished and its liberties unimpaired'. It is in effect a confirmation of the charter of November 1214 granting freedom of elections. There are no other grants to the church, but chapter 22 protected clergy from being the victims of disproportionate amercements and chapter 27 stated that in the event of a free man dying intestate his chattels should be distributed to his nearest and dearest under the supervision of the church. Stephen Langton is named in chapter 55 as having a role, 'if he can be present', in helping to deal with unjust fines and amercements.

It is hardly possible to state with any confidence the precise part that Langton and his fellow bishops actually did play in the formulation of *Magna Carta*, for the evidence does not exist. However it can be stated with some confidence that Langton was the force behind the first chapter.[56] Roger of Wendover gave Langton an heroic role as leader of the baronial movement against a tyrant king, but no reputable historian would today take Wendover at his face value. Nevertheless some statements about the part Langton played after he came to England in July 1213 can be made with confidence. When he received John back into the church at Winchester the king assured him of his intention to reform and observe just laws. Then it is almost certain that he curbed John's impetuosity in autumn that year. It is beyond doubt that in the period from that autumn to June 1215 he was the chief mediator between John and his opponents and he continued to play a significant part in events until he left England for Rome. Innocent III certainly expected him to play a leading part in negotiations, even if he did not do so in the way that the pope intended.

As Painter wrote,[57] *Magna Carta* is a document 'carefully worked over by highly intelligent men with a thorough knowledge of the English government'. It is not a piece of special pleading on behalf of a selfish and violent baronage. It is an attempt to put in writing general principles rather than an expression of a series of personal grievances. Among the barons were intelligent men of principle. They were not formally educated and they were not accustomed to think in abstract sophistications or the language of lawyers, but they had a clear concept of what was just royal behaviour, the correct practice of relationships and the idea of the realm as a community. They were well able to grasp that peace and order in the land depended on a grant not just to the tenants-in-chief but to all the freemen of the community of the realm. Chapter 20 even gave the villeins a look-in although, as Carpenter has pointed out, this was not as favourable towards the villeins as it appears at first reading.[58] Such men could work harmoniously with Langton. They respected his office, for they were well aware that no community could function without due respect being given to those who properly held positions of authority, but they could also respect Langton as the holder of the office on account of his personal integrity. This personal integrity was enhanced by an intellectual integrity, the product of his university education and teaching. Langton, with the support perhaps of some of the other bishops, and a group of barons led by William Marshal, could work together. The chancery clerks could work on *The Articles of the Barons* to produce the final version for their approval.

The essence of *Magna Carta* was that the king was under the law. The problem facing everyone, whether royalists, moderates or affirmed enemies, was how to keep the king under the law. The essential weakness of *Magna Carta* lay in its attempt to resolve this problem. It was faced in *The Articles of the Barons*. There, in addition to a committee of lay enforcers, it was proposed that the archbishops, bishops and the papal nuncio Pandulf would undertake to ensure that John would not look to Innocent to release him from whatever he had ostensibly agreed to. The 'sanctions' clause of *Magna Carta*, chapter 61, did not include any of the clergy. The charter was to be enforced by 25 barons who are not mentioned by name and who were probably hostile to the king. In the event of any breach of the Charter coming to the attention of four of the 25, those 4 were to approach the king or, in his absence, the chief justiciar, and seek immediate redress. If nothing was done within 40 days the four barons should refer the problem to the other 21, and they, 'with the commune of the whole land' (*cum communa tocius terrae*), should put every possible pressure on the king short of harming his person or the persons of his queen and children until amends had been made. The clergy were given no part to play in the charter's enforcement. All that is said regarding them occurs in the penultimate chapter. Here John undertakes to proclaim an amnesty for all breaches of the peace since Easter 1215, and to remit all ill will and rancour incurred since the beginning of his quarrel with the barons. The chapter continues: 'We have caused letters patent of the Lord Stephen, Archbishop of Canterbury, the Lord

Henry, Archbishop of Dublin, the aforesaid bishops [i.e. those who are listed in the preamble] and Master Pandulf to be made for them [the barons] on this security and the aforesaid concessions.' Essentially the clergy are limited, in Cheney's words, to 'preventing an untrustworthy king from tampering with the text of his charter'.

Those who hoped that the charter might bring peace to England were soon disappointed. In response to the inevitable appeal from John, the pope sent his envoys back to England with an open letter dated 24 August addressed to 'all the faithful in Christ who will see this document'. Innocent had absorbed all the propaganda that had been fed to him.[59] In reality neither John nor the leaders of the baronial opposition really wanted peace. Before this denunciation of the charter reached England two developments had materialised. The country had drifted back into civil war and Stephen Langton had been suspended. Despite the fact that the papal commissioners knew the truth of the situation in England far better than the pope could ever hope to, and despite the fact that Peter des Roches was one of Langton's suffragans, and that he and Pandulf had allowed their names to appear in the preamble to *Magna Carta*, they acted on the papal mandate of 7 July.[60] Putting self-serving loyalty to the king before principled loyalty to his archbishop and ignoring the manifest ambiguities in Innocent's mandate, des Roches suspended Langton. Just as Archbishop Laud discovered four and a half centuries later, John was as impossible to work with as Charles I proved to be. At least Langton kept his head, but he must have been thoroughly dispirited and disillusioned. One of his few supporters was Gerald of Wales, who himself had had his share of humiliating experiences. So distressed was Langton that he considered abandoning public life altogether and joining a Carthusian monastery. At the end of September he left England to attend the Lateran Council and hoped to plead his case with Innocent himself. If he looked for understanding from the pope he must have been profoundly disappointed. Far from listening sympathetically, and despite some pressure from the cardinals, who were more favourably disposed to the archbishop, Innocent confirmed the sentence of suspension on 4 November. He later relaxed it but on the understanding that Langton should not return to England. John's relationship with his archbishop of Canterbury was at an end.

Had it ended there, Stephen Langton's career as archbishop of Canterbury might be judged something of a tragic disaster. Civil war continued in England, and the following year Louis of France invaded. John died in October 1216. But two years later Innocent's successor Honorius III allowed Langton to return to England as its archbishop of Canterbury. In the final period of his life, working with Hubert de Burgh and remarkably, in view of his earlier experiences, with Peter des Roches, he played a significant part in ensuring that the minority of Henry III and his transition to king in his own right went smoothly. That is another story, but ultimately the judgement of history must be that Stephen Langton was not a failure but one of the great churchmen of the Middle Ages.

Epilogue

The relationship of the kings of England with their bishops was influenced by the fact that from the Norman Conquest to the early years of King John's reign they were also lords of considerable territories in France and, theoretically at least, subjects of the French kings for their French lands. Consequently, with the exception of William II before his brother mortgaged Normandy to him, and Stephen, kings of England spent a considerable part of their reigns governing and defending their continental territories. Richard I's absence from England for all but six months of a ten-year reign was exceptional, but nevertheless he maintained a considerable interest in English affairs. Likewise many members of the aristocracy held territories in France and England, and of few bishops could it be said 'he is an Englishman'. As late as 1205 foreigners filled the majority of English sees; eight were held by Frenchmen, Bernard of Ragusa, the unconsecrated bishop of Carlisle, was an Italian, and there were only four English bishops, including the Anglo-Norman Giles of Briouse. Nevertheless, by the end of the twelfth century the concept of Englishness was developing and bishops like William Longchamp and Peter des Roches were seen as aliens in English politics. The northern borders of England were not precisely defined and fluctuated depending on the relative strengths and weaknesses of the kings of England and Scotland. Nor were English politics, secular and ecclesiastical, uninfluenced by events in Wales and Ireland.

Cosmopolitanism rather than insularity was reinforced by the development of the centres of European learning. Men were drawn to the emerging universities according to their pre-eminence as centres of study for particular disciplines. Bologna became pre-eminent for legal studies, Montpellier for medicine, and Paris was renowned for theology. There students of different nationalities mingled and were taught by masters, some of whom might be from their own country and others who were foreigners. All were united by the desire for study, either for its own sake or as a means of professional advancement, and the common language of scholarship, Latin, was also the common language of the western Church.

In the course of the twelfth century increasing numbers of English bishops had a master's degree from Paris. This degree was the essential teaching qualification. Able student that he was, Becket was well aware that he had not taken a master's. Stephen Langton had been a Paris master, and among his contemporaries as a student had been Lothar of Segni, the future Pope Innocent III. Innocent was the first pope to impose on England an archbishop of Canterbury of his choice. That was not on his initiative but in response to the fact that John, suffragan bishops and the monks of Christ Church were in conflict. Previously Eugenius III had significantly influenced the Angevin succession, but he too had been drawn into English affairs by Stephen. At no time did kings of England claim that England was anything but part of Christendom under papal authority. No king in this period remotely contemplated anything like a Henrician breach with Rome, and John went so far as to formally accept Innocent as his overlord.

As papal government and canon law became more sophisticated, papal authority was extended throughout Western Christendom through legates and judge delegates, while appeals to Rome greatly increased. William I had established barriers against papal influence in England but they had never been impenetrable, and it should be remembered that there had been papal incursions in English affairs well before the Conquest. Metropolitan archbishops were required to receive their symbol of office, the pallium, from the pope, and popes expected to authorise the translation of a bishop from one see to another. English kings were not completely successful in forbidding legates to enter the country, appeals continued to go to Rome and English bishops and abbots attended church councils. Moreover English clergy and laymen could be subject to ecclesiastical sanctions imposed by papal authority. In practice the papacy was weakened in the twelfth century by the fact that several popes died soon after their election, and for long periods the pope was faced by a rival anti-pope supported by the emperor. The papacy was drawn into the complexities of European secular politics and at times kept out of Rome. Kings of England could attempt to exploit the situation to their advantage. The decline in Hohenstaufen power after the premature death of the Emperor Henry VI helped ease the papacy's entanglement in European politics.

Although the kings of England spent long periods of their reigns out of the country, government did not break down in their absence. In the course of the twelfth century, building on Anglo-Saxon foundations, England created a sophisticated system of governmental institutions and legal administration. This century saw the development of bureaucratic government and the creation of a 'common law'. The practical part played by highly intelligent laymen in these developments must not be underestimated, but fundamental to it all was the work of clerics, some of whom, like Ranulf Flambard, Roger of Salisbury and Hubert Walter, were creative geniuses. The ablest and most ambitious of these clerical administrators, whether working for episcopal households, cathedrals or the king, could expect to be rewarded with high office such as archdeacon or promotion to a bishopric. Of the 133 bishops appointed between 1070 and 1216 it is known that 42 had been ecclesiastical clerks and 62 royal clerks .[1] The remainder were distinguished monks. The fact that a bishop might have considerable secular responsibilities did not necessarily make him a poor bishop, neglectful of his responsibilities to his flock.

A fundamental issue in medieval Christendom was that of who had the last word. Were anointed kings ultimately superior to consecrated bishops, or were bishops, charged as they were with the care of kings' souls, the spiritual lords of kings? From the fourth century onwards Christian intellectuals faced this problem. St Augustine wrote of two cities, a City of God and a City of the World.

He acknowledged that the tendency of the human race to sin led to a need for civil governments with coercive powers, but the loyalty of a true Christian was not ultimately to such an authority. At the end of the fifth century Pope Gelasius introduced the doctrine of the two swords derived from Luke's words: 'Lord, behold there are two swords.' He was pope from 492 to 496, and although he stated that he loved, respected and honoured the Roman emperor, by then ruling from Constantinople, he had no intention of being subservient to him. He declared that there were two authorities by which the world is ruled, the sacred authority of the priesthood and the royal power. The responsibility of priests was weightier in that they answer for kings at the day of judgement.[2] Three and a half centuries later Hincmar, archbishop of Rheims, took the line derived from Gelasius and proclaimed in those celebrated forgeries *The Donation of Constantine* and the *Pseudo-Isidorian Decretals* that the church, led by the bishops, had the right and duty to censure lay moral conduct. All power, secular and spiritual, was granted by God to the pope, who delegated secular power to the emperor. If he misused that power he could be deposed.

This view was proclaimed with great vigour by the Gregorian reformers, who unequivocally asserted the superiority of all priests to laymen. They were challenged by an unnamed writer once called 'The Anonymous of York' and now known as 'The Norman Anonymous'. His line was that the priestly authority and the royal authority together have ultimate responsibility for sacred government, and it was wrong to claim that the priesthood has the care of souls and the king bodies, for bodies and souls are indivisible. A king is no ordinary layman, for he is the anointed of the Lord, the supreme ruler and shepherd. The fact that a king is consecrated by a bishop does not make a bishop superior, for he is not the author of the consecration but the minister.[3]

These were excellent debating points in the propaganda war associated with the papal reform movement, but tension between *regnum* and *sacerdotium* should not be exaggerated. As Lanfranc had pointed out to Bishop Odo and Bishop William of Durham, they functioned in two capacities. They were spiritual lords with considerable pastoral, moral and spiritual responsibilities for those in their care, and they also had the responsibility of maintaining the integrity of their episcopal estates, but, as a very spiritual bishop like Anselm was well aware, their lives were lived in this world, and to ensure that the world of which they were part functioned reasonably effectively they had to accept the conventions and practices of their time. As great tenants of the king they had the worldly responsibilities of any secular lord, political, financial and military. Kings, for their part, had a spiritual dimension conferred on them by their anointing. Although this did not make them priests – ordination actually disqualified a man from becoming a king – they enjoyed a sacred quality which set them apart from other laymen and which their bishops recognised.

In reality the king had the last word and he made sure that when a see became vacant he secured the appointment of the man he wanted. True, he had to be politic, particularly when national and international circumstances made it necessary; he could leave sees vacant when it suited him but not for ever, and he could be flexible over particular appointments. He might be threatened with excommunication and in the face of it might capitulate in the interests of political expediency. But no king was exiled, deposed or murdered by a bishop. In fact, despite tensions and occasional quarrels, kings and bishops were mutually dependent. Mediation and compromise were accepted in this period as ways of resolving disputes, and a settlement from which all parties concerned might gain something was considered preferable to an absolute victory for one party which would leave the other humiliated.[4] A wise and politic bishop could challenge a king without causing him to lose face or feel his royal dignity was threatened. Some, like Lanfranc or Thurstan, could use humour to relax a tense situation.

In a Christian society kings and bishops were mutually dependent. Although there were examples of serious conflict, made the more notorious by their rarity and the fluent pens of episcopal champions, kings and bishops could work constructively together in forming medieval England. In practice Anselm saw himself as a feeble old sheep yoked to an untamed bull, but his ideal was expressed in his words to the bishops and nobles at the time that the episcopal office was forced upon him: 'You must think of the church as a plough … drawn by two oxen outstanding above the rest, the King and the Archbishop of Canterbury. These two drawing the plough, rule the land, one by human justice and sovereignty, the other by divine doctrine and authority.'[5] 'No bishop, no King', declared James I to a delegation of Presbyterians in the early seventeenth century. Five centuries before that it was clear that while every bishop needed his king, owed his office and much that went with it to him and relied on him to maintain law and order, no king could do without his bishops.

Notes

Introduction

1. *HM-H* 184–5.
2. J. Blair, *Minsters and Parish Churches: The Local Church in Transition 950–1200* (Oxford University Committee for Archaeology Monograph no. 17, 1988).
3. Barlow, *Edward the Confessor*, 66–77.
4. *RW* 153–9.
5. Knowles, *The Monastic Order in England* (Cambridge University Press, 1963); Burton, *Monastic and Religious Orders in Britain 1000–1300* (Cambridge University Press, 1994).
6. C.H. Lawrence, *Medieval Monasticism* (Longman, 2001), 68, 80.
7. Southern, *The Making of the Middle Ages*, 122–4.
8. Douglas, *William the Conqueror* (Eyre and Spottiswoode, 1964), 341–2.
9. G. Tellenbach, trans. R.F. Bennett, *Church, State and Christian Society at the Time of the Investiture Contest* (Blackwell, 1959); Ullmann, *A Short History of the Papacy*; Barraclough, *The Medieval Papacy*; Morris, *The Papal Monarchy*.
10. Tierney, *The Crisis of Church and State*, 49–50.
11. *SLI* 107–9.
12. Brundage, *Medieval Canon Law, passim*.
13. Robinson, *The Papacy 1073–1198*, 312–18.
14. King, *King Stephen* (Yale University Press, 2012), 43–9.
15. *RW* 79–81.
16. John Gillingham, *Richard I* (Yale University Press, 1999), 107.
17. *HH* 48.
18. For a detailed description of Westminster Hall and its purpose see Mason, *William II, Rufus the Red King* (Tempus, 2005), 186–90.
19. See below, Ch. 4 and Truax, *Archbishops Ralph d'Escures, William of Corbeil and Theobald of Bec – Heirs of Anselm and Ancestors of Becket* (Ashgate, 2012), 62–3.
20. *WMVW* 51.
21. *HM-H* 67.
22. Mason, *William II*, 207.
23. *ASC* 1137.
24. *HM-H* 120–1; see also *HC* 51.
25. Bartlett, *England under the Norman and Angevin Kings*, 395–408.

26. Green, *Henry I: King of England and Duke of Normandy* (Cambridge University Press, 2006), 264; *WMGP* 196.
27. M. Brett, *The English Church under Henry I* (Oxford University Press, 1975), 110–11.
28. Barlow, *William Rufus* (Methuen, 1983), 348–51.
29. *HH* 70–2.
30. Truax, *Archbishops*, 6.
31. Brett, *The English Church under Henry I*, 116–17.
32. Crosby, *Bishop and Chapter in Twelfth-Century England*.
33. Truax, *Archbishops*, 66–9.
34. *HH* 98.
35. Southern, *The Making of the Middle Ages*, Ch. 4, 187–8 (1993 edn).
36. Green, *Henry I*, 265.

1   The Norman Conquest and the Church in England

1. Bates, *William the Conqueror*, 57.
2. Douglas, *William the Conqueror*, 121.
3. *WMGP* 168–9.
4. Ibid., 26.
5. F.M. Stenton, *Anglo-Saxon England*, 652 n.6.
6. *WMGP* 122.
7. Ibid., 203–4.
8. Ibid., 184.
9. Ibid., 95.
10. Ibid., 95.
11. Ibid., 98.
12. *The Letters of Lanfranc* no. 40; *EHD* ii 683–9; Cowdrey, *Lanfranc*, 142–3.
13. *WMGP* 209–10.
14. Ibid., 172–3.
15. Ibid., 172–3.
16. See the story of lambskins and catskins in *WMVW* 68–9 and *WMGP* 190.
17. *EHD* ii 449–51.
18. Members of the Anglo-Saxon lesser aristocracy below the great lords and above free men.
19. *WMVW* bk 3 ch. 6.
20. *EHD* ii 897.
21. *EHD* ii docs 93, 94, 96–102.
22. *EHNA* 9–10.
23. Bates, *William the Conqueror*, 44.
24. *EHD* ii 631–5, *The Acts of Lanfranc*.
25. Gibson, *Lanfranc of Bec*, 174–5; Cowdrey, *Lanfranc*, 151–5.

26. *EHD* ii 628.
27. Quoted Cowdrey, *Lanfranc*, 185.
28. *HM-H* 37, 119; Knowles, *The Evolution of Medieval Thought* (Longman, 1962), ch. 8.
29. *EHNA* 12, 24–5; *WMGR* bk 3 para. 269.
30. *WMGR* bk 4 para. 305.
31. *ASC* D&E for 1075.
32. For this episode see Cowdrey, *Lanfranc*, 189–92; *The Letters of Lanfranc* nos 31–5. Although historians often refer to 'Florence' of Worcester it is now generally accepted that the chronicle attributed to him was actually written by another monk of Worcester, John. See *OV* ii 186–9).
33. Gibson, *Lanfranc of Bec*, 141.
34. *EHD* ii 631–5.
35. *WMVW* 81.
36. *WMGP* 88.
37. Loyn, *The English Church*, 78.
38. *WMGP* 89.
39. See the valuable short survey of the career of Remigius written by David Bates, published by Lincoln Cathedral.
40. *HH* 34.
41. Ibid., 99.
42. *WMGP* 211.
43. *EHNA* 11.
44. *HH* 33–4.
45. Ibid., 99–100.
46. *WMGP* 211–12.
47. Loyn, *The English Church*, 67.
48. *WMVW* 29, 36–9.
49. *WMGP* 190–1.
50. *EHNA* 26; *WMGP* 49.
51. *WMGR* bk 4 para. 306, p. 272.
52. Barlow, *William Rufus*, 70–82.
53. *ASC* for 1088, p. 223 and *HH* based on it, 35, 129.
54. *WMGP* 49.

2 The Sons of the Conqueror and their Bishops

1. Barlow, *The Feudal Kingdom of England 1042–1216* (Longman, 1955), 170.
2. Barlow, *William Rufus*, 433–4.
3. *EHNA*.
4. *HH* 49.
5. Mason, *William II*, 139.

6. *HH* 104.

7. Brett, *The English Church under Henry I*, 110–11.

8. When his 17-year-old son William, along with many of his friends and relatives, was drowned off the coast of Normandy after the ship, travelling at excessive speed, hit a rock (*WMGR* bk 5 para. 419).

9. Quoted in Hollister, *Henry I*, 214–16; but see Southern, 'King Henry', in *Medieval Humanism*.

10. *WMGR* bk 5 para. 412; *EHD* ii 294–6.

11. *EHNA* 48–50.

12. Ibid., 149–52.

13. *EHD* ii 400.

14. *WMGR* bk 5 para. 413.

15. *OV* ii 260–3.

16. *EHNA* 31.

17. Ibid., 33–43.

18. Vaughn, *Anselm of Bec*.

19. *EHNA* 44.

20. Ibid., 53.

21. Vaughn, *Anselm of Bec*; Mason, *William II*.

22. *EHNA* 55 et seq.

23. *WMGP* 58–60.

24. *EHD* ii 609–24.

25. Southern, *St Anselm: A Portrait*, 269.

26. *WMGP* 60.

27. *EHNA* 72–7.

28. Southern, *St Anselm: A Portrait*, 270.

29. *WMGP* 61.

30. *EHNA* 84.

31. Ibid., 89.

32. Ibid., 90–1.

33. Mason, *William II*, 175.

34. *EHNA* 42.

35. Ibid., 108–11.

36. Ibid., 116–19.

37. Barlow, *William Rufus*, 193 et seq.; Hollister, *Henry I*, 307.

38. *WMGR* 344 para. 393.

39. *HH* 38.

40. Southern, 'Ranulf Flambard', in *Medieval Humanism*, 184–5.

41. Fyrd service was the obligation of all free men in Anglo-Saxon times to defend their country at their own expense.

42. *ASC* 1094.

43. *WMGP* 184.

44. *OV* v 312–13; Hollister, *Henry I*, 133–4.

45. Southern, *Medieval Humanism*, 205.

46. For Paschal II and the investiture issue see *EHNA* 124–49; *WMGP* 70–1; Vaughn, *Anselm of Bec*, ch. 6 *passim*, 230ff.
47. *EHNA* 146.
48. Ibid., 149–52.
49. *WMGP* 77–9.
50. *EHNA* 166–7.
51. A.L .Poole, *From Domesday Book to Magna Carta* (Oxford University Press, 1955), 178.
52. See *HM-H* 51–4; *HC* 13–14.

3 The Struggle for the Primacy

1. Hollister, *Henry I*, 280–1; Brett, *The English Church under Henry I*, 69–70; Green, *Henry I*, 168–9. Truax, *Archbishops*, 216–19.
2. Ibid., 62–3.
3. Bede, *The Ecclesiastical History of the English People* (Oxford World Classics edn), 55–6.
4. *WMGP* 32–41.
5. Southern, *St Anselm: A Portrait*, ch. 14, 352–62.
6. Southern, *Western Society and the Church in the Middle Ages* (Penguin, 1990), 91–3.
7. *HC* 3.
8. Nicholl, *Thurstan*, 7.
9. *WMGP* 172–3.
10. *EHD* ii 633–4.
11. Southern, *St Anselm: A Portrait*, 344–5.
12. See also Hollister, *Henry I*, 123.
13. *EHNA* 218.
14. Hollister, *Henry I*, 148; Vaughn, *Anselm of Bec*, 236.
15. *EHNA* 43.
16. *HC* 8.
17. Southern, *St Anselm: A Portrait*, 342.
18. HC 13.
19. *EHNA* 149.
20. *EHNA* 215–16; Southern, *St Anselm: A Portrait*, 343.
21. *WMGP* 174–5.
22. Ibid., 196.
23. Quoted Southern, *St Anselm: A Portrait*, 345.
24. Nicholl, *Thurstan*, passim.
25. *WMGP* 74.
26. *EHNA* 217.
27. *HC* 15.

28. *WMGP* 175–6; *EHNA* 218–26; Vaughn, *Anselm of Bec*, 336–51.
29. *WMGP* 84.
30. Green, *Henry I*, 135.
31. *WMGP* 86.
32. Green, *Henry I*, 135.
33. *HC* 43.
34. *WMGP* 84.
35. Ibid., 85.
36. Nicholl, *Thurstan*.
37. *WMGP* 177.
38. Nicholl, *Thurstan*, 72.
39. *ASC* 1123; Kealey, *Roger of Salisbury – Viceroy of England* (University of California Press, 1972), 130–3.
40. *WMGP* 95.
41. *ASC* 1123.
42. *HC* 114–15.
43. *ASC* 1124.
44. *HH* 58.
45. *ASC* 1125.
46. *HC* 127; *HH* 104.
47. Robert Bartlett, *England under the Norman and Angevin Kings 1075–1225* (Oxford University Press, 2000), 92.
48. *EHNA* 64.
49. C.H. Lawrence, *Medieval Monasticism* (3rd edn, Pearson Education, 2001), 45.
50. Barlow, *The English Church 1000–1066*, 232.
51. *EHNA* 79–81.
52. Ibid., 79–80.
53. Cowdrey, *Lanfranc*, 145.
54. Brett, *The English Church under Henry I*, 29.
55. Cowdrey, *Lanfranc* 148.
56. Brett, *The English Church under Henry I*, 29.
57. *EHNA* 76.
58. Vaughn, *St Anselm: A Portrait*, 159–60.
59. Green, *Henry I*, 134.
60. David Carpenter, *The Struggle for Mastery: Britain 1066–1284* (Allen Lane, 2003), 147.
61. Bartlett, *England under the Norman and Angevin Kings*, 93.
62. Brett, *The English Church under Henry I*, 29–30.
63. Ibid.; Green, *Henry I*, 173.
64. *HM-H* 48.
65. Bartlett, *England under the Norman and Angevin Kings*, 94.
66. Carpenter, *The Struggle for Mastery*, 144–5.
67. Nicholl, *Thurstan*, 79–82.
68. *RH* ii part 1 261.

4 Mitred Civil Servants: The Rise and Fall of the Salisbury Dynasty

1. *EHD* ii 400–2.
2. *Constitutio Domus Regis* in *Dialogus de Scaccario*, 130–45 (NMT, 1950).
3. Chibnall, *Anglo-Norman England*, 122.
4. Ibid., 110.
5. *SC* (1913 edn) 95; *EHD* ii 851.
6. Chibnall, *Anglo-Norman England*, 127.
7. Southern, *The Making of the Middle Ages* (1993 edn), 187 et seq.
8. Chibnall, *Anglo-Norman England*, 128.
9. Barlow, *The Feudal Kingdom of England 1042–1216* (Longman, 1955), 263–6.
10. Green, *The Government of England under Henry I* (Cambridge University Press, 1986), 50.
11. *WMGP* 27, 98–9.
12. *WMGP* 203.
13. *HEA* bk 1, 57.
14. *Eadmer, Vita Anselmi*, ed. and trans. Southern (OMT 1972), 8.
15. *WMGR* 354–5 para. 408.
16. *EHNA* 153–4.
17. *WMGP* 72.
18. Kealey, *Roger of Salisbury*, 26.
19. *HH* 52.
20. *ASC* 1124, 1125.
21. *HH* 58.
22. *ASC* 1125.
23. Chibnall, *The Empress Matilda*, 84–7.
24. *WMHN* 2.
25. *ASC* 1126.
26. *HH* 61, 102.
27. Ibid., 63, 64.
28. *HC* 129.
29. *WMHN* 3.
30. *WMHN; WNHEA;* John of Worcester, *Chronicle*, ed. and trans. P. McGurk (Oxford University Press, 1998), vol. 3, 176–8.
31. *WNHEA* 59.
32. *ASC* 1123.
33. King, *King Stephen*, 30–1.
34. *WMHN* 10.
35. King, *King Stephen*, 36.
36. Kealey, *Roger of Salisbury*, 152.
37. *GS* 7.
38. *WMHN* 5.
39. Ibid., 15.

40. *WMGP* 71; *WMHN* 5.
41. Truax, *Archbishops*, 105.
42. Quoted King, *King Stephen*, 72.
43. Davis, *King Stephen*, 146; King, *King Stephen*, 88n.
44. *HH* 66.
45. *WMHN* 25.
46. Crouch, *The Beaumont Twins*.
47. *WMGR* 353 para. 406.
48. *HH* 77.
49. Ibid., 73.
50. *GS* 48.
51. Ibid., 46.
52. *WMHN* 25, 26.
53. *GS* 50.
54. *WMHN* 26.
55. *GS* 49.
56. *WMHN* 26.
57. Ibid., 26, 27.
58. *GS* 51.
59. Ibid., 52.
60. *HH* 73.
61. *OV* v, 120, 121. Quoted Kealey, *Roger of Salisbury*, 186.
62. Ibid.
63. *WMHN* 27.
64. *HH* 74.
65. *WMHN* 37–9.
66. Ibid., 29–34.
67. *GS* 53.
68. White, *Restoration and Reform*, 23–4.
69. K. Yoshitake, *JMH* vol. 14; *EHR* ciii.

5 King Stephen and His Bishops

1. *WMHN* 53.
2. *GS* 74–5.
3. *EHD* ii 21; Cronne, *The Reign of Stephen*, 125–6.
4. Matilda was never actually crowned empress, claiming the title by association with her first husband, the emperor Henry V. To avoid confusion with Stephen's wife Matilda she will be referred to as Empress Matilda or 'the empress' throughout.
5. Cronne, *The Reign of Stephen*, 125–8; Crouch, *The Reign of Stephen*, 298–300; Stringer, *The Reign of Stephen*, 63.

6. King, *King Stephen*, 102–5; Chibnall, *The Empress Matilda*, 75–6.
7. King, *King Stephen*, 39.
8. White, 'The Governance of England in Stephen's Reign', in *Restoration and Reform*, ch. 2.
9. Loyn, *The English Church 940–1154* (Longman, 2000), 135.
10. Saltman, 'The Archiepiscopal Household', in *Theobald, Archbishop of Canterbury*, ch. 5.
11. *HH* 69.
12. *WNHEA* 99.
13. Saltman, *Theobald, Archbishop of Canterbury*, 125.
14. *HH* 86.
15. Knowles, *The Monastic Order*, 255.
16. *WNHEA* 111–15.
17. See Knowles, *The Episcopal Colleagues of Archbishop Thomas Becket* (Cambridge University Press, 1951), 34.
18. *WNHEA* 65.
19. Riall, *Henry of Blois*.
20. *HH* 108.
21. Quoted Saltman, *Theobald, Archbishop of Canterbury*, 15–16.
22. *GS* 78.
23. *WMHN* 52–6.
24. *GS* 79.
25. Ibid., 78.
26. *WMHN* 62.
27. Chibnall, *The Empress Matilda*, 138.
28. Saltman, *Theobald, Archbishop of Canterbury*, 20, 23.
29. *EHD* ii 680.
30. Ibid., ii 681.
31. Truax, *Archbishops*, 134–8.
32. *ASC* 1137.
33. *GS* 103–4.
34. Ibid., 104.
35. Quoted King, *King Stephen*, 222.
36. *EHD* ii 314–21.
37. Nicholl, *Thurstan: Archbishop of York 1114–1140* (Stonegate Press, 1964), 222–3.
38. *EHD* ii 314–21.
39. *HH* 70–2.
40. Truax, *Archbishops*, 145–50.
41. *GS* 76, 104–6.
42. Saltman, *Theobald, Archbishop of Canterbury*, 93.
43. *EHD* ii 682.
44. White, *Restoration and Reform*, 67.
45. Ibid., 66–7.

46. F.M. Stenton, *The First Century of English Feudalism* (Clarendon Press 1954), 249–52.
47. *HH* 82.
48. Ibid., 87.
49. Saltman, *Theobald, Archbishop of Canterbury*, 34, 547–9; Truax, *Archbishops*, 129.
50. Ibid., 19.
51. *HH* 88.
52. Ibid., 88–96.
53. *EHD* ii 407.
54. Quoted in Saltman, *Theobald, Archbishop of Canterbury*, 41.

6 The Becket Conflict in Perspective

1. *LTB* 45.
2. Ibid., 45, 46.
3. John of Salisbury, letter 127, quoted in Jean Truax, *Archbishops Ralph d'Escures, William of Corbeil and Theobald of Bec – Heirs of Anselm and Ancestors of Becket* (Ashgate, 2012), 180.
4. Duggan, 'Henry II, the English Church and the Papacy 1154–76', in Christopher Harper-Bill and Nicholas Vincent, *Henry II: New Interpretations* (Boydell Press, 2007).
5. *ECP* 189.
6. Chibnall, 'Canon Law and the Church Courts', in *Anglo-Norman England 1066–1166* (Blackwell, 1993), ch. 8.
7. Ibid., 198–9.
8. Saltman, *Theobald, Archbishop of Canterbury*, 126–32.
9. Ibid., 45–52; Truax, *Archbishops*, 177–80.
10. *LTB* 46–53, 55–9.
11. Ibid., 51.
12. Ibid., 52.
13. Ibid., 83.
14. Saltman, *Theobald, Archbishop of Canterbury*, 95.
15. Ibid., 156–8; Warren, *The Governance of Norman and Angevin England 1086–1272* (Arnold, 1994), 429–32; Guy, *Thomas Becket*, 100–5.
16. Guy, *Thomas Becket*, 371.
17. *LTB* 59–60.
18. J.E.A. Jolliffe, *Angevin Kingship* (A&C Black, 1963), ch. 4.
19. Warren, *The Governance of Norman and Angevin England*, 163–4; Guy, *Thomas Becket*, 242–3.
20. *EHD* ii 386–90, *Gerald of Wales* and *Walter Map*.
21. *LTB* 122–3.

22. *ECP* 192–6; A.L .Poole, *From Domesday Book to Magna Carta* (Oxford University Press, 1955), 198.
23. *LTB* 54–5.
24. Ibid., 53.
25. Knowles, *The Episcopal Colleagues of Archbishop Thomas Becket;* Knowles, *Thomas Becket,* 64–70.
26. *LTB* 46.
27. Knowles, *Thomas Becket,* 65.
28. Barlow, *Thomas Becket,* 33–4; Guy, *Thomas Becket,* 127, 374–5.
29. *LTB* 223–37.
30. D.M. Stenton, *English Justice between the Norman Conquest and the Great Charter* (Allen & Unwin, 1965), 22.
31. *LTB* 79–83.
32. Cheney, *Roger, Bishop of Worcester,* 15.
33. *LTB* 83–99.
34. Duggan, *Thomas Becket,* 44.
35. *HM-H* 83.
36. *EHD* ii 718–22; *LTB* 91–6.
37. Ibid., ii 720.
38. *HM-H* 76–84; Duggan, *Thomas Becket,* 48–56.
39. *CTB* i 78–9 quoted Duggan, *Thomas Becket,* 45.
40. *LTB* 100–15; see also Barlow, *Thomas Becket,* 109–14; Duggan, *Thomas Becket,* 61–83; Knowles, *Thomas Becket,* 94–100; Warren, *Henry II,* 485–8.
41. But see the complete para.: Warren, *Henry II,* 488–9.
42. *LTB* 120–8.
43. Ibid., 136–7.
44. Ibid., 138, 149.
45. Duggan, *Thomas Becket,* 101.
46. *LTB* 144–5.
47. Smalley, *The Becket Conflict and the Schools,* 182.
48. *LTB* 154–62.
49. Ibid., 166–72.
50. Ibid., 174–80.
51. *HM-H* 94.
52. For full accounts see *LTB* 188–205; Barlow, *Thomas Becket,* 225–50; Duggan, *Thomas Becket* 201–15; Guy, *Thomas Becket,* 298–322; Knowles, *Thomas Becket,* 135–49.
53. *LTB* 211–15; *EHD* ii 771–6.
54. *EHD* ii 770-1.
55. Ibid., 773–4; *LTB* 215–16.
56. Ibid., ii 351.
57. *LTB* 217–29; *EHD* ii 775–6.
58. For Richard see Charles Duggan, *ODNB.*
59. *ODNB.*

60. *EHD* ii 361.
61. *ODNB*.
62. *EHD* ii 480–2.
63. Cheney, *From Becket to Langton: English Church Government 1170–1213* (Manchester University Press, 1965), 23–4.
64. Frederick Pollock and F.W. Maitland, *The History of English Law* (2nd edn, Cambridge University Press, 1968), vol. I, 132–3.
65. *Dialogue of the Exchequer, NMT* 17, 26–7, 74.
66. *HM-H* 84.
67. Warren, *Henry II*, 633.
68. *LTB* 238.
69. Quoted in *LTB* 38.

7   England Without a King

1. Cheney, *From Becket to Langton*, 41.
2. Gillingham, *Richard I*.
3. Ibid., 70–82.
4. Clanchy, *England and its Rulers* (Fontana, 1983), 142.
5. Cheney, *From Becket to Langton*, 90–1.
6. Ibid., 93.
7. *RH* ii part I, 231–8.
8. Gillingham, *Richard I*, 228.
9. See Frances Ramsey, *ODNB*.
10. See Ralph V. Turner, *ODNB*.
11. *RH* 238; see also *EHD* iii docs 1, 2.
12. *RW* 111; *RH* 225 et seq.
13. *RH* 228–9.
14. *RW* 113–14.
15. *RH* 231–8.
16. Ibid., 238–41.
17. Ibid., 242–3.
18. Ralph V. Turner, *ODNB*.
19. *RH* 230.
20. William of Newburgh, *EHD* ii 362.
21. Cheney, *Hubert Walter*; Robert C. Stacey, *ODNB*.
22. Cheney, *Hubert Walter*, ch. 3; C. Tyerman, *God's War: A New History of the Crusades* (Penguin, 2007), 428–30.
23. *The Autobiography of Gerald of Wales*, ed. and trans. H.E. Butler (Boydell Press, 2005), 98–104.
24. Quoted in Cheney, *Hubert Walter*, 35.
25. Ibid., 36–7.

26. Quoted in Cheney, *Hubert Walter*, 46.
27. *RH* 295–7.
28. Ibid., 371.
29. Ibid., 395, 396–8.
30. Ibid., 394.
31. Ibid., 334–9.
32. Ibid., 368.
33. Ibid., 388; *RW* 146.
34. *RH* 389
35. Ibid., 396–7; *RW* 156–7.
36. *RH* 432.
37. Ibid., 420–1.
38. Cheney, *Hubert Walter*, 46; Clanchy, *From Memory to Written Record: England 1066–1307* (Blackwell, 1993), 68–9.
39. *RW* 141–2.
40. *RH* 361–6.
41. Ibid., 490–500.
42. Ibid., 393–4.
43. Ibid., 410–11.
44. Cheney, *Hubert Walter*, 137–50.
45. *RH* 422.
46. Cheney, *Hubert Walter*, 99.
47. *MV*; Henry Mayr-Harting, *ODNB*.
48. *EHD* ii 335.
49. *MV* ii 78.
50. Ibid., ii 110–14.
51. Ibid., ii 34–7.
52. Ibid., ii 98–100.
53. Ibid., ii 101–2.
54. Ibid., ii 105.
55. *RH* 321–2.
56. *MV* ii 134–7
57. Ibid., ii 137–44.
58. Ibid., ii 188–9.

8   Stephen Langton, the Bishops and *Magna Carta*

1. Warren, *King John*, pp. 230–1, based on *Histoire de Guillaume le Maréchal*.
2. *RW* 207.
3. Ibid., 293–303.
4. Quoted in Carpenter, *The New Cambridge Medieval History*, ed. David Abulafia (Cambridge University Press, 1999), vol. v, 319.

5. D.M. Stenton, *English Justice between the Norman Conquest and the Great Charter* (Allen & Unwin, 1965), 88–114.
6. John Hudson, *The Formation of the English Common Law* (Pearson Education, 1996), ch. 8.
7. Ibid., 223.
8. Quoted in RW 283 et seq.
9. Knowles, *The Monastic Order in England* 281–97 (Cambridge University Press, 1963), 659.
10. Painter, *The Reign of King John*, 155.
11. C. Harper-Bill, 'John and the Church of Rome', in Church (ed.), *King John: New Interpretations*.
12. Vincent, *Peter des Roches*.
13. Clanchy, *England and its Rulers* (Fontana, 1983), 183–5.
14. *EEA* ix, ed. Vincent.
15. Janet Burton, *Monastic and Religious Orders in Britain 1000–1300* (Cambridge University Press, 1994), 112, 229.
16. *SLI* 86.
17. Powicke, *Stephen Langton*, 81.
18. Painter, *The Reign of King John*, 155.
19. *RW* 215–16.
20. *SLI* no. 29.
21. *RW* 257–9.
22. Ibid., 259–60.
23. Cheney, 'The Alleged Deposition of King John', in *Studies in Medieval History Presented to F.M. Powicke* (Oxford University Press, 1948).
24. *SLI* no. 45.
25. *RW* 268–70.
26. Ibid., 273–4.
27. Powicke, *Stephen Langton*, 3.
28. *SLI* nos 53–5.
29. *RW* 292–3.
30. *SC* 283–4; *SLI* no. 76; Cheney, *Pope Innocent III and England*, 363–5.
31. *SLI* no. 45.
32. Ibid., nos 82, 83.
33. Ullmann, *Principles of Government and Politics in the Middle Ages* (Barnes & Noble, 1961), 162–3.
34. *RW* 257–8.
35. *SLI*.
36. *RW* 275.
37. Ibid., 276–8.
38. Powicke, *Stephen Langton*, 116 et seq.
39. *HER*, October 2011.
40. Powicke, *Stephen Langton*, 43.
41. *RW* 276–8.

42. Warren, *King John*, 228.
43. Painter, *The Reign of King John*, 276.
44. For the text see Warren, *King John*, 215–16.
45. *SLI* nos 60–2.
46. *RW* 293.
47. Cheney, *Pope Innocent III and England*, 362; Warren, *King John*, 225.
48. Recent research by Cristian Ispir shows that *Walter of Coventry* is actually *The Crowland Chronicle*.
49. *SLI* no. 76.
50. *RW* 304.
51. *SLI* no. 74.
52. Ibid., no. 75.
53. Painter, *The Reign of King John*, 249–51.
54. *RW* 308.
55. Carpenter, in *The Reign of Henry III* (Hambledon Press, 1996), argues that it was; see also his *Magna Carta*, 361–6.
56. Carpenter, *Magna Carta*, 347–52.
57. Painter, *The Reign of King John*, 316.
58. Carpenter, *Magna Carta*, 107–15, 354.
59. *SLI* no. 82.
60. *SLI* no. 80.

Epilogue

1. Bartlett, *England under the Norman and Angevin Kings* (Oxford University Press, 2000), 375.
2. Tierney, *The Crisis of Church and State 1050–1300* (Prentice-Hall, 1964), ch. 1; Duffey, *Saints and Sinners: A History of the Popes* (Yale University Press, 1997), 40–1.
3. Tierney, *Crisis*, 74–8.
4. Truax, *Archbishops Ralph d'Escures, William of Corbeil and Theobald of Bec – Heirs of Anselm and Ancestors of Becket* (Ashgate, 2012), 8–9.
5. *EHNA* 37. It may be that these words were actually a literary artefact created by Eadmer rather than a literal account of what exactly happened.

Further Reading

In addition to the books included here there are others in the reference section at the end of each chapter. Extensive bibliographies will be found in many of the works cited. Where not included here, full publication details can be found in the List of Abbreviations.

Primary sources

Attention will be drawn to specific sources under the appropriate heading. With very few exceptions, all the sources referred to are English translations of the original Latin.

Indispensable is the second volume of *English Historical Documents* (*EHD*). The third volume contains some material relevant to the reigns of Richard I and John.

All students of the period are indebted to the series of Oxford Medieval Texts (*OMT*), edited and translated by distinguished scholars with the original Latin on one page and a translation on the facing page. Originally published as Nelson's Medieval Texts (*NMT*), with the first volume appearing in 1949, from 1966 they were taken over by Oxford University Press. Unfortunately, as they are very expensive they may well be beyond the reach of most sixth-formers and undergraduates and it is unlikely that many school libraries will be able to afford copies. It is sometimes possible to buy second-hand editions, perhaps as *NMT* publications, at a reasonable price.

Invaluable, therefore, are the Oxford University Press editions of modern trans-lations of medieval texts in the Oxford World's Classics series. Unfortunately very few have been published.

All those interested in medieval studies who have little or no Latin are indebted to the Llanerch Press for their facsimile editions of a number of medieval texts mainly translated in the nineteenth century. They have not been modified for twenty-first-century readers but they are nevertheless very useful and affordable.

It is possible to download a range of translations of medieval sources.

Introduction and background

Stimulating and beautifully written introductions to the medieval period and the medieval church are two books by Sir Richard Southern, *The Making of the Middle Ages*, first published by Hutchinson in 1953 and *Western Society and the*

Church in the Middle Ages in the Penguin History of the Church series (1990). Also recommended are *A History of the Church in the Middle Ages* by F. Donald Logan (Routledge, 2002) and Joseph H. Lynch, *The Medieval Church: A Brief History* (Pearson Education, 1992). For the papacy, readable introductions are E. Duffey, *Saints and Sinners: A History of the Popes* (Yale University Press, 1997) and G. Barraclough, *The Medieval Papacy* (Thames & Hudson, 1968). Very important are Colin Morris, *The Papal Monarchy: The Western Church from 1050 to 1250* (Oxford University Press, 1991) and I.S. Robinson, *The Papacy 1073–1198: Continuity and Innovation* (Cambridge University Press, 1990). Challenging and idiosyncratic is Walter Ullmann, *A Short History of the Papacy in the Middle Ages*, with a new introduction by George Garnett (Routledge, 2003). An essential collection of source material in translation is Brian Tierney, *The Crisis of Church and State 1050–1300* (Prentice-Hall, 1964). For developments in canon law see James A. Brundage, *Medieval Canon Law* (Longman, 1995).

For the English background, David Carpenter, *The Struggle for Mastery: Britain 1066–1284* (Allen Lane, 2003) is an essential introduction. Exciting and remarkably wide-ranging is Robert Bartlett, *England under the Norman and Angevin Kings 1075–1225* (Oxford University Press, 2000). Readable and stimulating is M.T. Clanchy, *England and its Rulers* (Fontana, 1983). First published in 1955, Frank Barlow, *The Feudal Kingdom of England 1042–1216* (Longman) remains helpful. Invaluable is Henry Mayr-Harting, *Religion, Politics and Society in Britain 1066–1272* (Pearson Education, 2011).

Two recently published books that readers may wish to turn to are Everett Crosby, *The King's Bishops: The Politics of Patronage in England and Normandy 1066–1216* (Palgrave Macmillan, 2013) and Hugh M. Thomas, *The Secular Clergy in England 1066–1216* (Oxford University Press, 2014).

The Oxford Dictionary of National Biography (*ODNB*) and volumes in the *English Episcopal Acta* series often contain up-to-date biographical material about the bishops discussed. The *ODNB* can be accessed online at http://www.oxforddnb.com.

Chapters 1 and 2

General

F.M. Stenton, *Anglo-Saxon England* (3rd edn, Clarendon Press, 1971), H.R. Loyn, *The English Church 940–1154* (Longman, 2000), Frank Barlow, *The English Church 1000–1066* (Longman, 1979), Frank Barlow, *The English Church 1066–1154* (Longman, 1979), David Bates, *Normandy before 1066* (Longman, 1982), M. Brett, *The English Church under Henry I* (Oxford University Press, 1975), Judith A. Green, *The Government of England under Henry I* (Cambridge University Press, 1986) and R.W. Southern, *Medieval Humanism* (Basil Blackwell, 1970), especially the chapters on Ranulf Flambard and Henry I.

Kings

D.C. Douglas, *William the Conqueror* (Eyre & Spottiswoode, 1964), David Bates, *William the Conqueror* (Tempus, 2001), Frank Barlow, *William Rufus* (Methuen, 1983), Emma Mason, *William II, Rufus the Red King* (Tempus, 2005), Judith A. Green, *Henry I: King of England and Duke of Normandy* (Cambridge University Press, 2006) and C. Warren Hollister, *Henry I* (Yale University Press, 2001).

Bishops

Margaret Gibson, *Lanfranc of Bec* (Clarendon Press, 1978), H.E.J. Cowdrey, *Lanfranc* (Oxford University Press, 2003), David Bates, *Bishop Remigius of Lincoln 1067–1092* (Lincoln Cathedral Publications, 1992), Emma Mason, *St Wulfstan of Worcester c.1008–1095* (Oxford University Press, 1990), R.W. Southern, *St Anselm and his Biographer: A Study of Monastic Life and Thought 1059–c.1130* (Cambridge University Press, 1966), R.W. Southern, *St Anselm: A Portrait in a Landscape* (Cambridge University Press, 1990), Sally N. Vaughn, *Archbishop Anselm 1093–1109* (Ashgate, 2012) – the documents in Latin and in translation are particularly helpful – and Sally N. Vaughn, *Anselm of Bec and Robert of Meulan: The Innocence of the Dove and the Wisdom of the Serpent* (University of California Press, 1987).

Primary sources

English Historical Documents, vol. ii 1042–1189 (*EHD*); *The Anglo-Saxon Chronicles* (*ASC*); William of Malmesbury, *The Deeds of the Bishops of England* (*WMGP*); William of Malmesbury, *A History of the Norman Kings 1066–1125* (*WMGR*); William of Malmesbury: *Vita Wulfstani* (*WMVW*); Henry of Huntingdon, *The History of the English People 1000–1154* (*HH*); Eadmer, *History of Recent Events in England* (*EHNA*); *The Ecclesiastical History of Orderic Vitalis* (*OV*); *The Letters of Lanfranc*, ed and trans H. Clover and M. Gibson (*OMT*, 1979); *The Letters of St Anselm of Canterbury*, ed. and trans. W. Frohlic (Cistercian Studies series, 1990); Eadmer, *Vita Anselmi*, ed. and trans. R.W. Southern (*OMT*, 1972).

Chapter 3

Much of the material cited under Chapters 1 and 2 is relevant to this chapter. Eadmer's *Historia Novorum* (History of Recent Events) is outclassed by the brilliant propaganda of Hugh the Chantor's *History of the Church of York*, ed. and trans. C. Johnson (*NMT*, 1961). William of Malmesbury's *Gesta Pontificum* (*WMGP*) is also essential. Helpful too is the letter of Archbishop Ralph of Canterbury to Pope Calixtus and the extracts from the *Actus Pontificum* of Gervase of Canterbury printed in Latin and English as appendices 2 and 3 to Jean Truax, *Archbishops Ralph d'Escures, William of Corbeil and Theobald of Bec – Heirs of Anselm and*

Ancestors of Becket (Ashgate, 2012). Essential reading is Donald Nicholl, *Thurstan: Archbishop of York 1114–1140* (Stonegate Press, 1964).

Chapters 4 and 5

For introductory material on government and administration readers should begin with S.B. Chrimes, *An Introduction to the Administrative History of Medieval England* (Blackwell, 1959), R. Bartlett, *England under the Norman and Angevin Kings* (Oxford University Press, 2000) and M.T. Clanchy, *England and its Rulers* and *From Memory to Written Record, England 1066–1307* (Blackwell, 1993). Also important are Marjorie Chibnall, *Anglo-Norman England 1066–1166* (Blackwell, 1993) and W.L. Warren, *The Governance of Norman and Angevin England 1086–1272* (Arnold, 1994).

King Stephen

The reign of Stephen is remarkably well covered by historians. The starting point for modern works was R.H.C. Davis, *King Stephen 1135–54* (Longman, 1967, 3rd edn 1990). Further studies of the reign followed: H.A. Cronne, *The Reign of Stephen: Anarchy in England 1135–54* (Weidenfeld & Nicolson, 1970), K. Stringer, *The Reign of Stephen* (Routledge, 1993) and David Crouch, *The Reign of Stephen* (Pearson Education, 2000). A masterly work with a very extensive bibliography, written with a sense of humour, is Edmund King, *King Stephen* (Yale University Press, 2012). For Stephen's adversary Matilda see Marjorie Chibnall, *The Empress Matilda: Queen Consort, Queen Mother and Lady of the English* (Blackwell, 1994). Also important is D. Crouch, *The Beaumont Twins: The Roots and Branches of Power in the Twelfth Century* (Cambridge University Press, 1986). Graeme White's *Restoration and Reform 1153–65: Recovery from Civil War in England* (Cambridge University Press, 2000) focuses on the first 12 years of the reign of Henry II, but the first two chapters are very helpful.

The bishops

There is an invaluable and very readable study of Bishop Roger by Edward J. Kealey: *Roger of Salisbury – Viceroy of England* (University of California Press, 1972). Essential, too, is Avrom Saltman, *Theobald, Archbishop of Canterbury*, with its collection of charters (Athlone Press, 1956). See also Jean Truax, *Archbishops*. Unfortunately there is to date no modern biography of Henry of Winchester and no biography in English, but see David Knowles, *The Monastic Order in England* 281–97 (Cambridge University Press, 1963) and Nicholas Riall, *Henry of Blois, Bishop of Winchester: A Patron of the Twelfth-Century Renaissance* (Hampshire County Council, 1994). More generally, Stephen Marritt's *Reeds Shaken by the Wind? Bishops in Local and Regional Politics in King Stephen's Reign 1135–54*, ed.

Paul Dalton and Graeme White (Boydell Press, 2008) is important, as is Christopher Holdsworth, 'The Church', in Edmund King, *The Anarchy of Stephen's Reign* (Oxford University Press, 1994).

Sources

The reign of Stephen is particularly well documented, with four invaluable chronicle sources readily available to the student and the enthusiast. A significant part of Henry of Huntingdon's *History* is about Stephen's reign, and William of Malmesbury's *Historia Novella* is available in the *NMT/OMT* series. The latter covers the period from the recall of Matilda from Germany by Henry I in 1125 to her escape from Oxford Castle in 1141. It was written for Robert of Gloucester. Also in the *NMT/OMT* series is the *Gesta Stephani*, written possibly by the Bishop of Bath, Robert of Lewes, a firm but critical royalist. Until around 60 years ago historians had only a text which ended in 1148. The final part, to 1154, was discovered in 1955. Some passages are missing, but it is an invaluable contemporary account of the reign. A fourth chronicle source is the first book of William of Newburgh's *History of English Affairs*. There are a few references in *The Anglo-Saxon Chronicle*, the most notorious being the entry for 1137. Recommended to those comfortable with Latin is *The Letters and Charters of Gilbert Foliot*, ed. Adrian Morey and C.N.L. Brooke (Cambridge University Press, 2008). Those with no Latin can gain something from it. The *Historia Pontificalis* of John of Salisbury is important. For those with no access to it there is an excerpt in *EHD* ii, no. 114.

Chapter 6

Henry II

For the reign the brilliant, extensive survey by W.L. Warren, *Henry II* (Yale University Press, 2000), is an essential work of reference. Part III – *Henry II and the Church* – sets the Becket conflict in the broader context. See also Graeme White, *Restoration and Reform 1153–1165* (Cambridge University Press, 2000) and E. Amt, *The Accession of Henry II in England: Royal Government Restored, 1149–56* (Boydell Press, 1993).

Becket

There are four works that are essential for an appreciation of the issues at stake between Henry II and Becket and the different ways that historians interpret them: David Knowles, *Thomas Becket* (A&C Black, 1970), Frank Barlow, *Thomas Becket* (Weidenfeld & Nicolson, 1986) and Anne Duggan, *Thomas Becket* (Arnold, 2004) are very readable studies by eminent scholars. A different style of book is John Guy, *Thomas Becket – Warrior, Priest, Rebel, Victim: A 900-Year-Old Story Recalled* (Penguin, 2013). It is thoroughly grounded in scholarship, with very extensive notes and references, and is an impressive narrative account of the reign. For Becket's apprenticeship see Avrom Saltman, *Theobald, Archbishop of Canterbury* (Athlone Press, 1956); for his fellow bishops see David Knowles, *The Episcopal Colleagues of Archbishop Thomas Becket* (Cambridge University Press, 1951). See also Mary G. Cheney, *Roger, Bishop of Worcester 1164–79* (Oxford University Press, 1980). Beryl Smalley, *The Becket Conflict and the Schools: A Study of Intellectuals in Politics in the Twelfth Century* (Oxford University Press, 1973) sets the conflict in the context of contemporary intellectual developments. A judicious assessment is Henry Mayr-Harting, 'The Conflict between Henry II and Thomas Becket', Chapter 4 of his *Religion, Politics and Society in Britain 1066–1272* (Pearson Education, 2011).

Sources

Fundamental is *The Lives of Thomas Becket*, ed. and trans. Michael Staunton, in the Manchester Medieval Sources series (Manchester University Press, 2001). *EHD* ii, Part 3 C, *The Church in England 1154–89*, contains material not found in *LTB*. Anne Duggan's *Thomas Becket* quotes a range of sources in translation, and her edition of *The Correspondence of Thomas Becket*, 2 vols (*OMT*, 2000) is an essential collection of source material made accessible to the modern reader.

Chapter 7

John Gillingham, *Richard I* (Yale University Press, 1999) is erudite, readable and entertaining (he twice refers to Walt Disney's *Robin Hood* and quotes from *1066 and All That*). Also by Gillingham: *Richard Coeur de Lion: Kingship, Chivalry and War in the Twelfth Century* (Hambledon Press, 1994) and *The Angevin Empire* (Holmes & Meier, 1984).

For the bishops, two studies by C.R. Cheney are essential: *From Becket to Langton: English Church Government 1170–1213* (Manchester University Press, 1965) and *Hubert Walter* (Nelson, 1967). Also important is Henry Mayr-Harting, 'Archbishop Hubert Walter and St Hugh of Lincoln: Church and King in the Late Twelfth Century', Chapter 7 of his *Religion, Politics and Society in Britain 1066–1272* (Pearson Education, 2011).

Sources

Roger of Wendover, *Flowers of History*, vol. 2, part I, trans. J.A. Giles (Llanerch Press); *The Annals of Roger de Hoveden*, vol. 2, parts 1 and 2; *Magna Vita S. Hugonis:*

The Life of St Hugh of England, ed. and trans. Decima Douie and Hugh Farmer, 2 vols, Nelson Medieval Texts (Nelson, 1961–2).

Chapter 8

King John

A classic work is Kate Norgate, *John Lackland* (Macmillan, 1901); the first modern work is Sidney Painter, *The Reign of King John* (Baltimore Press, 1949). In 1961 W.L. Warren wrote his celebrated attempt to rehabilitate John in *King John* (Eyre & Spottiswoode, 1961). It remains highly regarded and is now available in the Yale English Monarchs series. Before Warren, V.H. Galbraith had been very critical of two of the principal chronicle sources for John's reign in *Roger Wendover and Matthew Paris* (University of Glasgow, 1944). Ralph V. Turner, *King John* (Longman, 1994) is also recommended. An important collection of essays is *King John: New Interpretations*, ed. S.D. Church (Boydell Press, 2007). Since the compilation of this bibliography another relevant book has appeared: Stephen Church, *King John: England, Magna Carta and the Making of a Tyrant* (Macmillan, 2015).

The church

Crucial to an understanding of John's relationship with the church is C.R. Cheney, *Innocent III and England* (Hiersemann, 1979). For Pope Innocent III, Jane Sayers, *Innocent III: Leader of Europe 1198–1216* (Longman, 1994) is a very important study; see also John C. Moore, *Pope Innocent III: To Root Up and to Plant* (Indiana University Press, 2009). Nicholas Vincent, *Peter des Roches: An Alien in English Politics 1205–38* (Cambridge University Press, 1996) is an essential study of one of the key figures in John's reign. F.M. Powicke, *Stephen Langton,* the Ford Lectures for 1927 (reprinted by the Merlin Press, 1965) has not been superseded. Langton's thought is discussed in J.W. Baldwin, *Masters, Princes and Merchants: The Social Views of Peter the Chanter and his Circle,* 2 vols (Princeton University Press, 1970).

Magna Carta

An excellent starting point is Nicholas Vincent, *Magna Carta: A Very Short Introduction* (Oxford University Press, 2012). From there anyone with a serious interest in the subject must turn to the works of J.C. Holt: *The Northerners: A Study in the Reign of King John* (Oxford University Press, 1961, 2nd edn 1992), *Magna Carta* (Cambridge University Press, 1965, 2nd edn 1992) and collected essays in *Magna Carta and Medieval Government* (Hambledon Continuum, 1985). David Carpenter's *Magna Carta,* published in 2015 in the *Penguin Classics Series,* is indispensable. It is scholarly, encyclopedic and written with a lightness of touch that makes it very readable.

Sources

C.R. Cheney and W.H. Semple, *Selected Letters of Pope Innocent III concerning England (1198–1216)* (Nelson, 1953), Roger of Wendover's *Flowers of History, vol. 2, part 1, 1170–1215*. Translations of *Magna Carta* are available in a number of publications. Sources in translation relevant to the reign of John are found in the third volume of *EHD* for 1189–1327, ed. H. Rothwell (Eyre & Spottiswoode, 1975).

Index

Note: Historical figures are listed with their personal names first, otherwise surnames are printed first.

William de Ferrers, earl of Derby
(d. 1190)　138
William Giffard, bishop of Winchester
(1107–29)　xv, 38, 40, 41, 44, 51,
60, 69, 70
William the Lion, king of the Scots
(1165–1214)　62, 159
William, bishop of London (1051–75)
4, 10
William Longchamp, chancellor,
bishop of Ely (1189–97)　xxix,
129, 130, 131, 132–6, 137, 139,
141, 159, 169
William Longsword, earl of Salisbury
(1197–1226)　158
William of Malmesbury, chronicler
xxii, xxviii, 4, 5, 13, 15, 16, 17,
18, 21, 24, 29, 30, 33, 34, 35, 38,
45, 46, 49, 50, 51, 55, 70, 74, 75,
76, 79, 80, 81, 82, 84, 94
William de Mandeville, earl of Essex
(d. 1189)　133
William Marshal, earl of Pembroke
(1199–1219)　134, 149, 162, 164,
167
William of Newborough, Augustinian
canon, chronicler　68, 69, 76,
88, 92, 124, 125, 127, 133,
139, 145
William de Northall, bishop of
Worcester (1186–90)　145
William, bishop of Norwich
(1146–74)　99, 113
William fitz Osbern　13, 64
William fitz Osbert　142, 144
William of Poitiers, chronicler　2
William de Pont de l'Arche,
treasurer　74, 75
William of Roumare, earl of Lincoln
(d. c.1198)　93
William of Sainte-Mère-Église,
exchequer clerk, bishop of
London (1198–1221)　139,
166

William de St Barbe, bishop of
Durham (1143–52)　91
William of St Calais, bishop of
Durham (1080–96)　5, 21, 29, 34,
40, 171
William fitz Stephen, biographer of
Becket　110, 112, 117
William de Tracy　123
William de Turbe, bishop of Norwich
(1146–74)　115
William de Vere, bishop of Hereford
(1186–98)　145
William of Volpiano, abbot of Dijon
2, 3
William Warelwast, bishop of Exeter
(1107–37)　xxix, 30, 32, 33, 39,
41, 55
William of Warenne, earl of Surrey
(d. 1138)　77
William of the White Hands,
archbishop of Sens　118, 123
William d'Ypres　79, 99, 108, 141
Winchester
Councils of (1072)　13, 47; (1076)
13, 14; (1139) 80 196
Rout of 1141　96
Treaty of 1153　84, 105
Windsor　158, 162, 163, 166
Council of (1072)　13, 47; (1100)
48; (1141) 95
Witan　xx
Woden　xx
Woodstock, Council of (1163)　114
Wordsworth, Elizabeth　148
Wulfric of Haselbury　84
Wulfstan I, bishop of Worcester,
London, archbishop of York
(1002–23)　xxviii; *Institutes of
Polity* xxviii
Wulfstan II, St, bishop of Worcester
(1062–95)　xxix, 4, 5, 6, 11, 14,
18–20, 21, 46, 143, 151

York, canons of　43–62 *passim*, 138